Treasure House

Year 6
Teacher's Guide

Author: Abigail Steel

William Collins' dream of knowledge for all began with the publication of his first book in 1819. A self-educated mill worker, he not only enriched millions of lives, but also founded a flourishing publishing house. Today, staying true to this spirit, Collins books are packed with inspiration, innovation and practical expertise. They place you at the centre of a world of possibility and give you exactly what you need to explore it.

Collins. Freedom to teach.

Published by Collins
An imprint of HarperCollins*Publishers*
The News Building
1 London Bridge Street
London
SE1 9GF

Browse the complete Collins catalogue at
www.collins.co.uk

© HarperCollins*Publishers* Limited 2015

10 9 8 7 6 5 4 3 2 1

ISBN 978-0-00-813355-9

All rights reserved. No part of this publication may be reproduced, stored in a retrieval system, or transmitted in any form or by any means, electronic, mechanical, photocopying, recording or otherwise, without the prior written permission of the Publisher or a licence permitting restricted copying in the United Kingdom issued by the Copyright Licensing Agency Ltd, 90 Tottenham Court Road, London W1T 4LP.

While every effort has been made to trace the copyright holders of text extracts, in cases where this has been unsuccessful or if any have inadvertently been overlooked, the Publishers will be pleased to make the necessary arrangements at the first opportunity.

British Library Cataloguing in Publication Data

A Catalogue record for this publication is available from the British Library

Publishing Managers: Tom Guy and Lizzie Catford
Project Managers: Dawn Booth and Sarah Thomas
Development editor: Jessica Marshall
Copy editor: Catherine Dakin
Cover design and artwork: Amparo Barrera
Internal design: Linda Miles and Hugh Hillyard-Parker

Printed in Great Britain by Martins the Printers

Contents

	Page
Welcome to the Treasure House Teacher's Guide for Year 6	5
About Treasure House	6
The National Curriculum for English	12
Using a Treasure House teaching sequence	15
Differentiation in Treasure House	17
Accessing achievement strategies	18
Assessment in Treasure House	19
Progression in Treasure House	21
Sequence overview chart	23
Curriculum map	24
Sequence 1: Fiction: Creating tensions	31
Sequence 2: Fiction: Traditional stories	41
Sequence 3: Non-fiction: Persuasive writing	51
Sequence 4: Non-fiction: Email conventions	61
Sequence 5: Poetry: Free verse	71
Sequence 6: Poetry: Descriptive techniques	81
Sequence 7: Poetry: Narrative techniques	91
Sequence 8: Non-fiction: Journalism	101
Sequence 9: Non-fiction: Reports	111
Sequence 10: Contrasting perspectives	121
Sequence 11: Fiction: Creating atmosphere	131
Sequence 12: Fiction: Plotting problems	141

Contents

Sequence 13: Fiction: Alternative perspectives	151
Sequence 14: Fiction: Comparing forms	161
Sequence 15: Non-fiction: Biographies	171
Sequence template	181
Editor's checklist	191
My writing checklist	192
Story planner	193
Non-fiction planner	194
Poetry planner	195
Challenge questions	196
Challenge question answers	205
Pupil Book answers	209

Welcome

Welcome to the Treasure House Teacher's Guide for Year 6

Welcome to this Treasure House Teacher's Guide. We have created this guide, with our expert authors, to provide a framework that will support you in planning your literacy teaching across Year 6. In the 15 engaging teaching sequences it contains, we have woven together the four core dimensions of the National Curriculum for English:

- Comprehension
- Composition
- Vocabulary, Grammar and Punctuation
- Spelling.

Word reading, speaking and listening, and transcription skills are integral throughout all sequences, as this is fundamental to the development of all literacy learning.

All of these elements are covered in each of the teaching sequences, as we have always found that applied learning is by far the most effective. Our experience is that this approach allows children to practise their skills purposefully and improves retention, particularly of spelling, vocabulary, grammar and punctuation. It is also considerably more fun!

The teaching sequences can be used as the basis of your literacy planning, providing potentially 30 weeks of teaching inspiration. They feature a range of different literary genres, both fiction and non-fiction. We have also included a wide range of poetry as, in addition to featuring prominently in the National Curriculum, its comprehension and composition can have a profound impact on a child's more general reading, writing and thinking skills. The sequences and the Curriculum Coverage Charts suggest which National Curriculum objectives will be covered by each unit so that full curriculum coverage can be achieved.

We all know, however, that formative assessment provides the most effective guidance for planning. Therefore, we have designed the units to be adaptable to the needs of different classes, according to your professional judgement. The sequences can be used in any order and the activities can be adjusted, to meet the needs of your class and to fit with your broader teaching scheme. Their flexibility allows you to draw upon your own experiences, and apply your own imagination, as frequently as you wish. This is a handbook that seeks to support and enhance teachers', as well as children's, skills and creativity.

Christine Chen and **Lindsay Pickton**
Primary Education Advisors
Series Editors, Treasure House Teacher's Guides

About Treasure House

Treasure House is a comprehensive and flexible bank of print and digital resources covering the 2014 English Programme of Study.

Treasure House comprises of:
- Print Pupil Books
- Print Teacher's Guides and Anthologies
- Online digital resources hosted on the Collins Connect Platform.

Treasure House Teacher's Guides and Anthologies

There are six Treasure House Teacher's Guides and six Anthologies. Each Teacher's Guide provides 15 teaching sequences. The sequences weave together all four dimensions of the National Curriculum for English – Comprehension; Composition; Vocabulary, Grammar and Punctuation; and Spelling – into a complete unit of work: Comprehension; Composition; Vocabulary, Grammar and Punctuation; and Spelling. The Anthologies contain the source texts for each sequence.

Chart of Treasure House Teacher's Guides and Anthologies

Year	Teacher's Guides	Anthologies	Year	Teacher's Guides	Anthologies
1	978-0-00-813360-3	978-0-00-816044-9	4	978-0-00-813357-3	978-0-00-816047-0
2	978-0-00-813359-7	978-0-00-816045-6	5	978-0-00-813356-6	978-0-00-816048-7
3	978-0-00-813358-0	978-0-00-816046-3	6	978-0-00-813355-9	978-0-00-816049-4

Inside the Treasure House Teacher's Guides and Anthologies

The Teacher's Guides contain 15 teaching sequences. Every teaching sequence follows the same four phases:

- **Enjoy and immerse** engages children with a source text through discussion and comprehension activities.
- **Capture and organise** uses discussion, drama and writing to help children analyse the text in more depth and record ideas for written work.
- **Collaborative composition** supports group and classwork exploring the process of writing.
- **Independent writing** provides opportunities for children to construct their own texts independently.

The Anthologies contain fully illustrated, extended extracts from all the text types specified in the curriculum, including classic fiction and leading contemporary children's authors. The extracts should be used as source texts for the teaching sequences.

About Treasure House

Teacher's Guide

Extra source text details provide information on the Anthology texts for each sequence.

Big Picture outlines success criteria for the sequence.

Diagnostic assessment options support an effective teaching and learning cycle by assessing children's knowledge and understanding at the start of a sequence.

Cross-curricular links gives details of Curriculum Objectives that are covered from other areas of the National Curriculum.

Year 5, Sequence 4
Non-fiction: News reports

Sequence 4
Non-fiction: News reports

Approximate duration: Two weeks

Big Picture

Through this teaching sequence, children will explore the way in which journalists present information in news reports. Understanding how journalists construct news reports will help children to use the conventions of report writing in their own work. Children will be able to write a newspaper article, using an impersonal style, which effectively conveys information.

Phase 1: Enjoy and immerse
Children analyse the techniques used in the model text, 'Cubs and Brownies to the Rescue'.

Phase 2: Capture and organise
Children begin to develop ideas for creating their own newspaper articles, using report-writing techniques.

Phase 3: Collaborate and compose
Children undertake supported writing sessions to develop the writing features of their newspaper articles.

Phase 4: Write independently
Children write, edit and present their own newspaper articles using an impersonal style.

Main source text
Treasure House Online, Year 5, Comprehension Unit 4: Non-fiction (news report): 'Cubs and Brownies to the rescue'

Extra source texts
'4-Year-Old Survives 11 Days Alone in Siberian Forest' (see Anthology)

Background knowledge
'Cubs and Brownies to the rescue' is an example of a local good-news story that details a community coming together to clean up their local area; '4-Year-Old Survives 11 Days Alone in Siberian Forest' exemplifies a global good-news story about a young girl and her puppy being found after surviving against the odds. In this sequence, the children make an investigation into how to write news reports, using the source texts as models. They observe and utilise characteristics common to news reports such as headlines, by-lines, quotes, captioned photographs, summary introductions (explaining who, what, when and where) and body text (further explaining how and why).

Spoken outcome
To present a news article as an oral performance to an audience of peers or parents

Writing outcome
To write a newspaper article, using an impersonal style, that conveys information effectively

Prior knowledge
Check the children's knowledge and understanding of:
- what Cubs and Brownies are
- the location and climate of Siberia
- the characteristics common to reports
- what might constitute a good news story.

Year 5, Sequence 4
Non-fiction: News reports

Diagnostic assessment options

Before starting the sequence, you may want to conduct an initial diagnostic assessment of the children's understanding of characteristics common to a news report.

Ideas for initial diagnostic assessment options include:
- discussion about news reports, their purpose and characteristics
- a brief, unsupported writing activity creating a short news report
- practising speaking and listening skills in aural reports, in the style of TV or radio news reports
- a short reading comprehension activity / quiz on a news report.

Cross-curricular links

KS2 Geography – Geographical skills and fieldwork
Use maps, atlases, globes and digital / computer mapping to locate countries and describe features studied.

KS2 Geography – Locational knowledge
Locate the world's countries, using maps to focus on Europe (including the location of Russia) and North and South America, concentrating on their environmental regions, key physical and human characteristics, countries and major cities.

Treasure House links

All digital and pupil book units have the same names and numbers, but different questions.
- Treasure House, Year 5, Comprehension Unit 4: Non-fiction (news report): 'Cubs and Brownies to the rescue'
- Treasure House, Year 5, Composition Unit 5: Writing reports
- Treasure House, Year 5, Composition Unit 12: Behind the news
- Treasure House, Year 5, Grammar Unit 1: Formal and informal language
- Treasure House, Year 5, Punctuation Unit 1: Using commas for clearer meaning
- Treasure House, Year 5, Punctuation Unit 5: Colons to introduce lists
- Treasure House, Year 5, Punctuation Unit 6: Punctuating bulleted lists
- Treasure House, Year 6, Grammar Unit 2: Using the passive voice
- Treasure House, Year 5, Spelling Unit 9: Words with 'silent' letters

Resources
Source texts – see Anthologies; My writing checklist; Editor's checklist

---

Background knowledge contains contextualising information on the text type and content of the text.

Spoken outcome and **Written outcome** provide oral and written outcomes for each sequence.

Prior knowledge lists questions to help elicit what children already know.

Treasure House links lists details of relevant units in the Pupil Books and Treasure House Digital.

Anthology

Extended extracts provide quality source texts for use during the teaching sequences.

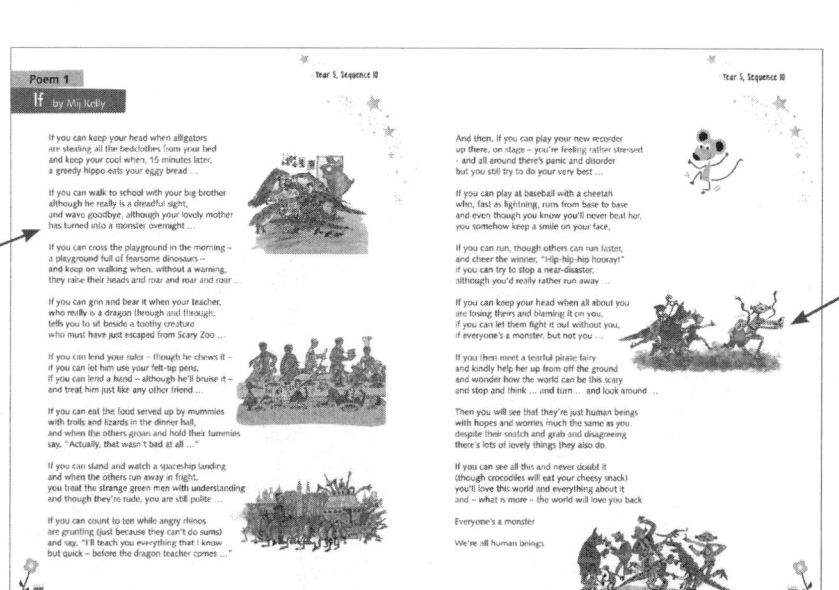

Beautiful illustrations engage children with the text.

About Treasure House

Treasure House Pupil Books

There are four Treasure House Pupil Books for each year group, based on the four dimensions of the National Curriculum for English: Comprehension; Composition; Vocabulary, Grammar and Punctuation; and Spelling.

Chart of Treasure House Pupil Books

Year	Comprehension	Composition	Vocabulary, Grammar and Punctuation	Spelling
1	978-0-00-813348-1	978-0-00-813354-2	978-0-00-813336-8	978-0-00-813342-9
2	978-0-00-813347-4	978-0-00-813353-5	978-0-00-813335-1	978-0-00-813341-2
3	978-0-00-813346-7	978-0-00-813352-8	978-0-00-813334-4	978-0-00-813340-5
4	978-0-00-813345-0	978-0-00-813351-1	978-0-00-813333-7	978-0-00-813339-9
5	978-0-00-813344-3	978-0-00-813350-4	978-0-00-813332-0	978-0-00-813338-2
6	978-0-00-813343-6	978-0-00-813349-8	978-0-00-813331-3	978-0-00-813337-5

About Treasure House

Inside Treasure House Print Pupil Books

Comprehension

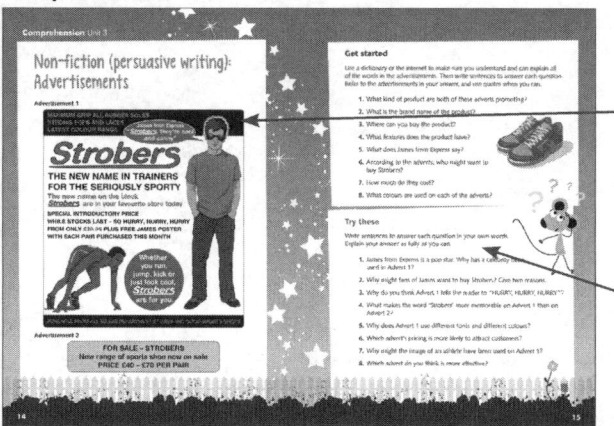

Includes high-quality, annotated text extracts covering poetry, prose, traditional tales, playscripts and non-fiction.

Pupils retrieve and record information, learn to draw inferences from texts and increase their familiarity with a wide range of literary genres.

Composition

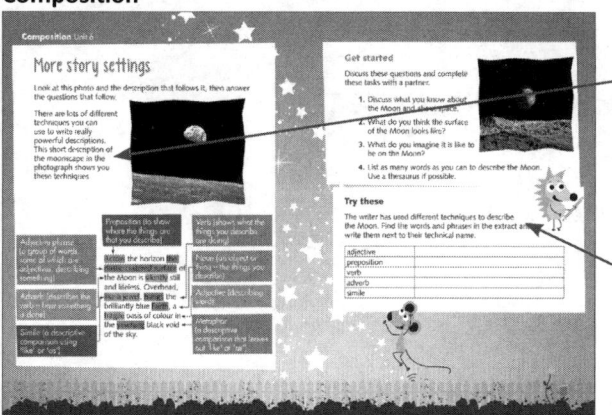

Includes high-quality, annotated text extracts as models for different types of writing.

Children learn how to write effectively and for a purpose.

Vocabulary, Grammar and Punctuation

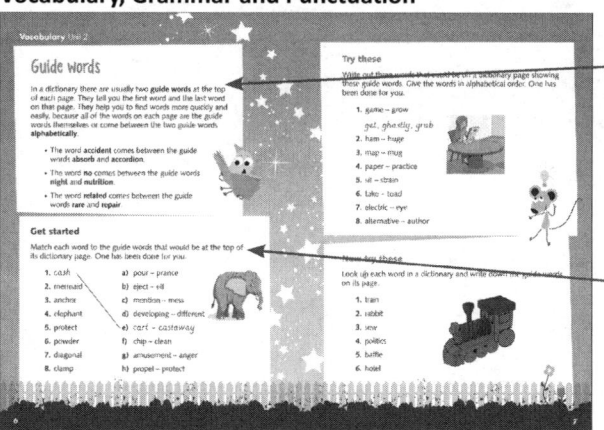

Develops children's knowledge and understanding of grammar and punctuation skills.

A rule is introduced and explained. Children are given lots of opportunities to practise using it.

Spelling

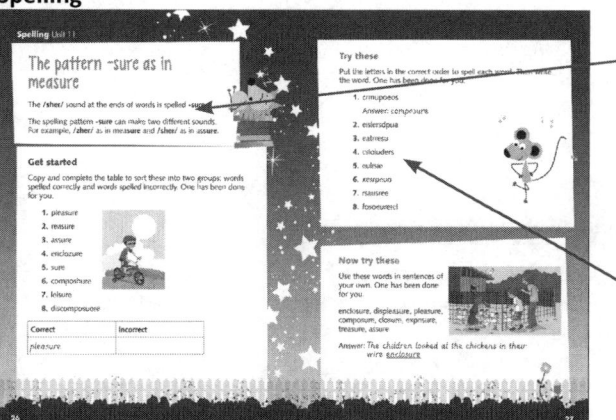

Spelling rules are introduced and explained.

Supports children to remember key spelling rules by investigating how they work.

About Treasure House

Treasure House Digital on Collins Connect

Digital pupil resources for Treasure House are available on Collins Connect, an innovative learning platform designed to support teachers and pupils by providing a wealth of interactive activities.

Treasure House is organised into six core areas on Collins Connect:

- Comprehension
- Composition
- Vocabulary, Grammar and Punctuation
- Spelling
- Reading Attic
- Teacher's Guides and Anthologies.

Features of Treasure House Digital on Collins Connect

Treasure House Digital enhances children's comprehension, composition, vocabulary, grammar and punctuation, and spelling skills through providing:

- a bank of varied and engaging interactive activities so children can practise their skills
- audio support to help children access the texts and activities
- auto-mark functionality so children receive instant feedback and have the opportunity to repeat tasks.

Digital Comprehension

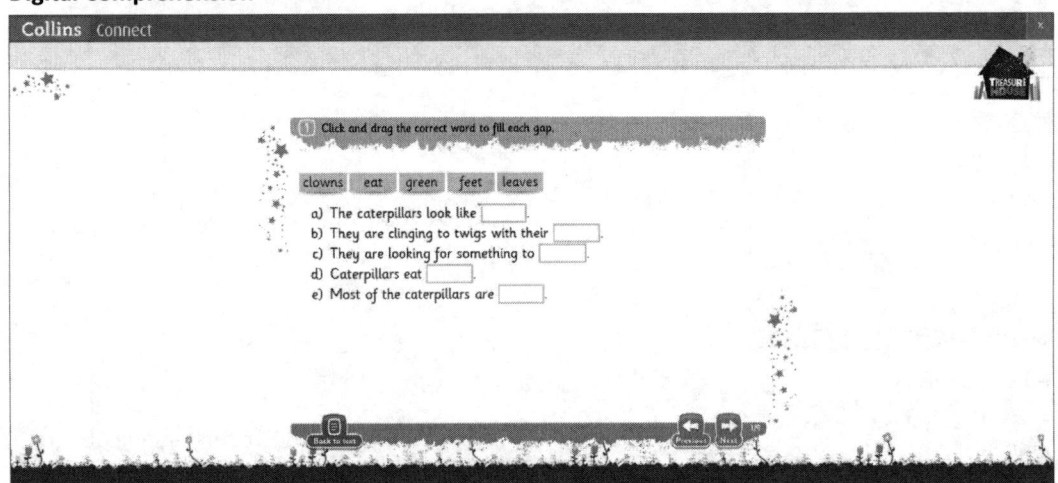

- Includes high-quality, annotated text extracts covering poetry, prose, traditional tales, playscripts and non-fiction.
- Audio function supports children to access the text and the activities.

Digital Composition

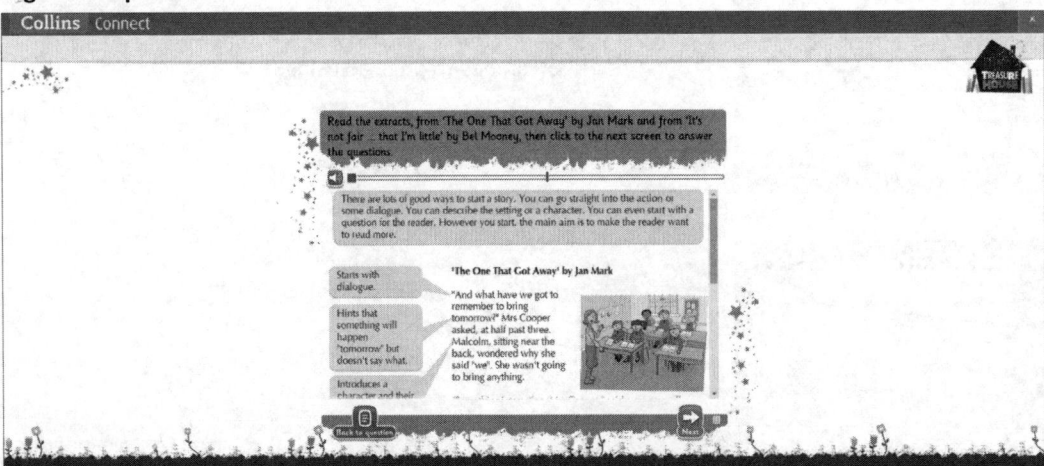

- Activities support children to develop and build more sophisticated sentence structures.
- Every unit ends with a longer piece of writing that can be submitted to the teacher for marking.

About Treasure House

Digital Vocabulary, Grammar and Punctuation

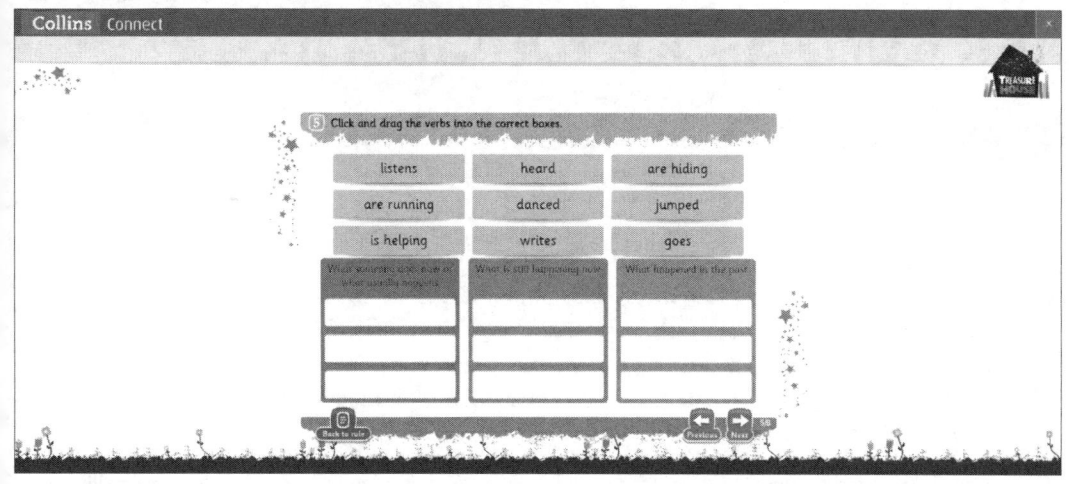

- Fun, practical activities develop children's knowledge and understanding of grammar and punctuation skills.
- Each skill is reinforced with a huge, varied bank of practice questions.

Digital Spelling

- Fun, practical activities develop children's knowledge and understanding of each spelling rule.
- Each rule is reinforced with a huge, varied bank of practice questions

Digital Reading Attic

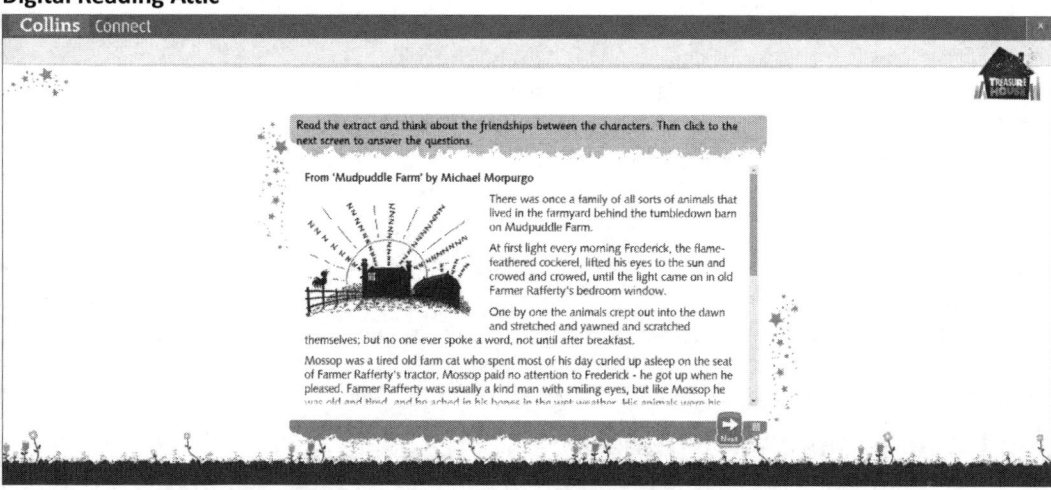

- Children's love of reading is nurtured with texts from the most exciting children's authors.
- Lesson sequences accompany the texts, with drama opportunities and creative strategies for engaging children with key themes, characters and plots.

Treasure House Digital Teacher's Guides and Anthologies
The teaching sequences and anthology texts for each year group are included as a flexible bank of resources on Collins Connect.

National Curriculum for English

The National Curriculum for English: An overview

Purpose and aims

The Treasure House Teacher Guides are designed not only to support teaching of the statutory programmes of study effectively but also as a response to the ethos of the National Curriculum for English. The overarching aim for English in the National Curriculum is to promote high standards of literacy by equipping pupils with a strong command of the written and spoken word, and to develop their love of literature through widespread reading for enjoyment. As the curriculum maintains, reading 'feeds pupils' imagination and opens up a treasure-house of wonder and joy for curious young minds'.

Treasure House encourages children to engage with a wide range of stories, poetry and non-fiction, to apply their literacy skills and develop their vocabulary and knowledge alongside their love of reading. In its study of these varied texts, it incorporates the four core dimensions of the National Curriculum for English:

- Comprehension
- Composition
- Vocabulary, Grammar and Punctuation
- Spelling.

Across these dimensions, it also provides thorough coverage of the underpinning principles and practices of literacy, from oracy and word reading to proofreading.

Spoken language

The National Curriculum states that spoken language is vital to the development of reading, writing and thinking: the quality and variety of language that pupils hear and speak are vital for developing their vocabulary and grammar, and their understanding for reading and writing. We have placed oracy at the heart of every sequence as we (like teachers everywhere) know that spoken language underpins the development of reading and writing. Each sequence, therefore, assists pupils to develop a capacity to explain their understanding of books and other reading, and to prepare their ideas, before they write. This assists them in making their thinking clear to themselves as well as to others.

Reading: Word reading

Alongside comprehension, the curriculum identifies the importance of speedy, accurate word reading. The development of speedy decoding of unfamiliar words and the rapid recognition of known words is utterly vital in every child's progression towards automatic word reading, and every opportunity across the curriculum must be seized to help children towards this goal. Treasure House includes phonics and word recognition in its 'Phonics and spelling' sessions in Phases 1 and 2, and its texts provide ample opportunity to implement the primary strategy for developing this fluency: one-to-one reading. Whole-class, shared reading of the source texts also benefits many children's development in this direction. At these points in the teaching sequences, you can use your knowledge of children's needs to emphasise particular word-reading skills. In the curriculum and in Treasure House, however, the goal of reading is making meaning from texts. Word reading supports comprehension; it is not an end goal independent of application.

Writing: Transcription (spelling and handwriting)

As the curriculum establishes, effective transcription enables composed ideas to flow onto a page in a manner that is legible to any reader.

The National Curriculum requires that children be taught to spell quickly and accurately, requiring phonics, knowledge of conventions and rules, and the learning and application of many words. For transcription, as for word reading, the development of speedy association between spoken and written words is vital. Treasure House includes phonics and word writing in its 'Phonics and

National Curriculum for English

spelling' sessions in Phases 1 and 2, which teach the statutorily required rules and patterns of the National Curriculum (see the core dimension of Spelling, below). Word transcription is furthermore necessary for every composition activity in Treasure House and, at these points in the teaching sequences, you can use your knowledge of children's requirements to emphasise particular word-writing skills as necessary.

Effective writing also requires fluent, legible and eventually speedy handwriting. Handwriting is a filter through which children's ideas must pass and a child with poor handwriting is at risk of achieving poor written outcomes, even if they have the best ideas in the room. Treasure House Teacher's Guides assume discrete teaching and practice of handwriting, as well as high expectations for application in children's own writing. We have not tried to define specific handwriting practices within the sequences, as each school has its own approach and policy designed best to suit the needs of their children. However, during the shared writing session of Phase 3 in each teaching sequence, expected handwriting styles may be modelled. Phase 4, in addition, provides the opportunity for children to edit and redraft their work: a second draft is a chance for a child to concentrate on their very best presentation, as their ideas have already been captured and organised.

The four core dimensions

Comprehension

The National Curriculum states: 'Comprehension skills develop through pupils' experience of high-quality discussion with the teacher, as well as from reading and discussing a range of stories, poems and non-fiction.' The comprehension teaching in Treasure House is built on questions that will stimulate children's ability to think more deeply, and enable dialogue necessary for them to explore meaning in both broader contexts and closer detail. High-quality questioning, as well as space for children to test their ideas about a text through discussion, is key to progressing children's comprehension skills. Phases 1 and 2 of the teaching sequences focus on developing these skills, and also identify appropriate points for drama, storytelling and oracy activities that will further develop children's grasp of the main and underlying ideas within and between texts.

Composition

As the National Curriculum states, composition is the generation, articulation and organisation of ideas in ways that are appropriate to different purposes and audiences. It is also deceptively complex. Some children appear to be natural writers, while others may struggle with ideas, organisation and/or the concept of an intended reader. However, all children have the potential to become effective writers. Imitation, even when unconsciously applied, is at the heart of learning to compose: children who can write stories also know stories. All children may be helped towards better writing if shown how to generate and organise ideas appropriately, for different purposes and audiences, and then how to transfer them successfully from plan to page.

Each Treasure House sequence builds towards children becoming competent writers. Phase 1 provides the inspiration and model for their eventual composition task, Phase 2 supports the generation and organisation of ideas and Phase 3 shows children how to apply vocabulary, grammar and punctuation skills to these ideas while composing collaboratively. In Phase 4, children demonstrate the composition skills they have accrued by planning, writing, redrafting and presenting or performing their own texts. They are encouraged to reflect on the effectiveness of their composition and compare it to the sequence's source texts in order to achieve the desired impact on their readers and learn from their choices for the future.

Vocabulary, Grammar and Punctuation

The Curriculum emphasises the use of Standard English, and growing mastery of grammar and punctuation in context. It also encourages the use of correct terminology for grammar and punctuation, enabling children and teachers to share a common language with which to talk about their reading and writing.

In Treasure House, stress is placed upon the applied use of grammar, rather than discrete grammatical exercises. National Curriculum objectives for vocabulary, grammar and punctuation are introduced in Phases 1 and 3, and woven into composition activities throughout Phase 3. In this way, children are able to implement their new knowledge immediately, and to see and discuss its effects of their writing. The suggested vocabulary, grammar and punctuation activities are not intended to constrain or restrict teachers' creativity: they can be changed or adapted to suit children's needs.

Spelling

Spelling, a priority in the National Curriculum, is a skill that many children find difficult. Ensuring that spelling is taught frequently, to all year groups, is essential. The Treasure House sequences cover all of the National Curriculum objectives, both from its

National Curriculum for English

programme of study and its spelling appendix (which are mainly on phonics, spelling patterns, and using prefixes and suffixes). The words on the word lists supplied for each year group in the curriculum, however, are not taught exhaustively. Encouraging the children to use these words in their own writing (perhaps with reference to these lists) will help to embed the vocabulary in their minds.

Treasure House suggests spelling activities in Phases 1 and 2, in discrete teaching sessions. Whilst we have found that grammar and punctuation is most effectively learnt when it is applied in writing in the very same lesson, we regard spelling as having a great deal in common with number bonds and times tables: it requires the frequency of regular 'starter' activities, and does not necessarily have a direct connection to the rest of the lesson. Seeing a particular word or spelling pattern in the model text is helpful, but it is not always possible in texts that have been chosen for their quality and relevance to young readers.

Because the spelling sessions are discrete, they can (like the vocabulary, grammar and punctuation sessions) be changed or adapted to suit children's needs. Each child's progress with spelling will be so variable that your knowledge of children's needs must take precedence, and will allow you to emphasise particular spelling skills as required. Personalised spelling strategies and learning targets, plus practice and application, are vital.

The flexibility inherent to Treasure House will allow you to customise your lessons to fit the needs of your class and your own teaching preferences. The goal of the Treasure House Teacher's Guides is to help you to help children become literate, literary and both confident and competent in English.

Using a Treasure House teaching sequence

This diagram reflects a literacy unit planning process that many schools use, and the process that we apply when supporting teachers with organising their literacy sequences. This is the route that every Treasure House teaching sequence follows.

The structure and content of a Treasure House sequence

Phase 1: Enjoy and immerse

- Firstly, choose a text that will both engage the class and provide the language style and overall structure that you want to see in the children's writing: this is 'the source text'. The source texts are prescribed for each Treasure House sequence, and are available in the anthology.
- Present the children with the 'Big Picture' from the outset: the reasons that they are looking at the source text, and the outcomes it will help them to achieve. The aim is that the children write texts in the style of the source text, but not usually on the same subject matter. Revealing this Big Picture early will help children to notice details that will help them to write their own texts in a similar style.
- Read the source text with the children, bringing it to life in ways that are appropriate to the purpose. The children should be given the chance to enjoy it and fully understand its purpose before they can truly appreciate how it works.
- After reading the text for enjoyment alone, discuss it, generating or researching ideas relating to its content, themes and/or genre. Explore the children's ideas using drama, storytelling and / or oracy activities.
- Help the children to expand their ideas further using incidental writing activities, which could include letters, diary entries, persuasive writing, character profiles or reviews. These are helpful for a range of reasons, including the consolidation of comprehension, the practice of writing in short bursts and the information available for formative assessment.
- Analyse the source text further, focusing on its style and structure and discussing *how* it achieves the effects it does.

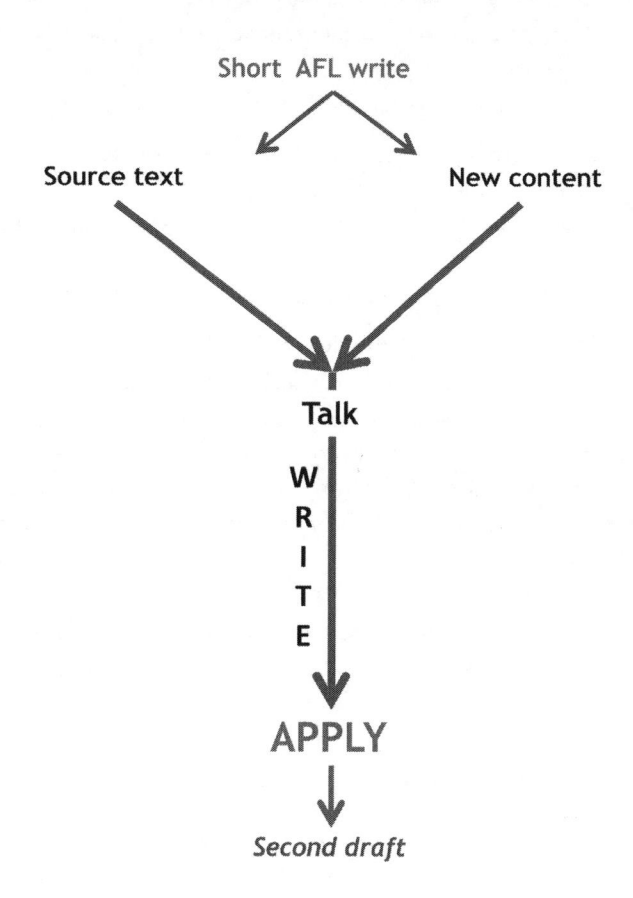

Phase 2: Capture and organise

- Remind the children of the Big Picture. This will help to keep them focused on the purpose of their task.
- Discuss ways in which the source text could be rewritten / used as inspiration for a class text. Ask probing questions of the children to assist them to think more deeply.
- Explore the children's ideas using drama, storytelling and / or oracy activities.
- Help the children to expand their ideas further using incidental writing activities.

Phase 3: Collaborate and compose

- Again, remind the children of the Big Picture. This will help to keep them focused on the purpose of their task.
- Teach the children to write, using their newly developed content and the style of the source text, one section at a time. Treasure House teaches vocabulary, grammar and punctuation (VGP) at this point of composition, as this allows for instant application: applied skills are much more likely to be remembered, and also improves the quality of the writing. Lessons in Phase 3 follow the same basic structure:

Using a Treasure House teaching sequence

- Teach a session on an appropriate VGP focus.
- Hold a shared writing session that models writing a section of the class text with reference to the source text, and demonstrates the VGP focus in context.
- Lead the children in an independent writing session, in which they compose their own versions of the modelled section of the class text, applying the VGP focus.
- Hold a plenary that allows children to discuss and assess their own and peers' writing.

* This structure is repeated, in Treasure House, over four lessons (but can, of course, be reduced or extended to suit the complexity of the composition task).
* Encourage the children to rehearse and present or perform their texts to their peers.

Phase 4: Write independently

* Again, remind the children of the Big Picture. This will help to keep them focused on the purpose of their task.
* Having completed the class text, and their own guided texts, the children must then be given the opportunity to apply everything that they have learnt, to plan and write an independent piece of their own, in a similar style. This is a chance for children to combine their literacy skills with their creative thinking. The resulting work may be viewed as an assessment piece: it will tell you what the children have learnt from the unit and the current quality of their writing. However, this aspect should not be emphasised to the children: rather, they should be encouraged to enjoy showing what they can do, and to make their texts their own.
* Give opportunities for editing and redrafting, in order that children work towards the best possible versions or their work they are able to achieve. Then allow the children to assess their own and each other's work using guiding questions.
* Encourage the children to rehearse and present or perform their texts to their peers, and then feedback on one another's work.

The duration of a sequence

To enable you to plan ahead and make decisions about the structure of literacy teaching over the term, a time-frame is suggested at the outset of each sequence. These time-frames are, however, only guidelines: each class will require different amounts of time at each phase, dependent on their particular needs and prior experiences. The only Treasure House phase that specifies a particular number of lessons is the third, as it focuses on the step-by-step teaching of vocabulary, grammar and punctuation applied to different sections of the class text. Even here, we encourage flexibility and adaptation according to need: if a class has experienced and / or composed text in a particular form already, fewer days of teaching may be required before the independence of Phase 4. On the other hand, if a class struggles with a particular concept, skill or style, the reverse may be true.

Differentiation in Treasure House

The Treasure House teaching sequences are structured around the principles of growth mindset, so every effort is made to avoid rigid methods of differentiation.

When differentiated activities are used as the default model of differentiation, it tends to place a ceiling on those identified as 'low ability', ensuring their abilities stay low. Treasure House Teacher's Guides adopt the high-ceiling, low-threshold approach to differentiation, enabling all children to access achievement: everyone can access the learning, but it can also be taken to very high levels. In every dimension of Treasure House, it is important that children master the threshold skills before considering acceleration.

Comprehension

In reading, all children should cross the threshold of reading the Treasure House source texts; however, the depth of their analysis and understanding will vary depending on prior experience, current interests and motivation. Some struggling readers have poor word-reading skills but sound comprehension; if they are always presented with simplified text, their comprehension, and enjoyment, is held back.

Where word reading interferes with comprehension, several tried-and-tested strategies can enable access:

- pre-teaching of concepts or vocabulary
- hearing the text read aloud
- paired reading
- use of visual prompts and dramatisations.

Once a source text has been read, all children can be encouraged to achieve their potential through open questions that pursue the children's own lines of enquiry: much of the teaching in Treasure House is built on questions that stimulate children's ability to think more deeply and enable dialogue. Again, formative assessment is crucial: effective starting-point questions have been provided, but subsequent questions depend entirely upon the children's responses. For example, children are working above age-related expectations may be given the challenge of making increasingly detailed comparisons between the main and extra source texts.

Composition and vocabulary, grammar and punctuation

All teaching of composition and vocabulary, grammar and punctuation should begin with the threshold of composing a simple sentence: all children should be assisted to master this skill and practise it often, to the point of automaticity. Where transcription interferes with composition, allocate extra handwriting practice rather than simplified composition activities: the expectation in Treasure House sequences is that children try to apply their newly acquired composition and vocabulary, grammar and punctuation skills to the best of their ability in their writing.

Levels of ability may then be differentiated through the complexity of changes and/or additions to the sentence, to achieve particular effects. For example, where children are working above age-related expectations, they may be asked to write from a different perspective or to manipulate the vocabulary, grammar and punctuation focus to create a particular effect on readers.

Spelling

Within spelling, all children must cross the threshold of learning new words, rules and patterns. The differentiation within this dimension of the Treasure House sequences should be focused upon application: for example, testing the rule on different root words and ensuring correct application in different writing contexts.

As each child's progress with spelling will be so variable, children should also be prompted to identify recurring personal spelling errors, with support as necessary, and to correct these in their writing during Phases 3 and 4. Where children require additional work on specific skills, Treasure House pupil books can provide additional independent consolidation.

Further ideas

For more ideas on providing access and challenge in Treasure House literacy sessions, please see Accessing achievement strategies.

Accessing achievement strategies

Strategy	Example
Differentiation within the task	- Must – Should – Could: Ensure all children achieve the basic requirement, but then go on to the best of their ability (a simple way of achieving a low-threshold, high-ceiling approach). - Changing targets: Set different success criteria (for example, writing from different viewpoints). - HOT: Prompt children to apply HOT (higher-order thinking) strategies to the main task (for example, extended analysis, comparison, creation of something new, design, investigation, organisation, summarisation or evaluation). - Use and apply: Vary the context of a task (such as describing a game) from familiar to fantastical. - Varied support: Provide varying degrees of support, from full scaffolding to complete independence.
Differentiation through flexible lesson structures	- Cut-aways: Allow the most able children less 'carpet time', starting them working independently but then giving them additional teaching part-way through the lesson. - Timed tasks: Give children varied lengths of time to complete tasks. - Waiting time: Wait a certain amount of time for others to respond before asking more able children for their responses to questions. - Time for review: Have children perform self- and peer evaluation.
Differentiation through choice	- Success selections: Have children self-select their success criteria - Pupil planning: Involve children in the planning process (for example, formatting writing outcomes). - Self-testing: Allow children to devise their own challenges or investigations (such as regarding spelling rules or choosing a research focus).
Differentiation through resourcing	- Vary task prompts to challenge children's responses. - Vary pictures or artefacts to provide more stimulation. - Provide more or fewer supporting resources. - Provide additional texts for comparison. - Provide ICT resources.
Differentiation through method of recording	- Assess learning through spoken responses. - Assess learning through written responses. - Use ICT for assessment (for example, dictation software). - Use graphic organisers to assist children with structural planning. - Use varied levels of formality for reports (oral or written). - Allow children their own choice of recording method.
Access through flexibility in groupings	- Vary the layout of the classroom and the location of resources. - Use guided learning groups or focus groups. - Create different near-ability and mixed-ability pairs, trios and small groups.
Access through pupils as experts	- Form reading, writing and/or response partnerships. - Ask children to think–pair–share ideas. - Allocate roles during group composition (such as spokesperson, scribe and director). - Create peer mentors. - Have children assist others using role-play (such as 'Ask the Expert' or hot seating). - Encourage self- and peer assessment.
Differentiation through questioning and dialogue	- Intervene by questioning, prompting and probing children. - Have sustained dialogues, discussions or debates with children. - Use higher-order questioning. - Have the children ask you questions. - Avoid giving answers that do the work for children.
Differentiated feedback	- Make developmental comments. - Give marks related (only) to children's next steps and targets. - Pose follow-up questions to move children's thinking onwards.

Assessment in Treasure House

Effective teaching is dependent on the assessment cycle delineated by the following questions.

- What can children already do?
- What do they need to learn?
- How is this best taught?
- What can they now do?

This cycle, although it should remain structured and led by the teacher, is most effective when children themselves understand and take an active part in the process. It is always important to keep in mind that, whether or not lesson objectives and intended learning outcomes have been met, children must always tackle their high-frequency errors, no matter how seemingly small. These errors will always hold children back even if, for example, they are mastering fronted adverbials and subordination.

The Treasure House sequences are designed to provide multiple opportunities for this ongoing system of formative assessment by making children's learning visible both to you and to them. By making learning visible, you can respond immediately to misconceptions and breakthroughs, capitalising on every opportunity for formative assessment, phase by phase. This information will help you to plan the course the current sequence should take and to appreciate what may be the most helpful topic for the next sequence.

Visible learning may be achieved through various incidental assessment opportunities (for example, use of mini-whiteboards to display knowledge) and is also attainable through numerous opportunities that are present in every Treasure House sequence.

Diagnostic assessment

Each sequence begins with prior knowledge and diagnostic assessment options that will guide both the starting point of the sequence and the necessary learning focuses as it progresses. You may undertake checks to explore children's current knowledge and understanding about the genre, form and wider context of the source text the text form, as well as the literacy skills to be studied, by engaging the children in discussions, quizzes and short writing activities. You may wish to alter spelling focuses or the sequence's schedule based on this feedback.

Open questions and discussion

In addition, each sequence contains guideline open questions as an integral feature of every phase. In Phase 1, these are comprehension focused; in Phase 2, they support idea generation and organisation; in Phase 3, the focus is on effective application of skills in writing; and in Phase 4 they require reflection and evaluation of independent writing outcomes. In each case, these questions are designed to open up discussion and provoke collaborative thinking; here, children's responses will provide further assessment information useful for tackling any misconceptions and informing the extent to which you adapt the suggested content of the sequence.

Drama, storytelling and performance

Children are encouraged to complete drama, storytelling and/or oracy activities in Phases 1 and 2, engaging with characters in role and with different forms of expression (such as TV news items and puppet shows). Children's responses to these activities will inform your understanding of their deeper appreciation of the content of the source texts and their own compositions, and your plans for when to move on to the next phase. The performance activities suggested at the ends of Phases 3 and 4 will also assist the children's self- and peer-assessment of their work.

Incidental writing

The incidental writing opportunities in Phases 1 and 2 will provide a wealth of information on each child's writing abilities, which can be used to alter the focus of the vocabulary, grammar and punctuation teaching within Phase 3 (the focus suggestions should never take precedent over your knowledge of the children's needs). Additionally, the incidental writing will tell you much

Assessment in Treasure House

about children's broader knowledge and competencies in the relevant text form(s), and this may be used to guide your selection of the next sequence once the current one is completed.

Independent composition

All of the Treasure House sequences, at Phases 3 and 4, result in independent compositions (potentially in more than one draft form). These enable assessment of writing and easy appreciation of the progress a child has made over the course of the Treasure House programme. These compositions may also inform your selection of the next sequence(s), and demonstrate the next steps required to progress children's spelling, grammar and vocabulary.

Preparation for summative assessment

The Treasure House sequences will help children to prepare for summative assessments against all of the National Curriculum English programmes of study by providing structured and contextualised understanding of all of the statutory requirements for learning.

Progression in Treasure House

Progression of source texts

The Treasure House source texts have been very carefully selected in order to stimulate and challenge children in an age-appropriate way, in relation to both their subject matter and their vocabulary choices. All titles have been assigned to year groups based on our pooled experience of what works well for a particular age range and, in some cases, on the age grades already allocated by the excellent Big Cat series from which some titles have been taken. They between those that children should be able to read themselves and more challenging texts that are intended to be explored as a whole class. The National Curriculum requires that children experience both, immersing themselves high-quality literature that is read to them as well as accessing texts independently. How children interact with the source texts is a decision to be informed by your assessment of your class's abilities and requirements.

Progression between year groups

For each year group, each Treasure House Teacher's Guide addresses the programmes of study for all four core dimensions of the National Curriculum for English:

- Comprehension
- Composition
- Vocabulary, Grammar and Punctuation
- Spelling.

In this way, Treasure House is built on the year-by-year progression required by the National Curriculum.

Progression between Key Stages

The English programmes of study are the same for Years 3 and 4 (Lower Key Stage 2) and for Years 5 and 6 (Upper Key Stage 2). We believe that, rather than dividing the statutory requirements between the year groups, it is more effective to teach the entire range of skills to each year group, revisiting skills in Years 4 and 6 to deepen children's understanding by applying them to more challenging texts.

Formative and summative assessments must inform such decisions, though, and you may wish not to revisit certain skills if they have been thoroughly understood by every child. The National Curriculum suggests that teachers should use the programmes of study with some flexibility, as required, so long as all required objectives are achieved by the end of each key stage. This is also our recommendation when using Treasure House: to use formative assessment to repeat of omit practice of skill sets as required.

Progression within year groups

In order to allow for as much flexibility as possible, we have purposely avoided building in a rigid progression between sequences in a given year. This will allow you better to fit the sequences into your school teaching plan, and to make cross-curricular links wherever relevant.

However, we have assigned programmes of study to particular texts so that these are met in context and them applied appropriately. Again, pace and progression within a year must be informed by formative and summative assessments, and you may wish to alter either the order of the sequences or the individual learning objectives within sequences to suit your class's requirements.

Comprehension and composition

Treasure House supports children's progression in reading comprehension within a year group by recommending a wide range of open questions, oracy and drama activities carefully composed to develop their grasp of the age-specific programmes of study. Although sequences can be taught in any order, the children's developing responses to open questions and activities will

Progression in Treasure House

prompt deeper, more complex and more inferential appreciation and adaptation of the texts, as well as more mature appreciation of linguistic and stylistic choices, as more sequences from one year group are completed.

Vocabulary, grammar and punctuation and spelling

The Treasure House progression in vocabulary, grammar and punctuation, and in spelling, within a year group is similarly adaptable, allowing children to progress in their application of the skills learned and to appreciate their effects on readers to a greater extent.

Sequence overview chart

Sequence number and heading	Anthology texts	Approximate duration
1. Fiction: Creating tensions	'The Snow Globe', in *Beyond the Stars* by Marita Conlon-McKenna *Tom's Midnight Garden* by Philippa Pearce *Trouble Half-Way* by Jan Marks	2 weeks
2. Fiction: Traditional stories	'The Discontented Fish', a Senegalese folk story 'The Tortoise and the Eagle', based on an Aesop fable	2 weeks
3. Non-fiction: Persuasive writing	Laughter Land	2 weeks
4. Non-fiction: Email conventions	'Climate Change, What Climate Change?' *Global Warming* by Seymour Simon *Fragile Earth* by Claire Llewellyn	2 weeks
5. Poetry: Free verse	'Shut Your Mouth' by Michael Rosen 'Crack-a-Dawn' by Brian Morse	2 weeks
6. Poetry: Descriptive techniques	'Hiawatha's Childhood' by H.W. Longfellow 'Hiawatha's Fishing' by H.W. Longfellow	2 weeks
7. Poetry: Narrative techniques	'The Listeners' by Walter de la Mare 'The Highwayman' by Alfred Noyes	2 weeks
8. Non-fiction: Journalism	'Warning: Oil Supplies are Running out Fast' by Steve Connor 'Save It!' by the Environment Correspondent	2 weeks
9. Non-fiction: Reports	*The Heart* by Seymour Simon 'Deserts'	2 weeks
10. Fiction: Contrasting perspectives	'Winter Morning' by Ogden Nash 'Christmas Landscape' by Laurie Lee 'Snow and Snow' by Ted Hughes	2 weeks
11. Fiction: Creating atmosphere	*Nightmare in Two Ghostly Tales* by Berlie Doherty *The Phantom Tollbooth* by Norton Juster *Alice in Wonderland* by Lewis Carroll	2 weeks
12. Fiction: Plotting problems	*The Railway Children* by E. Nesbit	2 weeks
13. Fiction: Alternative perspectives	*Gulliver's Travels* by Jonathan Swift	2 weeks
14. Fiction: Comparing forms	'Macbeth' edited by Roma Gill *Macbeth* by John Mayhew and Adrian Stone 'Compere Lapin and Compere Tig', a St Lucian folk story	2 weeks
15. Non-fiction: Biographies	*Virginia Hall WWII Spy* by Adrian Bradbury *Wild Swans* by Jung Chang	2 weeks

Curriculum map

Reading – comprehension	Sequence 1 Fiction: Creating tensions	Sequence 2 Fiction: Traditional stories	Sequence 3 Non-fiction: Persuasive writing	Sequence 4 Non-fiction: Email conventions	Sequence 5 Poetry: Free verse	Sequence 6 Poetry: Descriptive techniques	Sequence 7 Poetry: Narrative techniques	Sequence 8 Non-fiction: Journalism	Sequence 9 Non-fiction: Reports	Sequence 10 Poetry: Contrasting perspectives	Sequence 11 Fiction: Creating atmosphere	Sequence 12 Fiction: Plotting problems	Sequence 13 Fiction: Alternative perspectives	Sequence 14 Fiction: Comparing forms	Sequence 15 Non-fiction: Biographies
Continue to read and discuss an increasingly wide range of fiction, poetry, plays, non-fiction and reference books or textbooks.	✓	✓	✓	✓	✓	✓	✓	✓	✓	✓	✓	✓	✓	✓	✓
Read books that are structured in different ways and read for a range of purposes.		✓	✓	✓	✓	✓	✓	✓	✓	✓	✓	✓	✓	✓	✓
Increase their familiarity with a wide range of books, including myths, legends and traditional stories, modern fiction, fiction from our literary heritage, and books from other cultures and traditions.	✓	✓					✓								✓
Recommend books that they have read to their peers, giving reasons for their choices.	Cover this objective by allowing children to read and review books of their own choosing for homework.														
Identify and discuss themes and conventions in and across a wide range of writing.	✓	✓	✓	✓	✓	✓	✓	✓	✓	✓	✓	✓	✓	✓	✓
Make comparisons within and across books.	✓	✓	✓	✓	✓	✓	✓	✓	✓	✓	✓	✓	✓	✓	✓
Learn a wider range of poetry by heart.					✓	✓	✓			✓					
Prepare poems and plays to read aloud and to perform, showing understanding through intonation, tone and volume so that the meaning is clear to an audience.				✓	✓	✓	✓	✓			✓	✓			
Check that the book makes sense to them, discussing their understanding and exploring the meaning of words in context.	✓	✓	✓	✓	✓	✓	✓	✓	✓	✓	✓	✓	✓	✓	✓
Ask questions to improve their understanding.	✓	✓	✓	✓	✓	✓	✓	✓	✓	✓	✓	✓	✓	✓	✓
Draw inferences such as inferring characters' feelings, thoughts and motives from their actions, and justifying inferences with evidence.	✓	✓				✓	✓			✓	✓	✓	✓	✓	
Predict what might happen from details stated and implied.	✓											✓	✓	✓	

Curriculum map

Reading – comprehension [continued]

Objective	Seq 1: Fiction: Creating tensions	Seq 2: Fiction: Traditional stories	Seq 3: Non-fiction: Persuasive writing	Seq 4: Non-fiction: Email conventions	Seq 5: Poetry: Free verse	Seq 6: Poetry: Descriptive techniques	Seq 7: Poetry: Narrative techniques	Seq 8: Non-fiction: Journalism	Seq 9: Non-fiction: Reports	Seq 10: Poetry: Contrasting perspectives	Seq 11: Fiction: Creating atmosphere	Seq 12: Fiction: Plotting problems	Seq 13: Fiction: Alternative perspectives	Seq 14: Fiction: Comparing forms	Seq 15: Non-fiction: Biographies
Summarise the main ideas drawn from more than one paragraph, identifying key details that support the main ideas.			✓	✓				✓	✓	✓				✓	✓
Identify how language, structure and presentation contribute to meaning.	✓	✓	✓	✓	✓	✓	✓	✓	✓	✓	✓			✓	✓
Discuss and evaluate how authors use language, including figurative language, considering the impact on the reader.	✓	✓	✓	✓	✓	✓	✓	✓	✓	✓	✓	✓	✓		✓
Distinguish between statements of fact and opinion.			✓	✓				✓	✓						✓
Retrieve, record and present information from non-fiction.	✓		✓	✓				✓	✓						✓
Participate in discussions about books that are read to them and those they can read for themselves, building on their own and others' ideas and challenging views courteously.	✓	✓	✓	✓	✓	✓	✓	✓	✓	✓	✓	✓	✓	✓	✓
Explain and discuss their understanding of what they have read, including through formal presentations and debates, maintaining a focus on the topic and using notes where necessary.	✓	✓	✓	✓	✓	✓	✓	✓	✓	✓	✓	✓	✓	✓	✓
Provide reasoned justifications for their views.	✓	✓	✓	✓	✓	✓	✓	✓	✓	✓	✓	✓	✓	✓	✓

Curriculum map

Writing – transcription	Sequence 1 Fiction: Creating tensions	Sequence 2 Fiction: Traditional stories	Sequence 3 Non-fiction: Persuasive writing	Sequence 4 Non-fiction: Email conventions	Sequence 5 Poetry: Free verse	Sequence 6 Poetry: Descriptive techniques	Sequence 7 Poetry: Narrative techniques	Sequence 8 Non-fiction: Journalism	Sequence 9 Non-fiction: Reports	Sequence 10 Poetry: Contrasting perspectives	Sequence 11 Fiction: Creating atmosphere	Sequence 12 Fiction: Plotting problems	Sequence 13 Fiction: Alternative perspectives	Sequence 14 Fiction: Comparing forms	Sequence 15 Non-fiction: Biographies
Use further prefixes and suffixes and understand the guidance for adding them.	✓	✓	✓	✓	✓					✓			✓	✓	✓
Spell some words with 'silent' letters.				✓						✓					
Continue to distinguish between homophones and other words which are often confused.					✓	✓	✓				✓				✓
Use knowledge of morphology and etymology in spelling and understand that the spelling of some words needs to be learnt specifically, as listed in English Appendix 1.	✓	✓	✓	✓	✓	✓	✓	✓	✓	✓	✓	✓	✓	✓	✓
Use dictionaries to check the spelling and meaning of words.	✓	✓	✓	✓	✓	✓	✓	✓	✓	✓	✓	✓	✓	✓	✓
Use the first three or four letters of a word to check spelling, meaning or both of these in a dictionary.	✓	✓									✓	✓	✓	✓	✓
Use a thesaurus.	✓				✓						✓		✓		

Curriculum map

Writing – composition

Objective	Seq 1: Fiction: Creating tensions	Seq 2: Fiction: Traditional stories	Seq 3: Non-fiction: Persuasive writing	Seq 4: Non-fiction: Email conventions	Seq 5: Poetry: Free verse	Seq 6: Poetry: Descriptive techniques	Seq 7: Poetry: Narrative techniques	Seq 8: Non-fiction: Journalism	Seq 9: Non-fiction: Reports	Seq 10: Poetry: Contrasting perspectives	Seq 11: Fiction: Creating atmosphere	Seq 12: Fiction: Plotting problems	Seq 13: Fiction: Alternative perspectives	Seq 14: Fiction: Comparing forms	Seq 15: Non-fiction: Biographies
Identify the audience for and purpose of the writing, selecting the appropriate form and using other similar writing as models for their own.	✓	✓	✓	✓	✓	✓	✓	✓	✓	✓	✓	✓	✓	✓	✓
Note and develop initial ideas, drawing on reading and research where necessary.	✓	✓	✓	✓	✓	✓	✓	✓	✓	✓	✓	✓	✓	✓	✓
In writing narratives, consider how authors have developed characters and settings in what pupils have read, listened to or seen performed.	✓	✓					✓					✓	✓	✓	
Select appropriate grammar and vocabulary, understanding how such choices can change and enhance meaning.	✓	✓	✓	✓	✓	✓	✓	✓		✓	✓	✓	✓	✓	✓
In narratives, describe settings, characters and atmosphere and integrate dialogue to convey character and advance the action.	✓	✓					✓				✓	✓	✓		
Précis longer passages.	✓	✓					✓								
Use a wide range of devices to build cohesion within and across paragraphs.	✓	✓	✓	✓	✓	✓		✓	✓	✓	✓	✓	✓	✓	✓
Use further organisational and presentational devices to structure text and to guide the reader.	✓	✓	✓	✓	✓	✓	✓	✓	✓	✓	✓	✓	✓	✓	✓
Assess the effectiveness of their own and others' writing.	✓	✓	✓	✓	✓	✓	✓	✓	✓	✓	✓	✓	✓	✓	✓
Propose changes to vocabulary, grammar and punctuation to enhance effects and clarify meaning.	✓	✓	✓	✓	✓	✓	✓	✓	✓	✓	✓	✓	✓	✓	✓
Ensure the consistent and correct use of tense throughout a piece of writing.	✓	✓	✓	✓	✓	✓	✓	✓	✓	✓	✓	✓	✓	✓	✓
Ensure correct subject and verb agreement when using singular and plural, distinguishing between the language of speech and writing and choosing the appropriate register.	✓	✓	✓	✓	✓	✓	✓	✓	✓	✓	✓	✓	✓	✓	✓
Proof-read for spelling and punctuation errors.	✓	✓	✓	✓	✓	✓	✓	✓	✓	✓	✓	✓	✓	✓	✓
Perform their own compositions, using appropriate intonation, volume, and movement so that meaning is clear.	✓	✓	✓	✓	✓	✓	✓	✓	✓	✓	✓	✓	✓	✓	✓

Curriculum map

Writing – vocabulary, grammar and punctuation	Sequence 1 Fiction: Creating tensions	Sequence 2 Fiction: Traditional stories	Sequence 3 Non-fiction: Persuasive writing	Sequence 4 Non-fiction: Email conventions	Sequence 5 Poetry: Free verse	Sequence 6 Poetry: Descriptive techniques	Sequence 7 Poetry: Narrative techniques	Sequence 8 Non-fiction: Journalism	Sequence 9 Non-fiction: Reports	Sequence 10 Poetry: Contrasting perspectives	Sequence 11 Fiction: Creating atmosphere	Sequence 12 Fiction: Plotting problems	Sequence 13 Fiction: Alternative perspectives	Sequence 14 Fiction: Comparing forms	Sequence 15 Non-fiction: Biographies
Recognise vocabulary and structures that are appropriate for formal speech and writing, including subjunctive forms.		✓		✓	✓			✓	✓						
Use passive verbs to affect the presentation of information in a sentence.		✓						✓	✓		✓		✓		✓
Use the perfect form of verbs to mark relationships of time and cause.							✓						✓		
Use expanded noun phrases to convey complicated information concisely.						✓				✓		✓			
Use modal verbs or adverbs to indicate degrees of possibility.	✓	✓		✓	✓										
Use relative clauses beginning with who, which, where, when, whose, that or with an implied (i.e. omitted) relative pronoun.	✓	✓	✓	✓	✓	✓		✓	✓	✓	✓	✓	✓		✓
Learn the grammar for years 5 and 6 in English Appendix 2.	✓	✓	✓			✓		✓	✓		✓	✓	✓		✓
Use commas to clarify meaning or avoid ambiguity in writing.	✓							✓							
Use hyphens to avoid ambiguity.			✓							✓		✓			
Use brackets, dashes or commas to indicate parenthesis.											✓	✓			
Use semi-colons, colons or dashes to mark boundaries between independent clauses.								✓							✓
Use a colon to introduce a list.										✓					
Punctuate bullet points consistently.			✓												
Use and understand the grammatical terminology in English Appendix 2 accurately and appropriately in discussing their writing and reading.	✓	✓	✓	✓	✓	✓	✓	✓	✓	✓	✓	✓	✓	✓	✓

Curriculum map

English Appendix 1: Spelling

	Sequence 1 Fiction: Creating tensions	Sequence 2 Fiction: Traditional stories	Sequence 3 Non-fiction: Persuasive writing	Sequence 4 Non-fiction: Email conventions	Sequence 5 Poetry: Free verse	Sequence 6 Poetry: Descriptive techniques	Sequence 7 Poetry: Narrative techniques	Sequence 8 Non-fiction: Journalism	Sequence 9 Non-fiction: Reports	Sequence 10 Poetry: Contrasting perspectives	Sequence 11 Fiction: Creating atmosphere	Sequence 12 Fiction: Plotting problems	Sequence 13 Fiction: Alternative perspectives	Sequence 14 Fiction: Comparing forms	Sequence 15 Non-fiction: Biographies
Use words with endings which sound like /ʃəs/ spelt -cious or -tious.		✓											✓		
Use words with endings which sound like /ʃəl/.		✓													✓
Use words ending in -ant, -ance / -ancy, -ent, -ence / -ency.	✓		✓	✓	✓					✓				✓	
Use words ending in -able and -ible.	✓		✓	✓	✓										
Use words ending in -ably and -ibly.	✓														
Add suffixes beginning with vowel letters to words ending in -fer.			✓												
Use the hyphen [to join a prefix to a root word].						✓									
Use words with the /iː/ sound spelt ei after c.									✓						
Use words containing the letter-string ough.					✓		✓			✓	✓	✓			
Use words with 'silent' letters.											✓				
Use homophones and other words that are often confused.															✓

Curriculum map

English Appendix 2: Vocabulary, grammar and punctuation

Objective	Seq 1: Fiction: Creating tensions	Seq 2: Fiction: Traditional stories	Seq 3: Non-fiction: Persuasive writing	Seq 4: Non-fiction: Email conventions	Seq 5: Poetry: Free verse	Seq 6: Poetry: Descriptive techniques	Seq 7: Poetry: Narrative techniques	Seq 8: Non-fiction: Journalism	Seq 9: Non-fiction: Reports	Seq 10: Poetry: Contrasting perspectives	Seq 11: Fiction: Creating atmosphere	Seq 12: Fiction: Plotting problems	Seq 13: Fiction: Alternative perspectives	Seq 14: Fiction: Comparing forms	Seq 15: Non-fiction: Biographies
Understand the difference between vocabulary typical of informal speech and vocabulary appropriate for formal speech and writing.		✓		✓	✓			✓	✓						
Understand how words are related by meaning as synonyms and antonyms.		✓			✓										✓
Use the passive to affect the presentation of information in a sentence.		✓		✓	✓			✓	✓				✓		✓
Understand the difference between structures typical of informal speech and structures appropriate for formal speech and writing.		✓	✓												
Link ideas across paragraphs using a wider range of cohesive devices: repetition of a word or phrase, grammatical connections and ellipsis.								✓	✓						
Use layout devices.			✓												
Use the semi-colon, colon and dash to mark the boundary between independent clauses.	✓										✓	✓			✓
Use the colon to introduce a list and use semi-colons within lists.										✓					
Punctuate bullet points to list information.						✓		✓	✓						
Understand how hyphens can be used to avoid ambiguity.															

30

Year 6, Sequence 1
Fiction: Creating tensions

Sequence 1
Fiction: Creating tensions

Approximate duration: Two weeks

Big Picture

Through this teaching sequence, children will explore the way in which authors can create an atmosphere of tension between characters in a text, particularly through the characters' dialogue. Understanding the techniques used by real authors will help children to use these techniques within their own narrative writing. Children will be able to write text that has an impact on readers' responses.

Phase 1: Enjoy and immerse

Children analyse the tension portrayed in the opening scene from the model text, *Tom's Midnight Garden*.

Phase 2: Capture and organise

Children begin to develop ideas for creating their own scene containing tension between characters.

Phase 3: Collaborate and compose

Children undertake supported writing sessions to develop the writing features of their tension scene.

Phase 4: Write independently

Children write, edit and present their own narrative scenes showing tension between characters, using dialogue.

Main source text

Treasure House Anthology Sequence 1 text. *Tom's Midnight Garden*, Philippa Pearce, ISBN 978-0-19-279242-6, pp.1–3

Extra source texts

Treasure House Online, Year 6, Comprehension Unit 1: Fiction: 'Trouble Half-Way'

The Snow Globe, Marita Conlon-McKenna, ISBN 978-0-00-810337-8, pp.167–176

Background knowledge

Tom's Midnight Garden is a low fantasy children's novel first published in 1958. The plot focuses on Tom, a modern boy, living under quarantine with his aunt and uncle in a 1950s city apartment building that was a country house during the 1880s–1890s. At night, he sneaks into the garden where he meets a playmate from the past. In the extract used in this teaching sequence, Tom and his mother say goodbye to one another as she sends Tom to stay with his relatives. Tom is clearly unhappy about the situation and the atmosphere of tension is successfully portrayed through the characters' dialogue.

Spoken outcome

To perform a tense domestic scene to an audience of peers or parents

Writing outcome

To create a piece of narrative writing depicting a domestic scene that portrays an atmosphere of tension through the dialogue between family members

Prior knowledge

Check children's knowledge and understanding of:
- atmosphere and tension
- dialogue.

Diagnostic assessment options

- Before starting the sequence, you may want to conduct an initial diagnostic assessment of the children's understanding of the typical characteristics of a dialogue that portrays tension.

Year 6, Sequence 1
Fiction: Creating tensions

Ideas for initial diagnostic assessment options include:

- discussion about the meaning of tension and associated feelings and causes
- a brief, unsupported writing activity creating a short dialogue showing tension between two characters
- practising speaking and listening skills relating to a tension dialogue
- a short reading comprehension activity / quiz on a tension dialogue text.

Cross-curricular links

KS2 PSHE – Relationships

Treasure House links

All digital and pupil book units have the same names and numbers, but different questions.

- Treasure House, Year 6, Comprehension Unit 1: Fiction: 'Trouble Half-Way'
- Treasure House, Year 6, Composition Unit 1: Story planning
- Treasure House, Year 6, Composition Unit 2: Summaries
- Treasure House, Year 6, Composition Unit 13: Paragraphs in fiction
- Treasure House, Year 6, Grammar Unit 3: Relative clauses
- Treasure House, Year 6, Spelling Unit 4: The suffixes -able, -ible, -ably and -ibly
- Treasure House, Year 6, Spelling Unit 5: Adding suffixes beginning with vowel letters to words ending in -fer
- Treasure House, Year 6, Punctuation Unit 4: Boundaries between clauses
- Treasure House, Year 6, Vocabulary Unit 1: Using a thesaurus
- Treasure House, Year 4, Punctuation Unit 4: Punctuating direct speech (1)
- Treasure House, Year 4, Unit 5: Punctuating direct speech (2)
- Treasure House, Year 6, Punctuation Unit 1: Using commas for clearer meaning

Resources

Source texts – see Anthologies; Story planner; My writing checklist; Editor's checklst

Year 6, Sequence 1
Fiction: Creating tensions

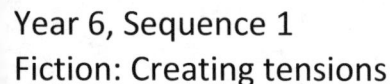

Phase 1: Enjoy and immerse

In Phase 1, the children are introduced to the opening scene from *Tom's Midnight Garden* which contains the tense dialogue between Tom and his mother as she sends him to stay with relatives while his brother is at home suffering from measles. Over several sessions, children are offered the opportunity to immerse themselves fully in the scene through comprehension and discussion activities, as well as exploring characters and structure through drama, storytelling, writing and analysis of the text.

Programmes of study: Year 6
- **Comprehension**: Continue to read and discuss an increasingly wide range of fiction, poetry, plays, non-fiction and reference books or textbooks.
- **Comprehension**: Draw inferences such as inferring characters' feelings, thoughts and motives from their actions, and justifying inferences with evidence.
- **Comprehension**: Discuss and evaluate how authors use language, including figurative language, considering the impact on the reader.
- **Composition**: Identify the audience for and purpose of the writing, selecting the appropriate form and using other similar writing as models for their own.
- **Vocabulary, grammar and punctuation**: Use relative clauses beginning with who, which, where, when, whose, that or with an implied (i.e. omitted) relative pronoun.
- **Spelling**: Use words ending in -able and -ible.
- **Spelling**: Use words ending in -ably and -ibly.

Sparking interest

Introduce the sequence by highlighting the overall Big Picture to the children: they will be working towards writing a scene showing tension, using dialogue and behaviour, independently. Use an opening question such as: 'How do you behave when you are feeling tense?'

Reading and discussion

Introduce the text, read it with the class and check the children's understanding of the language. Discuss children's understanding of the content of the extract.

Discuss the following with the children.
- Who are the characters in this extract?
- How do you think Tom feels?
- Why does Tom feel that way?
- How do you know how Tom is feeling?
- How do you think Tom's mother feels?
- Is this an effective story opening? Why?

Drama and storytelling

Use drama and storytelling activities to reinforce the children's understanding of the atmosphere in the scene. Select the activities that would suit your class or fit in with your lesson timing. Encourage mixed-ability grouping for the chosen activities.

- **Hot-seating Tom or his mother:** This activity can be done in pairs, small groups or as a class situation with different children representing the characters. Questions could include: 'Why are you sending Tom away?' 'How do you feel?' 'Why are you so upset?'
- **Role-play discussion:** Have a discussion to debate whether Tom's mother made the right decision to send him away. Encourage children to imagine how Tom felt and how his mother felt.
- **Storytelling:** Become a storyteller. The children could accompany your performance, either by using props for sound effects or by taking the roles of the characters.
- **Performance:** Encourage the children to rehearse and perform the scene in small groups, with one or two narrators.
- **Presentation ideas:** Create a newsflash related to the scene.

Incidental writing

A short writing activity would enhance the children's understanding of the text and characters. Select activities that you think are appropriate for the abilities and interests of your class.

Year 6, Sequence 1
Fiction: Creating tensions

Use the children's written outcomes to inform the emphases during the collaborative composition phase. Children could compose:

- a diary entry by Tom
- a newspaper article about the measles outbreak
- a short summary of the main source text.

Analysis

Show the text to the children and discuss the setting, characters and plot. Discuss the way the extract begins with the chapter title 'Exile' and ask the children what this word suggests. Discuss how, in the opening sentence, we are told straight away how Tom is feeling. The characters' feelings are shown throughout this scene. Highlight the early description of the garden and suggest that this forms links with the later plot and the title of the book. Make a list of vocabulary that highlights the tension or feelings in the scene such as 'raged' and 'bitterly'. Discuss the importance of the dialogue between Tom and his mother which, combined with the characters' actions, shows the tension between them. With the children, look at what the characters are saying and how they are saying it.

Grammar: Relative clauses

Tell the children that we use relative clauses to give more information about nouns. They can start with a relative pronoun ('that,' 'which,' 'who' or 'whose') or a relative adverb ('where' or 'when').

Explain that we use a comma before a relative clause if the information is not vital to the meaning of the noun it describes. If it is vital, we do not use a comma. We never use a comma before 'that', and always before 'which'.

Provide children with a copy of the model text and challenge them to find and highlight examples of relative clauses.

On pieces of A4 paper or card, write a selection of simple sentences (one per sheet). Then write a selection of relative pronouns and adverbs (one per sheet). Shuffle up the sentence sheets and hand them out to the children. Challenge the children to find a partner whose sentence could be joined to theirs by using a relative pronoun or adverb. The pair should then find the correct relative pronoun or adverb and hold up the cards to show the class their new sentence.

Phonics and spelling

Display the word 'reasonably' on the board and underline the 'ably' part. Explain to the children that the -able / -ably ending is more common than -ible / -ibly if a complete root word can be heard as a whole when the ending is removed. However, there are some exceptions.

For this list of ten -able / -ably words, ask the children to decide whether the root word can be heard as a whole or not. Discuss the meaning of each word, then look it up in a dictionary to check. Then write each word in a short sentence. You could link the sentences to the theme of the model text, Tom's Midnight Garden.

-able / -ably words: applicable, adorably, considerably, tolerable, noticeable, dependable, comfortable, reasonable, enjoyable, reliable

Review of the Big Picture

Once you have completed this phase, remind the children (or have them remind each other) of the sequence's Big Picture: they are working towards writing a scene showing tension, using dialogue and behaviour, independently.

Year 6, Sequence 1
Fiction: Creating tensions

Phase 2: Capture and organise

During Phase 2, children start to develop ideas about new content and the literary features needed to create a class narrative scene portraying tension between the characters. Working collaboratively, children decide on a domestic setting, characters and plot ideas.

Programmes of study: Year 6
- **Comprehension:** Identify and discuss themes and conventions in and across a wide range of writing.
- **Comprehension:** Participate in discussions about books that are read to them and those they can read for themselves, building on their own and others' ideas, and challenging views courteously.
- **Comprehension:** Identify how language, structure and presentation contribute to meaning.
- **Composition:** Note and develop initial ideas, drawing on reading and research where necessary.
- **Composition:** In writing narratives, consider how authors have developed characters and settings in what children have read, listened to or seen performed.
- **Spelling:** Add suffixes beginning with vowel letters to words ending in -fer.

Introduction

Remind the children of the Big Picture for the sequence and recap on the learning achieved through Phase 1. Read one or both of the additional texts to provide further examples of tension within a domestic scene.

Discussing ideas

As a class, discuss and make decisions to form the basis of their own tense scene.

- Who should the characters be?
- What is the problem causing tension?
- Why has the problem arisen?
- Will there be any other characters in the scene? If so, who are they?
- How will the situation be resolved? Will it be resolved?

Drama and storytelling

Use drama and storytelling to encourage children to develop their ideas further, especially their ideas for the dialogue between the characters.

- **Hot-seating the main character:** This activity will help the children to get to know their new characters as they must think carefully about the questions to ask and the answers to give.
- **Freeze-framing key moments:** Once there are sufficient ideas to start developing a scene, encourage children to act out their ideas either by improvising or scripting a brief scene. Children could work in small groups.

At regular intervals, ask the children to freeze and use thought-tracking to develop children's ideas about their characters' feelings, thoughts and actions.

- **Storytelling:** Ask children to work together in pairs or small groups to develop their ideas, then present them to a larger group using storytelling techniques. The class could sit in a large circle and use props, puppets or music to help them tell their stories.

Incidental writing

Before you select any incidental writing, make sure the children are able to orally articulate the main ideas for their tension scene. Select activities that you think are appropriate for the abilities and interests of your class. Children could compose:

- a description of the setting
- a character's diary entry
- a character profile
- a script.

Organising the class narrative into a structure

Once the children have thoroughly explored ideas for their class tension scene, bring them together. Use their final suggestions to model how to plot their new narrative in diagram or note form with the help of the Story planner. Once recorded, go through the frame and ask the children to evaluate the structure and organisation.

Year 6, Sequence 1
Fiction: Creating tensions

Phonics and spelling

Display the word 'prefer' on the board and underline the 'fer' part. Explain to the children that when we add suffixes beginning with a vowel letter to words ending in -fer, we need to think about whether to double the **r**.

Tell children the rule that the **r** is doubled if the -fer is still stressed when the ending is added. The **r** is not doubled if the -fer is no longer stressed.

For this list of ten -fer words, ask the children to underline the syllable that is stressed. Discuss the meaning of each word, then look it up in a dictionary to check. Then write each word in a short sentence. You could try to link the sentences to the theme of the model text, *Tom's Midnight Garden*.

-fer words: conference, conferred, referee, referred, offer, offered, suffering, suffered, transferred, transfer

Review of the Big Picture

Once you have completed all the lessons for this phase, remind the children of the sequence's Big Picture. Recap on the learning achieved in Phase 2.

Year 6, Sequence 1
Fiction: Creating tensions

Phase 3: Collaborate and compose

This phase focuses in detail on supporting children to draft and write individual sections of their tension scene.

Programmes of study: Year 6
- **Composition:** Identify the audience for and purpose of the writing, selecting the appropriate form and using other similar writing as a model for their own.
- **Composition:** Note and develop initial ideas, drawing on reading and research where necessary.
- **Composition:** In writing narratives, consider how authors have developed characters and settings in what children have read, listened to or seen performed.
- **Composition:** Select appropriate grammar and vocabulary, understanding how such choices can change and enhance meaning.
- **Composition:** In narratives, describe settings, characters and atmosphere and integrate dialogue to convey character and advance the action.

Introduction

Remind the children about the Big Picture and recap on the learning in Phases 1 and 2. Explain to children that through Phase 3 they will be learning how to write their own narrative scene that portrays tension between the characters through their dialogue and actions.

Lesson 1

Starter (VGP focus) – Punctuation: Boundaries between clauses

Explain to the children that we can use colons, semi-colons or dashes to separate main clauses. Semi-colons show linked clauses that are equally important; colons introduce reasons or examples; and dashes can be used in informal writing. On a screen, display the first few paragraphs of *Tom's Midnight Garden* (or provide children with copies). Ask children to identify the examples of different punctuation used between clauses.

Shared writing

Children remind themselves and each other of their planning ideas from Phase 2. Ask the children to make suggestions for the wording of the opening paragraph of the class narrative, revisiting the opening of *Tom's Midnight Garden* as an example. Model writing the opening paragraph with the children's input, focusing on the introduction of the main character, what they are doing and how they are feeling. The opening should set the scene by implying, through the main character's action, that they are upset or agitated by something but may not reveal what the problem is yet. Have the children make suggestions about how to incorporate a semi-colon, colon or dash to mark the boundary between clauses. Discuss 'seeding' in a piece of detail that will be referred to later in the narrative to give cohesion through the whole story / extract.

Independent writing

The children can now write their own first section, applying the VGP focus on punctuation for boundaries between clauses. Some children may benefit from guided group writing or peer-paired writing at this stage.

Plenary

At appropriate points throughout the lesson, invite children to share their writing with small groups, partners or the whole class. Ask the children questions to help them focus on their progress and what they have created during that lesson, for example: 'How have you set the scene?' 'How have you introduced the main character?' 'Have you used colons, semi-colons and / or dashes to separate clauses correctly?'

Lesson 2

Starter (VGP focus) – Vocabulary: Using a thesaurus

Remind the children that we can use a thesaurus to find words with similar meanings. It can help us to find new or better words for what we want to say. Ask children, working in pairs, to choose one sentence from the *Tom's Midnight*

Year 6, Sequence 1
Fiction: Creating tensions

Garden extract and alter it by replacing some of the words with alternatives found in the thesaurus. Share children's examples, checking that nuances of meaning are understood.

Shared writing

With the children's input, model writing the next part of the narrative which sets the scene by describing the setting and could introduce either the character that the main character will have tension with, or could provide more information about the problem that is bothering the main character. Encourage children to use the thesaurus to improve the vocabulary you are using as you write.

Independent writing

The children can now write their own second section, applying the VGP focus on using a thesaurus to source new or interesting vocabulary to improve their setting descriptions. Some children may benefit from guided group writing or peer-paired writing at this stage.

Plenary

At the end of the lesson, invite children to share their writing with groups or the whole class. Ask the children questions to help them focus on their progress and what they have created during that lesson, for example: 'How have you created tension in the scene?' 'What varied and effective vocabulary have you used?' 'What effect does your choice of vocabulary have?'

Lesson 3

Starter (VGP focus) – Punctuation: Revision of direct speech punctuation

Write a speech sentence on the board without any punctuation, such as: 'you know tom she said its not nice for you to be rushed away'. Invite children to correctly punctuate the sentence (adding all necessary punctuation marks). Remind children that if a statement in speech comes before an explanation like 'she said,' the speech ends in a comma. The explanation does not use a capital letter unless it is a proper noun.

Shared writing

With the children's input, model writing the next part of the narrative. Introduce the second character and develop the direct speech between the characters to show tension between them. Features could include narrative of the character's actions between the speech, for example, body language to show tension, in addition speech may be interrupted or informal, or use exclamation marks. Reinforce the correct use of punctuation for direct speech throughout.

Independent writing

The children can now write their own third section, applying the VGP focus on using correct punctuation for direct speech. Some children may benefit from guided group writing or peer-paired writing at this stage.

Plenary

At the end of the lesson, invite children to share their writing with groups or the whole class. Ask the children questions to help them focus on their progress and what they have created during that lesson, for example: 'Have you used action and description to show tension between the characters?' 'How have you used dialogue to show tension between the characters?' 'Have you used direct speech punctuation correctly?'

Lesson 4

Starter (VGP focus) – Punctuation: Using commas for clearer meaning

Remind the children that commas can be useful for making the meaning of sentences clearer. Provide children with copies of the *Tom's Midnight Garden* extract and ask them, in pairs, to find examples of commas used within sentences. Have the children use mini whiteboards to create sentences with similar structures. As individuals read their sentences aloud, have the class make notes of correct punctuation (capital letter(s), comma(s) and a full stop) as they listen.

Shared writing

With children's input, continue modelling how to write the ongoing dialogue between the characters, interspersed with narrative to help move the story along. Explain that sometimes when we write dialogue we can be caught up in the characters' conversation and forget to progress the story. Use techniques such as interrupting speech with narrative or a character's thoughts as an aside. Include some reported speech to enhance narrative flow. Show, rather than tell, how the main character feels. At the end of the section, leave the tension unresolved and discuss with the children how this can be a technique to make the reader feel uneasy (like the characters, thus creating empathy as well as suspense). Be sure to include at least one example of commas being used to aid clarity within a sentence.

Year 6, Sequence 1
Fiction: Creating tensions

Independent writing

The children can now write their own fourth section, applying the VGP focus on using dialogue.

Some children may benefit from guided group writing or peer-paired writing at this stage.

Plenary

At the end of the lesson, invite children to share their writing with groups or the whole class. Ask the children questions to help them focus on their progress and what they have created during that lesson, for example: 'How have you moved the story forward?' 'Have you used commas to make meaning clear?' 'Share your work. Is your partner's writing easily understandable?'

Rehearsing and performing

Once the children have written their scene, encourage them to retell it either as narrators or by creating a performance. Discuss how similar or different the scene is to the *Tom's Midnight Garden* extract or the additional texts.

Review of the Big Picture

Once you have completed all the lessons for this phase, remind the children of the sequence's Big Picture. Discuss what they have learned during Phase 3.

Year 6, Sequence 1
Fiction: Creating tensions

Phase 4: Write independently

This final phase brings all the children's learning and writing skills together so that they can write their own independent scene portraying tension through dialogue and behaviours. Through their writing, they will be able to utilise the different VGP focuses that they have been practising throughout previous phases.

> **Programmes of study: Year 6**
> - **Composition:** Select appropriate grammar and vocabulary, understanding how such choices can change and enhance meaning.
> - **Composition:** In narratives, describe settings, characters and atmosphere and integrate dialogue to convey character and advance the action.
> - **Composition:** Assess the effectiveness of their own and others' writing.
> - **Composition:** Propose changes to vocabulary, grammar and punctuation to enhance effects and clarify meaning.
> - **Composition:** Proofread for spelling and punctuation errors.
> - **Composition:** Perform their own compositions, using appropriate intonation, volume and movement so that meaning is clear.

Introduction

Introduce this phase by highlighting the overall Big Picture to the children. Recap on learning and progress through Phases 1–3 and explain that in Phase 4 they will be applying their learning to write their own scene independently. Discuss and list examples of situations that might be tense between family members or friends. Examples could include: a child being disappointed and let down when a parent couldn't keep a promise to go somewhere; bereavement, for example, the death of a family pet; friends being unkind and leaving someone out of a group situation. Recap on the structure used in the class writing sessions in Phase 3.

Writing

Give each child a My writing checklist and instruct them to start planning and writing each section of their own scene. Display the class story-structure and a copy of the extract from *Tom's Midnight Garden* for reference. All the children should be encouraged to try to write independently to the best of their ability. Ask open questions such as: 'How will you show how the character is feeling at this point?' Avoid telling children what to write. Some children may benefit from guided composition. Focus on perseverance and resilience in their independent application.

Proofreading and redrafting

Have the children proofread their work periodically as they write. Proofreading and improvement without support means the writing may happen over a few lessons. Offer the children the Editor's checklist or create your own checklist that includes the VGP and spelling focuses covered throughout this sequence. Highlight the importance of redrafting, linking their efforts to the overall Big Picture.

Self- and peer-assessment

Encourage the children to self-assess their own writing, as well as that of others in their group. Offer them a set of self-assessment questions such as: 'How does the writing convey tension between the characters?' 'How clearly is the writing structured?' 'Has correctly punctuated direct speech been used?' 'What impact does the writing have?' 'What changes would improve the reader's experience?'

Rehearsing and performing

Once the children have written their independent scene (which could be extended into an entire story provided the tension element has been included), encourage them to retell it either as narrators or by creating a performance. Discuss how similar or different the scene is from the *Tom's Midnight Garden* extract. Encourage the children to feed back on one another's writing and performances.

Final review of the Big Picture

Individually or with partners, have children reflect on what they have learned from this sequence and what they will apply in their future writing.

Year 6, Sequence 2
Fiction: Traditional stories

Sequence 2
Fiction: Traditional stories

Approximate duration: Two weeks

Big Picture

Through this teaching sequence, children will explore the way in which a traditional folktale with a clear message can be regenerated within a modern context. Through the process of evaluating and rewriting the tale, children will understand the technique used by authors of embedding deeper layers of meaning within a text. Children will be able to write text that has an impact on readers' responses.

Phase 1: Enjoy and immerse

Children analyse the structure and meaning of the model text, 'The Discontented Fish'.

Phase 2: Capture and organise

Children begin to develop ideas for creating their own version of the folktale within a modern context.

Phase 3: Collaborate and compose

Children undertake supported writing sessions to develop the writing features of their modern folktale.

Phase 4: Write independently

Children write, edit and present their own modern folktale that contains a message for readers.

Main source text

Treasure House Anthology Sequence 2 text. Treasure House Online, Year 6, Comprehension Unit 2: Fiction (traditional): 'The Discontented Fish'

Extra source texts

'The Tortoise and the Eagle', *Stories from Aesop*, ISBN 978-1-40-953887-5, pp.236–242

Background knowledge

'The Discontented Fish' is a tale about a fish who is unsatisfied with his life so goes to find a grander home. He is arrogant and believes he is better than his peers. When he gets to his new home, he realises the value of his original community. He returns and is thereafter a more appreciative fish. The moral of the story is to be content with what you have. This version originates from Senegal in West Africa but is representative of many similar traditional tales with the same message. A folktale is a story originating in popular culture, typically passed on by word of mouth. 'The Discontented Fish' is a type of folktale called a 'fable'. A fable is a short story, typically with animals as characters, conveying a moral.

Spoken outcome

To perform an oral version of children's written stories to an audience of peers or parents

Writing outcome

To rewrite 'The Discontented Fish' as a tale of a Year 6 child going to secondary school

Prior knowledge

Check children's knowledge and understanding of:
- what distinguishes folktales and fables
- the location of Senegal, West Africa
- the meaning of 'discontent'.

Year 6, Sequence 2
Fiction: Traditional stories

Diagnostic assessment options

Before starting the sequence, you may want to conduct an initial diagnostic assessment of the children's understanding of the typical characteristics of traditional folktales or fables.

Ideas for initial diagnostic assessment options include:
- discussion about traditional folktales or fables and their purpose
- a brief, unsupported writing activity to create a folktale or fable
- practise speaking and listening skills relating to a well-known short folktale or fable
- a short reading comprehension activity / quiz on a folktale or fable.

Cross-curricular links

KS2 Geography – Locational knowledge

Locate the world's countries, using maps to focus on Europe (including the location of Russia) and North and South America, concentrating on their environmental regions, key physical and human features, countries, and major cities.

KS2 Geography – Geographical skills and fieldwork

Use maps, atlases, globes and digital / computer mapping to locate countries.

Treasure House links

All digital and pupil book units have the same names and numbers, but different questions.

- Treasure House, Year 6, Comprehension Unit 2: Fiction (traditional): 'The Discontented Fish'
- Treasure House, Year 6, Composition Unit 1: Story planning
- Treasure House, Year 6, Composition Unit 2: Summaries
- Treasure House, Year 6, Composition Unit 13: Paragraphs in fiction
- Treasure House, Year 6, Composition Unit 15: Story endings
- Treasure House, Year 5, Grammar Unit 2: Adverbs and modal verbs showing possibility
- Treasure House, Year 6, Spelling Unit 1: The suffixes -cious and -tious
- Treasure House, Year 6, Spelling Unit 3: The suffixes -ant, -ance / -ancy, -ent and -ence / -ency
- Treasure House, Year 6, Vocabulary Unit 2: Synonyms and antonyms
- Treasure House, Year 6, Grammar Unit 1: Using the subjunctive
- Treasure House, Year 6, Grammar Unit 2: Using the passive voice
- Treasure House, Year 6, Grammar Unit 3: Relative clauses

Resources

Globe or atlas to show location of Senegal; Story planner; Editor's checklist

Year 6, Sequence 2
Fiction: Traditional stories

Phase 1: Enjoy and immerse

In Phase 1, the children are introduced to a traditional folktale from Senegal that contains the message 'Be content with what you have.' Over several lessons they are offered the opportunity to immerse themselves fully in the story through comprehension and discussion activities as well as exploring its characters and structure through drama, storytelling, writing and analysis of the text.

Programmes of study: Year 6

- **Comprehension:** Increase their familiarity with a wide range of books, including myths, legends and traditional stories, modern fiction, fiction from our literary heritage, and books from other cultures and traditions.
- **Comprehension:** Check that the book makes sense to them, discussing their understanding and exploring the meaning of words in context.
- **Comprehension:** Discuss and evaluate how authors use language, including figurative language, considering the impact on the reader.
- **Composition:** Identify the audience for and purpose of the writing, selecting the appropriate form and using other similar writing as models for their own.
- **Vocabulary, grammar and punctuation:** Use modal verbs or adverbs to indicate degrees of possibility.
- **Spelling:** Use words with endings which sound like /ʃəs/ spelt -cious or -tious.

Sparking interest

Introduce the sequence by highlighting the overall Big Picture to the children: they will be working towards writing their own modern version of the tale. Have a map or globe available, so that the children can locate Senegal and understand that it is an African country. If needed, show images of Senegal.

Use an opening question such as: 'Why do you think folktales and fables have stood the test of time?'

Reading and discussion

Introduce the text, read it with the class and check their understanding of the language and content.

Discuss the following with the children.

- What was the moral of the story?
- Why did the fish feel discontented?
- What situations might make people feel dissatisfied with their lives today?
- How did the fish in the small pool react to the big fish's complaints?
- In your opinion, how effective is the story in delivering its moral? Explain your thinking.
- Do you know of any similar stories?

Drama and storytelling

Use drama and storytelling activities to reinforce the children's understanding of 'The Discontented Fish'. Select the activities that would suit your class or fit in with your lesson timing. Encourage mixed-ability grouping for the chosen activities.

- **Storytelling:** Become a storyteller. Explain that storytellers would retell different traditional stories to people often sitting around them. The children could accompany your performance, either by using props to create sound effects or by taking the roles of the characters.
- **Puppet show:** Make puppets of the fish characters. Children can work in small groups, using the puppets to perform a retelling of the story to the class or to younger children.
- **Hot-seating the fish:** This activity can be done in pairs, small groups or as a whole class situation with different children representing the characters. Questions could include: 'What made you so unhappy in the small pool?' 'How did you feel when you arrived in the river?' 'Why did you decide to come back?' 'What do you imagine might have happened if you hadn't returned?'

Year 6, Sequence 2
Fiction: Traditional stories

- **Freeze-frame with thought-tapping:** Either in small groups or as a whole class, the children create a moment that shows the action in a narrative frozen in time, as if the pause button has been pressed. The teacher (or a child) gently taps a character on the shoulder to 'unfreeze' them. That child then voices their thoughts in character. This activity encourages children to engage with the actions and thoughts of the characters.

Incidental writing

A short writing activity would enhance the children's understanding of the text and characters. Select activities that you think are appropriate for the abilities and interests of your class. Use your children's written outcomes to inform the emphases during the collaborative composition phase. Children could:

- rewrite part of the tale from the perspective of a different character, for example, one of the other fish that live in the small pool
- write a short, one-paragraph summary of the story
- write a letter of complaint from the little fish to the older fish in the small pool when they feel fed up of the big fish's moaning.

Analysis

Show the text to the children and discuss the following characteristics commonly found in fables, either by pointing them out, asking children to find them or prompting children to discover them.

- Characters that are animals but behave like human stereotypes
- An opening that quickly establishes the setting and the main character
- The name of the main character as the title
- Simple dialogue that moves the story along and often takes a question and answer format or involves its characters reflecting on the situation
- A moral or message as the ending

Grammar: Adverbs and modal verbs showing possibility

Remind children that adverbs and modal verbs can show how likely the action of a verb is.

Adverbs: perhaps, maybe, possibly, probably, definitely, certainly, surely

Modal verbs: can, could, may, might, shall, should, will, would

Put the adverbs and modal verbs onto cards or sheets of A4 paper (one word per card). Each child takes one word. Challenge the children to organise themselves so they are standing in a line holding up their word cards in order of likelihood.

Provide children with a copy of 'The Discontented Fish' and challenge them, in pairs, to find and highlight as many examples of adverbs and modal verbs showing possibility as they can.

Offer the sentence, 'You _____ do your homework.' Have children try different modals in the space and discuss the changing meaning.

Phonics and spelling

Display the word 'cautious' on the board and underline the 'ious' part. Explain to the children that the ending -ious can be added to turn nouns into adjectives.

caution + ious = cautious

Explain that, because -cious and -tious both spell the /shus/ sound, it is sometimes difficult to remember whether to spell the ending -cious or -tious. If the root word ends in -ce, the ending is -cious (remove the **e** before adding -ious). If the root word ends in -tion, the ending is -tious (remove the -ion before adding -ious). There is one common exception word: 'anxious'.

For this list of -cious / -tious words, ask the children to discuss the meaning of each word, then look it up in a dictionary to check. Then write each word in a short sentence. You could link the sentences to the theme of the model text, 'The Discontented Fish'.

-cious / -tious words: spacious, vicious, infectious, gracious, ambitious, cautious, precious, nutritious, malicious

Review of the Big Picture

Once you have completed this phase, remind the children (or have them remind one another) of the sequence's Big Picture: they are working towards independently writing their own modern version of the tale.

Year 6, Sequence 2
Fiction: Traditional stories

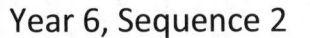

Phase 2: Capture and organise

During Phase 2, the children are able to use their knowledge from the previous lessons in Phase 1 to create their own class fable using the same moral as 'The Discontented Fish' (be content with what you have). The group and class discussions, as well as drama or short writing opportunities, offer chances for children of all abilities to contribute and use their skills towards designing a story-structure and developing characters for their fable. Their ideas can be recorded in picture, diagram or note form with the help from the Story planner..

Programmes of study: Year 6

- **Comprehension:** Identify and discuss themes and conventions in and across a wide range of writing.
- **Comprehension:** Participate in discussions about books that are read to them and those they can read for themselves, building on their own and others' ideas and challenging views courteously.
- **Comprehension:** Identify how language, structure and presentation contribute to meaning.
- **Composition:** Note and develop initial ideas, drawing on reading and research where necessary.
- **Composition:** In writing narratives, consider how authors have developed characters and settings in what children have read, listened to or seen performed.
- **Spelling:** Use words ending in -ant, -ance / -ancy, -ent, -ence / -ency.

Introduction

Remind the children of the Big Picture for this sequence and recap on the learning achieved through Phase 1. Read the additional text for the sequence, 'The Tortoise and The Eagle', and discuss the similarities and differences to 'The Discontented Fish' text.

Discussing ideas

As a class, discuss and make decisions to form the basis of their own class fable. Suggest that the class fable could be a tale with the same moral as 'The Discontented Fish': to be content with what you have. The storyline could involve animals that represent school children. An arrogant Year 6 child is fed up of primary school, then goes to secondary school and is suddenly not so brave. Discuss the following.

- What should the moral be?
- Who should the characters be?
- Where will the setting be?
- What will the problem be?
- How will the situation be resolved? Will it be resolved?

Drama and storytelling

Use drama and storytelling activities to allow the children to explore the suggestions for their new characters and story plot. Select the activities that would suit your class or fit in with your lesson timing. Encourage mixed-ability grouping for the chosen activities.

- **Hot-seating the main character:** This activity can be done in pairs, small groups or as a class situation. Encourage the children to think and, if necessary, write down their questions before the hot-seating session starts. Discuss the character's responses.
- **Freeze-framing key moments:** Once the structure of the story is created, try out the different scenes in the correct story order. Use thought-tracking by asking each child in the freeze-frame what they are thinking at a particular moment.
- **Storytelling:** Encourage the children to work in groups to devise a telling of the tale and then share it with the rest of the class. Discuss the differences between the different groups' stories and which parts worked better than others.

Incidental writing

Before you select any incidental writing, make sure the children are able to orally articulate the main events of their class fable. Select activities that you think are appropriate for the abilities and interests of your class. Children could compose:

- a diary entry
- a short description of a secondary school
- a character profile
- a blog entry or an email.

Year 6, Sequence 2
Fiction: Traditional stories

Organising the class fable into a structure

Once the children have thoroughly explored their ideas for their class fable, bring them together and use their final suggestions to model how to plot the new story in picture, diagram or note form, with the help of the Story planner and the Writing checkist. Once recorded, go through the frame and ask the children if they are happy with the tale.

Phonics and spelling

Write the following words on the board, including the missing letter space.

pati_nce; toler_nce; expect_nce; confid_nce; appear_nce; griev_nce; occur_nce; circumfer_nce; perform_nce; refer_nce; inherit_nce; resembl_nce; import_nce; evid_nce; obedi_nce; assist_nce; observ_nce; independ_nce; intellig_nce; confid_nce; innoc_nce

Challenge the children to use dictionaries to find the missing letter needed to spell the words correctly. Try 'beat the clock' and team-race strategies to encourage fun focus.

Review of the Big Picture

Once you have completed all the lessons for this phase, remind the children of the sequence's Big Picture. Recap on the learning achieved in Phase 2.

Year 6, Sequence 2
Fiction: Traditional stories

Phase 3: Collaborate and compose

This phase focuses on how to write a fable. There is one lesson per story part so that the children are taken through the writing of the whole piece, learning and applying new vocabulary, grammar and punctuation along the way. Children should have the planning framework from Phase 2: Capture and organise in front of them throughout, and should be able to revisit the original model text, 'The Discontented Fish'.

Within each lesson, the children will also be able to work interactively on vocabulary, grammar and punctuation focuses. The focus is initially looked at in detail as a whole-class activity at the beginning of the lesson and is then modelled and applied during the class shared writing element. The children will then be able to apply their learned VGP focus during their independent writing.

> **Programmes of study: Year 6**
> - **Composition:** Identify the audience for and purpose of the writing, selecting the appropriate form and using other similar writing as models for their own.
> - **Composition:** Note and develop initial ideas, drawing on reading and research where necessary.
> - **Composition:** In writing narratives, consider how authors have developed characters and settings in what children have read, listened to or seen performed.
> - **Composition:** Select appropriate grammar and vocabulary, understanding how such choices can change and enhance meaning.
> - **Composition:** In narratives, describe settings, characters and atmosphere and integrate dialogue to convey character and advance the action.

Introduction

Remind the children about the Big Picture and recap on the learning in Phases 1 and 2. Explain to children that through Phase 3, they will be learning how to write their own fable based on the model text, 'The Discontented Fish', and their own development ideas.

Lesson 1

Starter (VGP focus) – Vocabulary: Synonyms

Explain to the children that synonyms are words that have the same meanings as one another. They can be found using a dictionary or thesaurus. Ask children why they might need to find words that are similar. (To improve their writing by finding a more appropriate word; to extend their vocabulary knowledge.) Ask children, in pairs, to choose three sentences from 'The Discontented Fish' text and use synonyms to change the vocabulary in the sentences. Discuss the impact on the sentence / reader.

Shared writing

The children remind themselves and each other of their planning ideas from Phase 2. Ask the children to make suggestions for the wording of the opening paragraph of the class fable, revisiting the opening of 'The Discontented Fish' as an example. Model writing the opening paragraph with the children's input, focusing on the introduction of the setting and the main character, what they are doing and how they are feeling. Use a thesaurus to adjust and enhance the language for impact on readers.

Independent writing

The children can now write their own first section, applying the VGP focus on synonyms. Some children may benefit from guided group writing or peer-paired writing at this stage.

Plenary

At appropriate points throughout the lesson, invite children to share their writing with small groups, partners or the whole class. Ask the children questions to help them focus on their progress and what they have created during that lesson, for example: 'How have you introduced the setting / main character?' 'What varied and effective vocabulary have you used?' 'Share your work. What varied and effective vocabulary has your partner used?'

Year 6, Sequence 2
Fiction: Traditional stories

Lesson 2

Starter (VGP focus) – Grammar: Using the subjunctive

Explain to the children that the subjunctive form of verbs refers to what someone imagines, wishes or hopes will happen.

We usually use it in formal writing rather than everyday speech but it works well within the style of a fable. Write these expressions on the board: 'it is best that', 'it is desirable that', 'it is imperative that', 'I recommend that', 'I demand that', 'I propose that'. Ask children to work in pairs to choose two of the expressions to add clauses to in order to turn them into sentences that could be used in the class fable. Encourage children to use the verb 'to be', for example: 'It is best that you be there tomorrow.'

Shared writing

With the children's input, model writing the next part of the fable which describes the main character's dissatisfaction with their current situation. Introduce other characters and dialogue that includes a question and answer structure. Encourage children to help you build in at least one subjunctive example such as: 'If I were you …' 'I suggest that you …' 'Is it essential that I be here?'

Independent writing

The children can now write their own second section of the fable, applying the VGP focus (at least twice) on using the subjunctive form of verbs to give the language of their fable a traditional feel. Some children may benefit from guided group writing or peer-paired writing at this stage.

Plenary

At appropriate points throughout the lesson, invite children to share their writing with small groups, partners or the whole class. Ask the children questions to help them focus on their progress and what they have created during that lesson, for example: 'What is your character's situation and why are they dissatisfied with it?' 'Where have you used a subjunctive verb?' 'What effect has this had on the sentence?'

Lesson 3

Starter (VGP focus) – Grammar: Using the passive voice

Inform children that we often use the passive voice when an action is more important than who or what did it. Write the example on the board: 'The tail was nibbled by the Tiger fish.' The tail is the subject of the sentence. However, it did not perform the action in the sentence, the action happened to it.

Write these three sentences on the board and ask children to change them into sentences in the passive voice on their mini whiteboards: 'The rain flooded the river.' (The river was flooded by the rain.) 'The fish tasted the water in the river.' (The water in the river was tasted by the fish.) 'The black and white fish chased the big fish.' (The big fish was chased by the black and white fish.)

Shared writing

With the children's input, model writing the next part of the narrative. Focus on the part of the tale that shows how the main character transitions from their current setting (primary school) to the place they want to be (secondary school). Include dialogue with other characters and simple description of actions to help the story progress. Encourage children to contribute sentences in the passive voice, where appropriate.

Independent writing

The children can now write their own third section, applying the VGP focus as appropriate. Some children may benefit from guided group writing or peer-paired writing at this stage.

Plenary

At appropriate points throughout the lesson, invite children to share their writing with small groups, partners or the whole class. Ask the children questions to help them focus on their progress and what they have created during that lesson, for example: 'What dialogue and / or description of actions have you included to help the story progress?' 'Which language choices have helped you keep to the appropriate style?'

Lesson 4

Starter (VGP focus) – Grammar: Relative clauses

Remind children that we use relative clauses to give more information about nouns. A relative clause can start with a relative pronoun ('that', 'which', 'who' or 'whose'), for example: '… the good life **that** lay ahead.' '… the older fish, **who** was becoming irritated by the big fish's constant gripes.' A relative clause can also start with a relative adverb ('where' or 'when'), for example: '**When** he told the other fish in the pool …' Provide pairs of children with a copy of 'The Discontented Fish' and ask them to find and highlight

Year 6, Sequence 2
Fiction: Traditional stories

examples of relative clauses. Ask each pair to present one of their examples to a small group or the whole class.

Shared writing

With the children's input, continue modelling how to write the class fable. Focus on the main character's realisation that their new situation is worse than they had thought it would be. Include dialogue and comments on the main character's thoughts and feelings. Discuss the resolution of the fable with the children. In the class fable, the character cannot return to primary school, in the way that the fish in 'The Discontented Fish' returned to his small pool. Gather ideas for the ending but steer the children towards the idea that, although secondary school is far scarier for the main character than they had anticipated, it turns out well in the end. Perhaps they make new friends and settle in. However, end the fable by commenting that the main character had learned their lesson to be content with what they have. Include at least two examples of a relative clause.

Independent writing

The children can now write their own fourth section, applying the VGP focus to use relative clauses. Some children may benefit from guided group writing or peer-paired writing at this stage.

Plenary

At appropriate points throughout the lesson, invite children to share their writing with small groups, partners or the whole class. Ask the children questions to help them focus on their progress and what they have created during that lesson, for example: 'How effectively does your conclusion provoke the reader to reflect?' 'What relative clauses have you included in your writing?'

Rehearsing and performing

Once the children have written their modern version of the fable, encourage them to retell it either as narrators or by creating a performance. Discuss how different or similar the new fable is to the model text, 'The Discontented Fish', or the additional text, 'The Tortoise and The Eagle'.

Review of the Big Picture

Once you have completed all the lessons for this phase, remind the children of the sequence's Big Picture. Ask children to reflect on their learning within Phase 3.

Year 6, Sequence 2
Fiction: Traditional stories

Phase 4: Write independently

This final phase brings all the children's learning and writing skills together so that they can write their own modern version of the fable, 'The Discontented Fish'. Through their writing, they will be able to utilise the different VGP focuses that they have been investigating and applying to their shared writing in the previous phases.

> **Programmes of study: Year 6**
> - **Composition:** Select appropriate grammar and vocabulary, understanding how such choices can change and enhance meaning.
> - **Composition:** In narratives, describe settings, characters and atmosphere and integrate dialogue to convey character and advance the action.
> - **Composition:** Assess the effectiveness of their own and others' writing and suggest improvements.
> - **Composition:** Propose changes to vocabulary, grammar and punctuation to enhance effects and clarify meaning.
> - **Composition:** Proofread for spelling and punctuation errors.
> - **Composition:** Perform their own compositions, using appropriate intonation, volume and movement so that meaning is clear.

Introduction

Introduce this phase by highlighting the Big Picture to the children. Recap on learning and progress through Phases 1–3 and explain that in Phase 4 they will be applying their learning to write their own fable independently. Discuss and list examples of morals typically encountered in fables. Recap on the typical characteristics of fables from earlier in the sequence. Recap on the planning and writing structure used in Phase 3.

Writing

Give each child a Story planner and instruct them to start planning and writing each section of their own fable. Display the class story-structure and a copy of 'The Discontented Fish' text for reference. All the children should be encouraged to try to write independently to the best of their ability. Less confident children may wish to stick closely to the ideas developed as a class in Phases 2 and 3; more confident children may wish to develop independent ideas. Ask open questions such as: 'How will you show how the character is feeling at this point?' Avoid telling children what to write. Some children may benefit from guided composition. Focus on perseverance and resilience in their independent application.

Proofreading and redrafting

Have the children proofread their work periodically as they write. Proofreading and improvement without support means that the writing may happen over a few lessons. Offer the children the Editor's checklist or create your own checklist that includes the VGP focuses covered throughout this sequence. Highlight the importance of redrafting, linking their efforts to the Big Picture.

Self- and peer-assessment

Encourage the children to take time to self-assess their own writing as well as that of others in their group. Offer them a set of self-assessment questions, such as: 'How does the writing convey the moral of the tale?' 'How clearly is the writing structured?' 'How strongly stereotyped are the characters?' 'What changes would improve the reader's experience?'

Rehearsing and performing

Once the children have written their independent fable, encourage them to retell it either as narrators or by creating a performance. Discuss how similar or different the story is from 'The Discontented Fish'. Encourage children to feed back positively on one another's writing and performances.

Final review of the Big Picture

Individually or with partners, have children reflect on what they have learned from this sequence and what they will apply in their future writing.

Year 6, Sequence 3
Non-fiction: Persuasive writing

Sequence 3
Non-fiction: Persuasive writing

Approximate duration: Two weeks

Big Picture
Through this teaching sequence, children will explore the way in which writers of marketing materials attract readers to invest in their service or product, particularly through the techniques present in persuasive writing. Understanding how writers create persuasive texts will help children to use these techniques in their own writing. Children will be able to write a theme park brochure that effectively attracts and informs readers.

Phase 1: Enjoy and immerse
Children analyse the techniques used in the model text, a Disney Theme Park brochure.

Phase 2: Capture and organise
Children begin to develop ideas for creating their own theme park brochure using persuasive writing techniques.

Phase 3: Collaborate and compose
Children undertake supported writing sessions to develop the writing features of their theme park brochure.

Phase 4: Write independently
Children write, edit and present their own theme park brochures demonstrating persuasive writing techniques.

Main source text
Laughter Land theme park brochure

Background knowledge
The main source text is a theme park brochure for Laughter Land, comprising a 12-section format. The printed brochure is presented as an A3 sheet folded in half to form an A4 shape and then tri-folded. The sections comprise a front cover, an introduction and description section, a shows and events section, a ticket information section, an accommodation section, and a 'frequently asked questions' section. The interior of the leaflet, when opened out, shows a labelled map of the theme park covering the entire six-section spread. The extra source text provides a contemporary comparison with many similar and some different features.

Spoken outcome
To present a brochure to an audience of peers or parents

Writing outcome
To create a traditional 12-section folding brochure, or a multi-page e-brochure, to promote a theme park using persuasive techniques

Prior knowledge
Check children's knowledge and understanding of:
- what a theme park is
- the purpose of a brochure
- the concept of 'persuasive techniques'.

Year 6, Sequence 3
Non-fiction: Persuasive writing

Diagnostic assessment options

Before starting the sequence, you may want to conduct an initial diagnostic assessment of the children's understanding of the typical characteristics of persuasive writing in a brochure format.

Ideas for initial diagnostic assessment options include:
- discussion about brochures and their purpose
- a brief, unsupported writing activity to create a brochure
- practising speaking and listening skills relating to a brochure promoting a well-known place
- a short reading comprehension activity / quiz on a brochure-style persuasive text.

Cross-curricular links

KS2 Geography – Locational knowledge

Locate the world's countries, using maps to focus on Europe (including the location of Russia) and North and South America, concentrating on their environmental regions, key physical and human features, countries, and major cities.

Treasure House links

All digital and pupil book units have the same names and numbers, but different questions.

- Treasure House, Year 6, Comprehension Unit 3: Non-fiction (persuasive writing): Advertisements
- Treasure House, Year 6, Composition Unit 12: Paragraphs in non-fiction
- Treasure House, Year 6, Composition Unit 14: Writing for different purposes
- Treasure House, Year 6, Vocabulary Unit 2: Synonyms and antonyms
- Treasure House, Year 6, Spelling Unit 4: The suffixes -able, -ible, -ably and -ibly
- Treasure House, Year 6, Spelling Unit 6: Use of the hyphen after prefixes
- Treasure House, Year 6, Punctuation Unit 1: Using commas for clearer meaning
- Treasure House, Year 6, Punctuation Unit 4: Boundaries between clauses
- Treasure House, Year 6, Punctuation Unit 6: Punctuating bulleted lists

Resources

Treasure House Anthology Sequence 3 text. Source texts – see Anthologies; Non-fiction planner; Editor's checklist

Year 6, Sequence 3
Non-fiction: Persuasive writing

Phase 1: Enjoy and immerse

In Phase 1, the children are introduced to the brochure and they explore its many persuasive features. Over several sessions, children are offered the opportunity to immerse themselves fully in the design and contents of the brochure through comprehension and discussion activities, as well as exploring its features and structure through drama, writing and analysis of the text.

Programmes of study: Year 6
- **Comprehension:** Identify themes and conventions in and across a wide range of books.
- **Comprehension:** Summarise the main ideas drawn from more than one paragraph, identifying key details that support the main ideas.
- **Comprehension:** Discuss and evaluate how authors use language, considering the impact on the reader.
- **Composition:** Identify the audience for and purpose of the writing, selecting the appropriate form and using other similar writing as models for their own.
- **Vocabulary, grammar and punctuation:** Understand how words are related by meaning as synonyms and antonyms.
- **Spelling:** Use words ending in -able and -ible.
- **Spelling:** Use words ending in -ably and -ibly.

Sparking interest

Introduce the sequence by highlighting the overall Big Picture to the children: they will be working towards independently creating their own brochure or e-brochure to advertise a new theme park. Ask the children to imagine that an exciting new theme park has been created and they have been given the job of marketing executives and designers. It is their job to create a brochure that will successfully attract large crowds of people to the theme park.

Reading and discussion

Introduce the model brochure, read it with the class and check their understanding.

Discuss the following with the children.
- What is the purpose of this brochure?
- Who is the intended audience?
- What is the function of each section and how does each one help?
- What features can you identify within each section?
- How is the brochure effective in persuading readers to attend the theme park?
- Which part of the brochure do you think is most important?
- How would you describe the language used in the brochure?
- What would the impact be if the images and colours were removed?

Drama and storytelling

Use drama activities to reinforce the children's understanding of the contents and structure of the brochure. Select the activities that would suit your class or fit in with your lesson timing. Encourage mixed-ability grouping for the chosen activities.

- **Radio advert:** This activity can be done in pairs, small groups or as a class situation. Children imagine they are presenters on a radio show. They select information from the brochure to present as a radio advertisement.
- **Living brochure:** Children work in groups. Each child imagines that they are a video 'talking head' and presents one page of the brochure. Children take turns to present the information from their pages in the correct order to create the impression of an entire brochure.
- **News interview:** Children work in pairs. One child takes the role of news presenter and interviewer and their partner takes the role of theme park representative and interviewee. Present the contents of the brochure through a question and answer interview format.
- **Presentation ideas:** In groups, children take turns to imagine they are the project manager for the creation of a brochure for the theme park. The project manager presents and explains the features of the brochure to the team.

Year 6, Sequence 3
Non-fiction: Persuasive writing

Incidental writing

A short writing activity would enhance the children's understanding of the brochure contents and structure. Select activities that you think appropriate for the abilities and interests of your class. Children could compose:

- a design brief (instructions from the theme park owner to tell the design team what they want the brochure to contain and look like)
- a newspaper article to announce the opening of the new theme park
- a letter of complaint to the theme park owner about the increased traffic caused by visitors driving through the local area
- a diary entry by a visitor to the park.

Analysis

Show the brochure to the children and discuss the overall structure and the layout and contents of each section. Discuss the headings and subheadings. Highlight and note features such as: the use of rhetorical questions; language that speaks directly to the reader; adverbials of time; emotive and descriptive vocabulary; the use of colour, fonts and images; benefits and bonuses for visitors; imperative verbs; and a mixture of facts and persuasive comments.

Grammar: Synonyms and antonyms

Use the brochure to extract a selection of sentences that contain verbs, adverbs or adjectives that could be easily substituted with synonyms and antonyms to produce altered sentences. Explain to the children that synonyms are words that have the same meanings as one another and antonyms are words that have opposite meanings. Provide children with A4 plain or scrap paper that they can cut up into small word cards. Children choose a sentence from the brochure or from your pre-chosen list and write each word on a small word card. Children lay the word cards on the table in the correct order to form the sentence. Children choose a word from their sentence and use the thesaurus to find a synonym or antonym which they then write on a word card and swap with the chosen word in their sentence.

Phonics and spelling

Write the following words on the board, including the missing letter space.

suscept_ble; respect_ble; envi_ble; break_ble; identifi_ble; miser_ble; leg_ble; valu_ble; indestruct_ble; prob_ble; forgiv_ble; consider_ble; depend_ble

Challenge the children to use dictionaries to find the missing letter needed to spell each word correctly.

Review of the Big Picture

Once you have completed this phase, remind the children (or have them remind each other) of the sequence's Big Picture: they are working towards independently creating their own theme park brochure using persuasive techniques to appeal to the reader. Discuss and reflect upon the children's learning through Phase 1.

Year 6, Sequence 3
Non-fiction: Persuasive writing

Phase 2: Capture and organise

During Phase 2, children start to develop ideas about new content and the typical characteristics of persuasive writing needed to create a class brochure that would appeal to potential theme park visitors. Working collaboratively, children decide on the sections needed and the content of those sections.

> **Programmes of study: Year 6**
> - **Comprehension:** Identify how language, structure and presentation contribute to meaning.
> - **Comprehension:** Retrieve, record and present information from non-fiction.
> - **Comprehension:** Explain and discuss their understanding of what they have read, including through formal presentations and debates, maintaining a focus on the topic and using notes where necessary.
> - **Composition:** Identify the audience for and purpose of the writing, selecting the appropriate form and using other similar writing as models for their own.
> - **Composition:** Note and develop initial ideas, drawing on reading and research where necessary.
> - **Spelling:** Use the hyphen (to join a prefix to a root word).

Introduction

Remind children of the Big Picture for the sequence and recap on the learning achieved through Phase 1. Encourage children to bring in real-life examples of brochures designed to persuade people to visit attractions such as theme parks to compare with the model texts. (Brochures can be found in libraries, swimming pools and other public places as well as online.)

Discussing ideas

As a class, discuss and make decisions to form the basis of a plan to create a theme park brochure.

- What information should be included in the brochure?
- What makes this theme park better than others?
- How will the brochure persuade visitors to attend the theme park?
- Generate examples of language to be used.
- What else would visitors need to know about the theme park?
- How can we persuade visitors to book their tickets immediately?

Drama and storytelling

Use drama and oracy techniques to encourage children to develop their ideas further, especially developing the persuasive communication needed in the brochure.

- **Hot-seating the theme park owner:** Children could work in pairs or small groups to think of questions to ask the theme park owner, imagining that they are local residents or potential customers. The theme park owner should try to attract customers by persuading the audience about the benefits of the theme park.
- **Freeze-framing visitor reactions:** Children work in groups or as a whole class to role-play a visit to the theme park. When the teacher says 'freeze' children should imagine they are on a ride or looking at a ride and experiencing the park. The teacher could then use thought-tracking to ask individual children how they are feeling and what they are thinking whilst at the park.
- **Role-play advertising executives:** Encourage the children to work in groups to imagine they are the advertising executives responsible for promoting the theme park and attracting new customers. Role-play holding a board meeting to discuss promotional ideas and create slogans.

Incidental writing

Before you select any incidental writing, make sure the children are able to orally articulate their ideas, perhaps by telling a partner or group before writing. Select activities that you think appropriate for the abilities and interests of your class. Children could compose:

- a diary entry by someone who has just spent the day at the theme park
- a newspaper article announcing the grand opening of a brand new theme park

Year 6, Sequence 3
Non-fiction: Persuasive writing

- a letter from one friend to another telling them about their visit to the theme park.

Organising the class brochure ideas into a structure

Once the children have thoroughly explored ideas for their class brochure, bring them together and use their final suggestions to model how to plan an organisational structure in diagram or note with the help of the Non-fiction planner. Once recorded, go through the frame and ask children to evaluate the structure and organisation.

Phonics and spelling

Write the word 'mid-January' on the board.

Tell children that hyphens can be used to join a prefix to a root word if it helps the reader with pronunciation or meaning. Hyphens can help most with pronunciation if the prefix ends in a vowel and the root word also begins with a vowel. Ask: 'How might these words be pronounced differently or have a different meaning if the hyphen was removed?' Discuss each of the following words.

Hyphenated words: co-operate; co-exist; re-enter; co-ordinate; de-ice; anti-aging; re-elect; re-create; re-heat; re-sit; re-educate; re-examine; re-evaluate; co-author; co-own; re-energise; re-explain

Ask children to choose three of the hyphenated words and prepare to tell the class or group:
- how the word is pronounced with the hyphen
- how the word could be pronounced without the hyphen
- what the word means.

Review of the Big Picture

Once you have completed all the lessons for this phase, remind the children of the sequence's Big Picture. Recap on the learning achieved in Phase 2.

Year 6, Sequence 3
Non-fiction: Persuasive writing

Phase 3: Collaborate and compose

This phase focuses in detail on supporting children to draft and write individual sections of their persuasive brochure. It is presented as a series of four shared writing sessions covering: an introduction and general description section; a special events and opening hours section; a ticket prices, deals and offers section; a rides and attractions section. The series of lessons could be extended to include more support at your discretion. Through each lesson, persuasive writing techniques are modelled and practised.

> **Programmes of study: Year 6**
> - **Composition:** Identify the audience for and purpose of the writing, selecting the appropriate form and using other similar writing as a model for their own.
> - **Composition:** Note and develop initial ideas, drawing on reading and research where necessary.
> - **Composition:** Select appropriate grammar and vocabulary, understanding how such choices can change and enhance meaning.
> - **Composition:** Use a wide range of devices to build cohesion within and across paragraphs.
> - **Composition:** Use further organisational and presentational devices to structure text and to guide the reader.

Introduction

Remind the children about the Big Picture and recap on the learning in Phases 1 and 2. Explain to children that through Phase 3 they will be learning how to write persuasive content for a theme park brochure. Remind them that the purpose of the brochure is to persuade people to purchase tickets and visit the theme park.

Lesson 1

Starter (VGP focus) – Grammar: Using commas for clearer meaning

Display the following sentence on the board.

'For our younger visitors, Kids' Corner provides hours of fun on smaller rides such as the Teacups, and Mini Golf and Paddy's Paddling Pool.'

Explain that the sentence is taken from the model text. Ask the children to read the sentence and decide why the second comma has been placed where it is. How would the meaning be changed if we removed 'and' before 'Mini Golf'?

Read through the rest of the brochure. Ask children to find the sentences containing commas and take turns to read them to a partner, focusing on intonation and pauses.

Shared writing

Children remind themselves and each other of their planning ideas from Phase 2. Ask children to make suggestions for the wording of the opening paragraph of the brochure (the introduction section). Model writing the introduction section of the brochure with the children's input, focusing on using language that speaks directly to the reader, a rhetorical question, short paragraphs, and exaggerated, positive language to create a powerful first impression of the theme park. Have children make suggestions about where commas may aid the clarity of sentences and the flow of the text.

Independent writing

The children can now write their own first section, applying the typical characteristics of persuasive writing seen in the shared writing session along with the VGP focus to use commas. Some children may benefit from guided group writing or peer-paired writing at this stage.

Plenary

At appropriate points throughout the lesson, invite children to share their writing with small groups, partners or the whole class. Ask the children questions to help them focus on their progress and what they have created during that lesson, for example: 'What techniques have you used to make an impression on the reader?' 'What exaggerated, positive language have you used?' 'Where have you used commas to aid clarity in your writing?'

Lesson 2

Starter (VGP focus) – Punctuation: Boundaries between clauses (using dashes)

Ask the children to locate sentences in the model text that contain dashes and discuss with a partner the purpose of the

Year 6, Sequence 3
Non-fiction: Persuasive writing

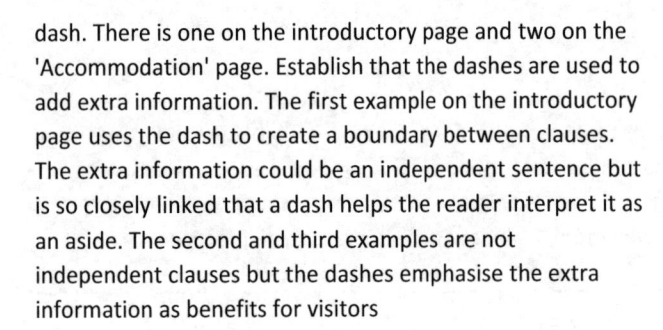

dash. There is one on the introductory page and two on the 'Accommodation' page. Establish that the dashes are used to add extra information. The first example on the introductory page uses the dash to create a boundary between clauses. The extra information could be an independent sentence but is so closely linked that a dash helps the reader interpret it as an aside. The second and third examples are not independent clauses but the dashes emphasise the extra information as benefits for visitors

Shared writing

With the children's input, model writing your class version of the special dates and events section of the brochure. Decide on a selection of dates and how the theme park might celebrate them. Use adjectives, adverbs and positive vocabulary to emphasise how amazing these celebrations will be. Sentences should combine factual information about the event mixed with persuasive comments to engage the reader. Include at least one example of using a dash to add extra information, either as a boundary between two clauses or as a positive comment or extra benefit for visitors.

Independent writing

The children can now write their own special dates and events section of the brochure, applying the VGP focus to include dashes for additional information. Some children may benefit from guided group writing or peer-paired writing at this stage.

Plenary

At points during the lesson, invite children to share their writing with groups or the whole class. Ask the children questions to help them focus on their progress and what they have created during that lesson, for example: 'How attractive does your theme park seem so far?' 'What adjectives, adverbs and positive vocabulary have you used to persuade and entice the reader?' 'Have you used a dash correctly to add extra information and, if so, what extra information did you add?'

Lesson 3

Starter (VGP focus) – Punctuation: Punctuating bulleted lists

Briefly look at the bulleted list on the introductory page of the model brochure.

Show the following bulleted list on the board and ask children to make comparisons between the punctuation used in this list and the list in the model brochure.

'Our theme park prices are:
- affordable
- frozen
- competitive.'

Explain that there are guidelines to help us correctly punctuate bulleted lists. If bulleted items are full sentences, start them with capital letters and end them with full stops, question marks or exclamation marks. If items are not full sentences, end them with commas, or semi-colons if any items already contain a comma, or no punctuation. End the last item in nothing or a full stop.

Shared writing

With the children's input, model writing the next part of the brochure: the ticket prices and special offers/deals section. Use children's planning and ideas from Phase 2 and the model brochure to make decisions about prices and packages. Use emotive language such as: 'Your children's happiness guaranteed for the price of less than a bunch of flowers!' Use imperative verbs such as: 'Buy Now!' Model using bullet-points to show a list of benefits included within a ticket package, for example:

'The family ticket includes:
- year round access to every part of the park
- free hotdogs at Sammy Jo's Cafe
- free parking in the red car park.'

Independent writing

The children can now write their own ticket prices section of the brochure, applying the VGP focus on a correctly punctuated bulleted list. They should also use emotive language and imperative verbs, where appropriate. Some children may benefit from guided group writing or peer-paired writing at this stage.

Plenary

At the end of the lesson, invite children to share their writing with groups or the whole class. Ask the children questions to help them focus on their progress and what they have created during that lesson, for example: 'How have you maintained the tone of the brochure for your intended audience?' 'What emotive language have you included?' 'What imperative verbs have you used?' 'Have you used a bulleted list and is it correctly punctuated?'

Year 6, Sequence 3
Non-fiction: Persuasive writing

Lesson 4

Starter (VGP focus) – Vocabulary: Synonyms and antonyms

Ask children to define 'synonym' and 'antonym', or remind them that synonyms are words that have the same meaning as one another and antonyms are words that have opposite meanings. Write the following words on the board (or your own selection of words) and challenge children to find three synonyms and three antonyms for each.

Suggested words: exciting, trip (noun), hungry, brave

Shared writing

With the children's input, continue modelling how to write the content of the brochure, focusing on the features and activities section. Ask children to contribute ideas for positive, persuasive, exciting and exaggerated language and use a thesaurus to find synonyms until the class agrees on the best words to use. The language used should be descriptive to help readers imagine how the rides or activities look, sound and feel. Examples of emotive language might include: 'Watch your children squeal in delight.' 'Your heart will melt.' Rhetorical questions could be included such as: 'When did you last have this much fun?' Decide with the children how many features and activities should be described.

Independent writing

The children can now write their own features and activities section of the brochure, applying the VGP focus on using a thesaurus to find synonyms where appropriate. Some children may benefit from guided group writing or peer-paired writing at this stage.

Plenary

At the end of the lesson invite children to share their writing with groups or the whole class. Ask the children questions to help them focus on their progress and what they have created during that lesson, for example: 'What positive, persuasive, exciting and exaggerated language have you used?' 'Share your writing. How effective is your partner's choice of vocabulary?' 'Have you included any rhetorical questions?'

Review of the Big Picture

Once you have completed all the lessons for this phase, remind the children of the sequence's Big Picture. Discuss what they have learned during Phase 3.

Year 6, Sequence 3
Non-fiction: Persuasive writing

Phase 4: Write independently

This final phase brings all the children's learning and writing skills together so that they can independently write their own theme park brochure using the persuasive techniques they have learned. Through their writing they will be able to utilise the different VGP focuses that they have been practising throughout the previous phases.

> **Programmes of study: Year 6**
> - **Composition:** Select appropriate grammar and vocabulary, understanding how such choices can change and enhance meaning.
> - **Composition:** Use a wide range of devices to build cohesion within and across paragraphs.
> - **Composition:** Use further organisational and presentational devices to structure text and to guide the reader.
> - **Composition:** Assess the effectiveness of their own and others' writing and suggest improvements.
> - **Composition:** Propose changes to grammar and vocabulary to enhance effects and clarify meaning.
> - **Composition:** Proofread for spelling and punctuation errors.
> - **Composition:** Perform their own compositions, using appropriate intonation, volume and movement so that meaning is clear.

Introduction

Introduce the phase by highlighting the overall Big Picture to the children. Recap on learning and progress through Phases 1–3 and explain that in Phase 4, they will be applying their learning to writing their own brochure independently. Discuss and list the contents of the theme park brochure that children might choose to include. Discuss and list the persuasive writing techniques that children could use. Recap on the structure used in the class writing sessions in Phase 3.

Writing

Give each child a Non-fiction planner and instruct them to start planning and writing each section for their own brochure. Display the class planning structure and a copy of the model brochures for reference. All the children should be encouraged to try to write independently to the best of their ability. Ask open questions such as: 'How will you engage readers to make them read more of the brochure?' 'How will you persuade readers to purchase their theme park tickets?' Avoid telling children what to write. Some children may benefit from guided composition. Focus on perseverance and resilience in their independent application.

Proofreading and redrafting

Have the children proofread their work periodically as they write. Proofreading and improvement without support means that the writing may happen over a few lessons. Offer the children the Editor's checklist or create your own checklist that includes the VGP and spelling focuses covered throughout this sequence. Highlight the importance of redrafting, linking their efforts to the overall Big Picture.

Self- and peer-assessment

Encourage the children to take time to self-assess their own writing as well as that of others in their group. Offer them a set of self-assessment questions, such as: 'How does the brochure attract and inform readers?' 'How does the brochure persuade readers to purchase tickets?' 'What impact does the writing have?' 'What changes would improve the reader's experience?'

Rehearsing and presenting

Once the children have written their independent brochure (including any design and illustration work), encourage them to present their final product to an audience. This could be in the form of a simple presentation, as a television advert, or in role as the owner of the theme park presenting a new brochure or new ride to potential visitors. Encourage children to feedback on one another's writing and presentations.

Final review of the Big Picture

Individually or with partners, have children reflect on what they have learned from this sequence and what they will apply in their future writing.

Year 6, Sequence 4
Non-fiction: Email conventions

Sequence 4
Non-fiction: Email conventions

Approximate duration: Two weeks

Big Picture

Through this teaching sequence, children explore the way in which many people communicate through the medium of email. Understanding the conventions involved in emailing, and the degree of formality or informality involved, will help children to use this approach in their wider life. Children will be able to communicate effectively and appropriately through the medium of email.

Phase 1: Enjoy and immerse

Children analyse the conventions used in a model fictional email exchange between a boy and his grandfather.

Phase 2: Capture and organise

Children begin to develop ideas for creating their own email exchange discussing an environmental issue.

Phase 3: Collaborate and compose

Children undertake supported writing sessions to develop the writing features common to emails.

Phase 4: Write independently

Children write, edit and present their own email exchange discussing an environmental issue.

Main source text

Treasure House Anthology Sequence 4 text. Treasure House Online, Year 6, Comprehension Unit 4: Non-fiction (emails): Climate change, what climate change?

Extra source texts

Global Warming, Simon Seymour, ISBN 978-0-06-114252-9

Fragile Earth, Claire Llewellyn, ISBN 978-0-00-723110-2

Background knowledge

The main source text is a series of eight short, fictional email exchanges between Josh (a fictional school boy) and his grandad. Written in an informal style, Josh asks his grandad for advice regarding a school project. Subsequently, Josh and his grandad debate the various arguments for and against climate change, which is the subject of Josh's project. The extra source texts provide further information about global warming and the fragility of planet Earth, which will enable children to access factual information to form their own email exchanges. This sequence provides an opportunity to explore the degrees of formality or informality that may be required when emailing a variety of recipients.

Spoken outcome

To perform the dialogue of an email exchange to an audience of peers or parents

Writing outcome

To write a series of emails discussing an environmental issue

Prior knowledge

Check children's knowledge and understanding of:
- the purpose of emails
- the conventions involved in writing emails
- global and local environmental issues.

Year 6, Sequence 4
Non-fiction: Email conventions

Diagnostic assessment options

Before starting the sequence, you may want to conduct an initial diagnostic assessment of the children's understanding of the features of emails.

Ideas for initial diagnostic assessment options include:

- discussion about emails and their purpose
- a brief, unsupported writing activity creating an email exchange between two characters
- practising speaking and listening skills relating to an email exchange
- a short reading comprehension activity / quiz on an email exchange.

Cross-curricular links

KS2 Geography – Human and physical geography

Describe and understand key aspects of:

- physical geography, including: climate zones, biomes and vegetation belts, rivers, mountains, volcanoes and earthquakes, and the water cycle
- human geography, including: types of settlement and land use, economic activity including trade links, and the distribution of natural resources including energy, food, minerals and water.

KS2 Computing

Understand computer networks, including the internet; how they can provide multiple services, such as the World Wide Web, and the opportunities they offer for communication and collaboration.

Treasure House links

All digital and pupil book units have the same names and numbers, but different questions.

- Treasure House, Year 6, Comprehension Unit 4: Non-fiction (emails): Climate change, what climate change?
- Treasure House, Year 6, Composition Unit 6: Factual writing
- Treasure House, Year 6, Composition Unit 12: Paragraphs in non-fiction
- Treasure House, Year 6, Vocabulary Unit 3: Our changing language
- Treasure House, Year 6, Spelling Unit 4: The suffixes -able, -ible, -ably and -ibly
- Treasure House, Year 6, Spelling Unit 9: Words with 'silent' letters
- Treasure House, Year 5, Grammar Unit 2: Adverbs and modal verbs showing possibility

Resources

Treasure House Anthology Sequence 4 text. Source texts – see Anthologies; Non-fiction planner; Editor's checklist

Year 6, Sequence 4
Non-fiction: Email conventions

Phase 1: Enjoy and immerse

In Phase 1, the children are introduced to the email exchanges of Josh (a school boy) and his grandad. Josh is working on a school project about climate change and he has emailed his grandad to ask for advice. Josh's friend has suggested that climate change does not really exist and that the concept of climate change has been created by journalists to generate a news story. Throughout the informal email conversation, Josh and his grandad explore different opinions on climate change. Over several lessons, children are offered the opportunity to immerse themselves fully in the exchange through comprehension and discussion activities, as well as exploring the content and structure of the emails through drama, storytelling, writing and analysis of the text.

Programmes of study: Year 6
- **Comprehension:** Identify themes and conventions in and across a wide range of writing.
- **Comprehension:** Identify how language, structure and presentation contribute to meaning.
- **Comprehension:** Discuss and evaluate how authors use language, considering the impact on the reader.
- **Composition:** Identify the audience for and purpose of the writing, selecting the appropriate form and using other similar writing as models for their own.
- **Vocabulary, grammar and punctuation:** Understand the difference between vocabulary typical of informal speech and vocabulary appropriate for formal speech and writing.
- **Spelling:** Use words ending in -able and -ible.
- **Spelling**: Use words ending in -ably and -ibly.

Sparking interest

Introduce the sequence by highlighting the overall Big Picture to the children: they will be working towards writing their own series of emails to explore an environmental issue independently.

Reading and discussing

Introduce the main source text, read it with the class and check their understanding. Discuss children's opinions of the contents of the emails as well as the typical characteristics of email writing.

Discuss the following with the children.
- Who were the email exchanges between?
- Why do you think they were using email as a medium for communication?
- What was the style of the writing like in the emails?
- How formal or informal is the language?
- How would the emails be written differently if they weren't between family members?
- Over what time period did the email exchange take place?
- How do / might you use emails?
- What are the benefits of using emails?
- Are there any disadvantages of using emails?

Drama and storytelling

Use drama and oracy activities to reinforce the children's understanding of the contents of the email exchange and the relationship between Josh and his grandad. Select the activities that would suit your class or fit in with your lesson timing. Encourage mixed-ability grouping for the chosen activities.

- **On the phone:** In pairs, children rehearse and then perform the emails as a phone conversation between Josh and his grandad. Children reflect on how the conversation might be different in a phone conversation to the email content.
- **Role-play discussion:** In pairs or small groups, children assume the roles of Josh and his school friend, Pete. Children should imagine that Josh goes back to school and relays the email exchange that he had with his grandad to Pete. Children then role-play the conversation Josh and Pete would have.
- **Hot-seating Grandad:** This activity can be done in pairs, small groups or as a whole-class situation with nominated children or the teacher assuming the role of Josh's grandad. Questions and answers could be derived from the email exchange.

Year 6, Sequence 4
Non-fiction: Email conventions

Incidental writing

A short writing activity would enhance the children's understanding of the content of the emails. Select activities that you think appropriate for the abilities and interests of your class. Use the children's written outcomes to inform the emphases during the collaborative composition phase. Children could compose:

- a diary entry by Josh
- a newspaper article about climate change
- a fact-file about an environmental issue.

Analysis

Show the model text to the children and discuss: the brief length of the emails; the informal nature of the conversation; the address used (Dear Grandad, My dear Josh), which then is omitted later in the exchange; the chatty style used; the period of time that the emails took place over; the differences to letter writing, such as no postal address and no sign off other than a name and kiss. Ask children whether these features would be the same if Josh were emailing a company to enquire about their environmental policies.

Grammar: Our changing language

Explain to the children that, although many email exchanges are less formal than letters, we need to have an awareness that the degree of formality required will depend on who the recipient of the email is. Similar to letter writing, an email to a friend or relative will be more informal but an email to someone you don't know well or to a company representative will need to be more formal.

Use large pieces of paper and coloured pens to create two posters that can be displayed on the classroom wall. In the centre of one, write 'informal language' and, in the centre of the other, write 'formal language'. Collect children's ideas which could include the following.

Informal language: shorter words, words missed out, slang, contractions, incomplete sentences, lots of exclamations

Formal language: careful word choices, polite and respectful language, no contractions and only complete sentences

Phonics and spelling

Write the following passage on the board for the children to copy and fill in the gaps with the correct spelling, -ible or -able. Alternatively, use the passage as a dictation.

Dear Grandad,

This is unbeliev____! Pete says it is poss____ for me to visit his dad's work with him. We must be sens____ though. The experience will be unforgett____. Pete's dad is knowledge____ and approach____. I am sure the information we get will be invalu____. I hope this terr____ weather clears up soon.

Love Josh x

Children should use a dictionary to check spellings.

Review of the Big Picture

Once you have completed this phase, remind the children (or have them remind each other) of the sequence's Big Picture: they are working towards writing their own series of emails about an environmental issue, independently.

Year 6, Sequence 4
Non-fiction: Email conventions

Phase 2: Capture and organise

During Phase 2, children start to develop ideas about new content and the features needed to create a class series of emails about an environmental issue. Working collaboratively, children research and decide on an environmental issue; think about whom the email exchanges will be between and therefore the degree of formality required; and think about and plan the content needed in the emails.

Programmes of study: Year 6

- **Comprehension:** Continue to read and discuss an increasingly wide range of fiction, poetry, plays, non-fiction and reference books or textbooks.
- **Comprehension:** Summarise the main ideas drawn from more than one paragraph, identifying key details that support the main ideas.
- **Comprehension:** Retrieve, record and present information from non-fiction.
- **Composition:** Identify the audience for and purpose of the writing, selecting the appropriate form and using other similar writing as models for their own.
- **Composition:** Note and develop initial ideas, drawing on reading and research where necessary.
- **Spelling:** Spell some words with 'silent' letters.

Introduction

Remind the children of the Big Picture for the sequence and recap on the learning achieved through Phase 1. Read one or both of the additional source texts to provide ideas for the subject of environmental issues.

Discussing ideas

As a class, discuss and make decisions to form the basis of the children's own email exchange. Explain that, in order to experience writing emails in an informal and a more formal way, the email exchange should take place between a variety of characters, some of whom know each other, such as between family members (like Josh and his grandad), and between characters who do not know each other, such as a school child and a company director. Discuss the following.

- Which environmental issue could we discuss in the emails?
- Who will the informal emails be between?
- Who will the formal emails be between?
- What might we want to ask in the emails?
- What environmental information do we need to research to enable us to write the emails, both for asking questions and for the responses to those questions?

Drama and storytelling

Use drama and oracy activities to encourage children to develop their ideas further.

- **Hot-seating an environmental expert:** After researching and gathering facts about the agreed environmental issue, children can take turns to assume the role of an environmental expert or scientist who answers questions on the environmental issue from the hot-seat.
- **Improvised role-play:** Create and act out an improvised role-play situation in groups. Assume the roles of a class teacher who sets the environmental issue project, some friends in the class who discuss the issue, and various family members or professionals who might be asked about the environmental issue by the school children.
- **News presenters:** In groups, children plan and present a television news item about the environmental issue. They could include interviews with civilians and / or experts.

Incidental writing

Before you select any incidental writing, make sure the children are able to orally articulate the main ideas for their email exchanges on an environmental issue. Select activities that you think appropriate for the abilities and interests of your class.

Year 6, Sequence 4
Non-fiction: Email conventions

Children could compose:
- a fact-file about the environmental issue
- a newspaper article
- a letter of complaint.

Organising the class email exchanges into a structure

Once the children have thoroughly explored ideas for the contents of their email exchanges, bring them together and use their final suggestions to model how to plot their new email series in diagram or note form with the help of the Non-fiction planner. Once recorded, go through the frame and ask the children to evaluate the contents and organisation.

Phonics and spelling

Display the word 'doubt' on the board.

Ask children to explain what makes 'doubt' a tricky word to spell (the silent letter). Tell children that silent letters are letters you cannot detect from the way a word is pronounced. They exist because the English language has been developing for hundreds of years and, over that time, the pronunciation of many words has changed. Some letters are no longer pronounced, even though they still exist in the spellings.

Read through the words below with the children and check that they understand what they mean.

Ask children to write each of the words in a sentence then underline the silent letter. The sentences could be linked to the theme of climate change or a simple email from Josh to his grandad.

Words with silent letters: doubt, gnarled, wrench, autumn, condemn, debt, writing, whistle, wrapper, gnash

Review of the Big Picture

Once you have completed all the lessons for this phase, remind the children of the sequence's Big Picture. Recap on the learning achieved in Phase 2.

Year 6, Sequence 4
Non-fiction: Email conventions

Phase 3: Collaborate and compose

This phase focuses in detail on supporting children to write individual sections of the series of email exchanges. Through four shared writing lessons, the children collaboratively compose two sets of email exchanges, one informal and one formal. Each set of email exchanges contain four emails, allowing for the development of authentic content on the topic of an environmental issue.

> **Programmes of study: Year 6**
> - **Composition:** Identify the audience for and purpose of the writing, selecting the appropriate form and using other similar writing as a model for their own.
> - **Composition:** Note and develop initial ideas, drawing on reading and research where necessary.
> - **Composition:** Select appropriate grammar and vocabulary, understanding how such choices can change and enhance meaning.
> - **Composition:** Use a wide range of devices to build cohesion within and across paragraphs.
> - **Composition:** Use further organisational and presentational devices to structure text and to guide the reader.

Introduction

Remind the children about the Big Picture and recap on the learning in Phases 1 and 2. Explain to children that through Phase 3 they will be learning how to write their own email exchanges in both a formal and an informal style, based on content focused on an environmental issue.

Lesson 1

Starter (VGP focus) – Grammar: Adverbs showing possibility

Remind children that adverbs of possibility can show how likely the action of a verb in a sentence is. Write adverbs of possibility on the board. Ask children to write each word on a small strip of paper then work with a partner to order the words from the least to the most certain. As an extension, ask children to write each word in a sentence to show how it can be used.

Adverbs of possibility: certainly, definitely, maybe, possibly, clearly, obviously, perhaps, probably

Shared writing

Children remind themselves and each other of their planning ideas from Phase 2. Explain to children that in this writing session you will be working as a team to write an informal email from a school child to a friend or relative in an informal tone, and a response email from the friend or relative to the school child. Ask the children to make suggestions for the salutation and opening sentence of the first email. Ideas for informal salutations could include: 'Hi,' 'Hey mate!' 'Hiya,' 'Dear …' Using the children's contributions, model writing an informal email to ask a question and / or give an opinion about the environmental issue. Include relevant small talk such as: 'I hope your party went well the other day.' 'How's your sore foot?' Discuss the use of appropriate informal language throughout. Show that the email is direct in manner and gets quickly to the point. Inform the children that the instantaneous transmission of emails usually means that people reply promptly, often within 24 hours. Ask children to contribute ideas for content and wording as you model writing the reply email.

Independent writing

The children can now write their own first email exchange, in an informal manner between the school child and their friend or relative. Children may work in pairs, taking on the role of each character as they write. Some children may benefit from guided group writing at this stage.

Plenary

At appropriate points throughout the lesson, invite children to share their writing with small groups / partners or the whole class. Ask the children questions to help them focus on their progress and what they have created during that lesson, for example: 'How well does your email exchange communicate the different ideas?' 'What language choices have you made to ensure the right tone for the characters involved?' 'What adverbs have you used to show possibility?'

Year 6, Sequence 4
Non-fiction: Email conventions

Lesson 2

Starter (VGP focus) – Vocabulary: Formal and informal language

Recap briefly on some of the typical characteristics of formal and informal language (see Phase 1). Ask children to turn these formal sentences into informal sentences:

'Pete's father and Josh's grandfather did not hold the same opinions.' 'Josh was undecided but remained open-minded regarding the climate change debate.' 'Josh's grandfather expressed his viewpoint with clarity and rationale.'

Shared writing

Remind the children of the email exchange they constructed between the school child and their relative or friend in Lesson 1 of this phase. Explain that this session will involve writing the continuation of the informal email exchange. Together with the children, model how to write another two short, informal emails: one from the school child to their friend or relative and one reply back to the school child. The content of the email could focus on new information to share about the environmental project or the purpose of the emails could be to make an arrangement to meet and carry out some research together. Again, ensure discussion to highlight the use of the typical characteristics of informal language such as contractions, exclamations and abbreviations, for example 'LOL' meaning 'laugh out loud'.

Independent writing

The children can now write their own second pair of emails in an informal manner. Encourage them to use as many typical characteristics of informal language as they can. Children may work in pairs, taking on the role of each character as they write. Some children may benefit from guided group writing at this stage.

Plenary

At the end of the lesson, invite children to share their writing with groups or the whole class. Ask the children questions to help them focus on their progress and what they have created during that lesson, for example: 'How well does your email exchange communicate the different ideas?' 'What language choices have you made to ensure the right tone for the characters involved?' 'What typical characteristics of informal language have you included?'

Lesson 3

Starter (VGP focus) – Grammar: Modal verbs showing possibility

Remind children that modal verbs of possibility can show how likely the action of a verb in a sentence is. Write the following modal verbs of possibility on the board.

Modal verbs of possibility: can, could, may, might, shall, should, will, would

Write the following sentence beginnings on the board.

'I can help you if…' 'You should have …' 'We might go …' 'I wouldn't do …' 'You ought to eat …' 'She will be late …'

Ask children to complete the sentences with their own endings or make up three of their own sentences using modal verbs to show how likely something is. Discuss the nuances of modal verb choices, for example, they may seem tentative, or perhaps bossy.

Shared writing

With the children's input, model writing an email exchange between the school child and a company representative such as a director. Show how the email has a more formal tone and uses formal language. Use an introductory sentence, for example: 'Dear Sirs, I am emailing you to enquire about your environmental policies.' Show that the email can still be direct and brief but maintains similarities to a formal letter. Include a sentence detailing the response you hope to receive from the company, for example: 'I hope that you will be able to email me back with the information I have requested.' When constructing the response, inform the children about the use of email signatures (the sender's job title and contact details or company logo shown under their sign off at the bottom of the email) and design an email signature for the company director's reply.

Independent writing

The children can now write their own formal email exchange between a school child and a company director, to request information about the environmental issue, using formal language. Some children may benefit from guided group or peer-paired writing at this stage.

Plenary

At the end of the lesson, invite children to share their writing with groups or the whole class. Ask the children questions to help them focus on their progress and what they have created during that lesson, for example: 'How well does your

Year 6, Sequence 4
Non-fiction: Email conventions

email exchange communicate the different ideas?' 'What language choices have you made to ensure the right tone for the characters involved?' 'What modal verbs showing possibility have you included?'

Lesson 4

Starter (VGP focus) – Vocabulary: Formal and informal language

Recap briefly on some of the typical characteristics of formal and informal language (see Phase 1). Ask children to turn these informal sentences into formal sentences:

'Josh jotted down a note to ping to the top dude in the company – he wanted to know what it was all about.' 'When he got the info he was gonna whack it together into a project folder.'

Shared writing

Remind the children of the email exchange they constructed between the school child and the company director in Lesson 3 of this session. Explain that this session will involve writing a continuation of the formal email exchange. Together with the children, model how to write another two short formal emails: one from the school child to the company director and one reply back to the school child. The content of the email could focus on asking another question about the environmental issue or the purpose of the emails could be to give an opinion about the reply from the last exchange. As this is not the first email to the company director, they could now be addressed by the name they gave when they replied in the last exchange, for example: 'Mrs Braithwaite'. With the reply from the company director you could include reference to an attachment (and then in a separate writing session create a report or document that could be the attachment).

Independent writing

The children can now write their own second pair of emails in a formal manner. Encourage them to use as many typical characteristics of formal language as they can. Some children may benefit from guided group or peer-paired writing at this stage.

Plenary

At the end of the lesson, invite children to share their writing with groups or the whole class. Ask the children questions to help them focus on their progress and what they have created during that lesson, for example: 'How well does your

email exchange communicate the different ideas?' 'What language choices have you made to ensure the right tone for the characters involved?' 'What typical characteristics of formal language have you included?'

Encourage reading-back to ensure consistency of formal tone.

Rehearsing and performing

Once they have written all of the email exchanges, encourage the children to present them by performing them either as a dialogue or as a performance. Discuss the similarities and differences to the email exchange between Josh and his grandad. Discuss any interesting points arising from the environmental topic.

Review of the Big Picture

Once you have completed all the lessons for this phase, remind the children of the sequence's Big Picture. Discuss what they have learned during Phase 3.

Year 6, Sequence 4
Non-fiction: Email conventions

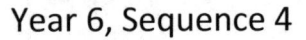

Phase 4: Write independently

This final phase brings all the children's learning and writing skills together so that they can write their own independent series of email exchanges. Through their writing, they will be able to utilise the different VGP focuses that they have been practising throughout the previous phases.

> **Programmes of study: Year 6**
> - **Composition:** Select appropriate grammar and vocabulary, understanding how such choices can change and enhance meaning.
> - **Composition:** Use a wide range of devices to build cohesion within and across paragraphs.
> - **Composition:** Use further organisational and presentational devices to structure text and to guide the reader.
> - **Composition:** Assess the effectiveness of their own and others' writing and suggest improvements.
> - **Composition:** Propose changes to grammar and vocabulary to enhance effects and clarify meaning.
> - **Composition:** Proofread for spelling and punctuation errors.
> - **Composition:** Perform their own compositions, using appropriate intonation, volume and movement so that meaning is clear.

Introduction

Introduce this phase by highlighting the overall Big Picture to the children. Recap on learning and progress through Phases 1–3 and explain that in Phase 4 they will be applying their learning to write their own email exchanges independently. Discuss and list examples of the possible contents of the emails related to the environmental issues topic. Recap on the typical characteristics of informal and formal email structures. Differentiate the independent writing task by altering the quantity of email exchanges expected.

Writing

Give each child a Non-fictionplanner and instruct them to start planning and writing each email in their series. Display the class planning structure and a copy of the model text for reference. All children should be encouraged to try to write independently to the best of their ability. Ask open questions such as: 'How will you achieve the purpose of the email?' Avoid telling children what to write. Some children may benefit from guided composition. Focus on perseverance and resilience in their independent application.

Proofreading and redrafting

Have the children proofread their work periodically as they write. Proofreading and improvement without support means that the writing may happen over a few lessons. Offer the children Editor's checklist or create your own checklist that includes the VGP and spelling focuses covered throughout this sequence.

Highlight the importance of redrafting, linking their efforts to the overall Big Picture.

Self- and peer-assessment

Encourage the children to take time to self-assess their own writing as well as that of others in the group. Offer them a set of self-assessment questions, such as: 'Does the email exchange sound authentic?' 'How clearly is the writing structured?' 'What impact does the writing have?' 'Have formal and informal language features been used appropriately?' 'What changes would improve the reader's experience?' 'How have you used modal verbs and adverbs to show possibility?' 'What words with silent letters have you used?'

Rehearsing and performing

Once the children have written their independent series of email exchanges, encourage them to work in pairs to perform their emails in role to one another and the whole class. Discuss how similar or different the emails are to the model text emails between Josh and his grandad. Encourage the children to feed back on one another's writing and performances.

Final review of the Big Picture

Individually or with partners, have the children reflect on what they have learned from this sequence and what they will apply in their future writing.

Year 6, Sequence 5
Poetry: Free verse

Sequence 5
Poetry: free verse

Approximate duration: Two weeks

Big Picture

Through this teaching sequence, children will explore the way in which poets write poems that portray the flow and natural rhythm of a conversation to engage and entertain readers. Understanding the techniques used by poets will help children to use these techniques within their own writing. Children will be able to write conversational poems that engage and entertain readers.

Phase 1: Enjoy and immerse

Children analyse the stylistic features of the model text, 'Shut Your Mouth When You're Eating' by Michael Rosen.

Phase 2: Capture and organise

Children begin to develop ideas for creating their own conversational poem.

Phase 3: Collaborate and compose

Children undertake supported writing sessions to develop the content and features of their conversational poem.

Phase 4: Write independently

Children write, edit and present their own conversational poem that will engage and entertain readers.

Main source text

Treasure House Anthology Sequence 5 text. 'Shut Your Mouth When You're Eating', *Quick, Let's Get Out of Here*, Michael Rosen, ISBN 978-0-14-031784-8, p.115

Extra source texts

Treasure House Online, Year 6, Comprehension Unit 5: Poetry: 'Crack-a-Dawn'

Background knowledge

Michael Rosen (born 7 May 1946) is a renowned British children's novelist and poet. His poem 'Shut Your Mouth When You're Eating' provides a classic example of free verse poetry, characterised by having no set metrical pattern and varying line lengths to convey the thoughts of the poet and the natural rhythms of speech. Suspensory pauses play an important role and are used to prevent the poem from turning into prose. The topic of the poem is a father nagging his son to close his mouth when eating; something many children will identify with. There is a humorous ending when the son catches his father talking with his mouth full. Both the main and extra source texts are examples of how language can be used powerfully in everyday contexts.

Spoken outcome

To perform poems to an audience of peers or parents

Writing outcome

To write a conversation poem set at home or school, in which someone is told what to do

Prior knowledge

Check children's knowledge and understanding of:
- poetry by Michael Rosen
- characteristics common to conversation poems
- characteristics common to poems in general.

Year 6, Sequence 5
Poetry: Free verse

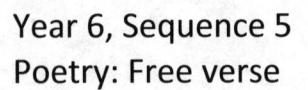

Diagnostic assessment options

Before starting the sequence, you may want to conduct an initial diagnostic assessment of the children's understanding of the style and structure of a conversation poem.

Ideas for initial diagnostic assessment options include:
- discussion about conversation poems, their purpose and form
- a brief, unsupported writing activity creating a short conversation poem
- practising speaking and listening skills relating to a conversation poem
- a short reading comprehension activity / quiz on a conversation poem.

Cross-curricular links

KS2 PSHE – Relationships

Treasure House links

All digital and pupil book units have the same names and numbers, but different questions.
- Treasure House, Year 6, Comprehension Unit 5: Poetry: 'Crack-a-Dawn'
- Treasure House, Year 6, Composition Unit 8: Humorous stories
- Treasure House, Year 6, Vocabulary Unit 3: Our changing language
- Treasure House, Year 6, Spelling Unit 4: The suffixes -able, -ible, -ably and -ibly
- Treasure House Year 6, Spelling Unit 13: Homophones and near-homophones (4)
- Treasure House, Year 6, Vocabulary Unit 1: Using a thesaurus
- Treasure House, Year 6, Vocabulary Unit 2: Synonyms and antonyms
- Treasure House, Year 5, Grammar Unit 2: Adverbs and modal verbs showing possibility

Resources

Source texts – see Anthologies; Poetry planner;

Year 6, Sequence 5
Poetry: Free verse

Phase 1: Enjoy and immerse

In Phase 1, the children are introduced to the humorous conversational poem, 'Shut Your Mouth When You're Eating' by Michael Rosen. The poem is written to sound like the natural conversation between a father and son as the father reprimands his son for eating with his mouth open. Over several sessions, children are offered the opportunity to immerse themselves fully in the poem through comprehension and discussion activities, as well as exploring the content and form through drama, writing and analysis of the text.

Programmes of study: Year 6

- **Comprehension:** Continue to read and discuss an increasingly wide range of fiction, poetry, plays, non-fiction and reference books or textbooks.
- **Comprehension:** Prepare poems and plays to read aloud and to perform, showing understanding through intonation, tone and volume so that the meaning is clear to an audience.
- **Comprehension:** Discuss and evaluate how authors use language, including figurative language, considering the impact on the reader.
- **Composition:** Identify the audience for and purpose of the writing, selecting the appropriate form and using other similar writing as models for their own.
- **Vocabulary, grammar and punctuation:** Understand the difference between vocabulary typical of informal speech and vocabulary appropriate for formal speech and writing.
- **Spelling:** Use words ending in -able and -ible.
- **Spelling**: Use words ending in -ably and -ibly.

Sparking interest

Introduce the sequence by highlighting the overall Big Picture to the children: they will be working towards creating their own conversation poem in which someone is being told what to do. Use an opening question such as: 'How can a poet make their poem sound like a conversation?'

Reading and discussing

Introduce the main source text, read it with the class and check their understanding.

Discuss the following with the children.

- Who is this poem about?
- What is this poem about?
- Why do you think the poet wrote this poem?
- Who do you think it was written for?
- How does the poet create humour?
- Why do you think it makes you feel like that?
- Why did Rosen choose this style for this theme?
- How would you describe the rhythm?
- Why is rhyme unnecessary here?

Drama and storytelling

Use drama and oracy activities to reinforce the children's understanding of the poem. Select the activities that would suit your class or fit in with your lesson timing. Encourage mixed-ability grouping for the chosen activities.

- **Performance poetry:** Give children the stage and invite them to read the poem by themselves or with a friend in a style they think is appropriate for the style of the poem. Encourage children to memorise some, or all, of the poem in preparation for performance.
- **Hot-seating the poet:** Research more about Rosen via his website, then imagine the poet has come to visit the class. Give children the opportunity, in pairs, groups or as a whole class, to ask the imaginary poet questions. The child or teacher playing the role of the poet should improvise their answers.
- **Act it out:** Have children turn the poem into an improvised role-pay scene. Use freeze-framing and thought-tracking to think about what the characters in the poem are thinking.

Year 6, Sequence 5
Poetry: Free verse

Incidental writing

A short writing activity would enhance the children's understanding of the poem. Select activities that you think appropriate for the abilities and interests of your class. Children could compose:

- a diary entry by the son
- an online article or blog about a decline in basic manners (such as eating with your mouth shut)
- a letter of complaint from father to son about the son's lack of manners.

Analysis

Show the poem to the children and discuss the content and the form. Ask children: 'How does it compare with dialogue found in a story?' Discuss the sentence lengths and presentation. Ask the children to decide whether there is a rhyming pattern. Have the children count the syllables in each line and see if there is a pattern. Ask: 'How does the poem flow?' Practise reading it out to listen to the rhythm. Establish that the natural pauses in speech play an important role in the flow and rhythm of the poem. Experiment reading the poem in different voices and discuss how it sounds when it is, for example, whispered, bellowed or sobbed.

Grammar: Our changing language

Tell children that we use informal language when we are speaking or writing casually to friends, family or people we know well. We use formal language when we are speaking or writing to a person we don't know. Ask the children whether the poem is written with informal or formal language and encourage them to explain how they know. Establish that the poem should largely be informal because it is a conversation between two family members. The title 'Shut Your Mouth When You're Eating' is a very informal way of speaking; some people would argue this is rude. Discuss the typical characteristics of informal and formal language.

Informal language: shorter words, words missed out, slang, contradictions and incomplete sentences

Formal language: careful word choices, polite and respectful language, no contractions and only complete sentences

Ask children to change lines from the poem to make them formal. Ask children: 'How has the poem changed?' 'How has the impact on the reader been affected?' 'What would the title of the poem be if it were changed into formal language?' Discuss the fact that some people tend to speak more formally or informally. Many people would say 'Please eat with your mouth closed' instead. Ask children why they think this is and whether they think it matters.

Phonics and spelling

Display the word 'horrible' on the board and underline the 'ible' part. Explain to the children that the -ible / -ibly ending is more common if a complete root word cannot be heard. However, there are some exceptions.

For the list of ten -ible words below, ask the children to decide whether the root word can be heard as a whole or not. Discuss the meaning of each word then look it up in a dictionary to check. Then write each word in a short sentence. You could link the sentences to the theme of the 'Shut Your Mouth When You're Eating' poem by writing sentences that are conversational or bossy, considering carefully which of the words are more likely to be used in informal and formal situations.

-ible words: illegible, responsible, reversible, flexible, plausible, convertible, susceptible, incredible, eligible, feasible

Review of the Big Picture

Once you have completed this phase, remind the children (or have them remind each other) of the sequence's Big Picture: they are working towards writing their own conversation poem.

Year 6, Sequence 5
Poetry: Free verse

Phase 2: Capture and organise

During Phase 2, children start to develop ideas about new content and the literary features needed to create a class conversation poem set at home or at school, in which someone is told what to do. Working collaboratively, children decide on the setting, characters and conversation ideas.

> **Programmes of study: Year 6**
> - **Comprehension:** Identify and discuss themes and conventions in and across a wide range of writing.
> - **Comprehension:** Identify how language, structure and presentation contribute to meaning.
> - **Comprehension:** Explain and discuss their understanding of what they have read, including through formal presentations and debates, maintaining a focus on the topic and using notes where necessary.
> - **Composition:** Identify the audience for and purpose of the writing, selecting the appropriate form and using other similar writing as models for their own.
> - **Composition:** Note and develop initial ideas, drawing on reading and research where necessary.
> - **Spelling:** Continue to distinguish between homophones and other words which are often confused.

Introduction

Remind the children of the Big Picture for the sequence and recap on the learning achieved through Phase 1. Read the extra source text, 'Crack-a-Dawn', for another example of a conversation poem in which a parent berates their child.

Discussing ideas

As a class, discuss and make decisions to form the basis of their own conversation poem.

- Where should the poem be set? Should it be set at home, at school or another familiar setting?
- Who will the two characters be?
- What will the characters be talking about?
- How do the characters feel?
- In what way will they speak to one another? Fondly? Grumpily? Rudely? Softly?
- What is the background story to their conversation?
- How will the conversation be resolved? Or will the conversation be left in suspense?

Drama and storytelling

Use drama and oracy activities to allow the children to explore the suggestions for their new characters and conversation development. Select the activities that would suit your class or fit in with your lesson timing. Encourage mixed-ability grouping for the chosen activities.

- **Hot-seating the main characters:** This activity can be done in pairs, small groups or as a class. Encourage the children to think and, if necessary, write down their questions before the hot-seat session starts. Discuss the characters' responses.
- **Freeze-framing key moments:** Once the structure of the conversation is created, try out the different scenes in the right story order. Use thought-tracking by asking each child in the freeze-frame what they're thinking at a particular moment.
- **Poetry rehearsal:** Have the children work in pairs to devise a retelling of the conversation and then perform it to the rest of the class. Discuss the differences between the different pairs' conversations and which parts worked better than others. Try retelling it in the first person and in the third person. Ask children: 'How does the impact change?' 'Which version do you prefer?'

Incidental writing

Before you select any incidental writing, make sure the children are able to orally articulate the main events of their class conversation poem. Select activities that you think appropriate for the abilities and interests of your class. Children could compose:

- a diary entry
- further dialogue
- a character profile
- a blog entry or email.

Year 6, Sequence 5
Poetry: Free verse

Organising the class conversation poem into a structure

Once the children have thoroughly explored ideas for their class conversation poem, bring them together and use their final suggestions to model how to plan their conversation into a diagram or note form with the help of the Poetry planner. Once recorded, go through the frame and ask the children to evaluate the structure and organisation.

Phonics and spelling

Explain to the children that homophones are words that sound the same but are spelt differently and have different meanings. You always need a context (a setting, for example, a sentence) to know how to spell homophones. Often the spellings of homophones just have to be learned.

Ask the children to use a dictionary to find the meaning of each word. Then use the definitions to create a quiz for a friend. For example: 'Clue 1) Some people eat this at breakfast time. (answer: cereal)'

Homophones: draft, draught, principal, principle, aisle, isle, serial, cereal, aloud, allowed, stationery, stationary

Review of the Big Picture

Once you have completed all the lessons for this phase, remind the children of the sequence's Big Picture. Discuss what they have learned so far.

Year 6, Sequence 5
Poetry: Free verse

Phase 3: Collaborate and compose

This phase focuses in detail on supporting children to draft and write individual sections of their conversation poem.

> **Programmes of study: Year 6**
> - **Composition:** Identify the audience for and purpose of the writing, selecting the appropriate form and using other similar writing as a model for their own.
> - **Composition:** Note and develop initial ideas, drawing on reading and research where necessary.
> - **Composition:** Select appropriate grammar and vocabulary, understanding how such choices can change and enhance meaning.
> - **Composition:** Use further organisational and presentational devices to structure text and to guide the reader.

Introduction

Remind the children about the Big Picture and recap on the learning in Phases 1 and 2. Explain to children that in Phase 3 they will be learning how to write their own conversation poem, set at home or school, in which someone is told what to do.

Lesson 1

Starter (VGP focus) – Vocabulary: Using a thesaurus

Begin the lesson by reminding children that we can use a thesaurus to find words with similar meanings. It can help us to find new or better words for what we want to say. Ask children to look up and note alternatives for the words 'talk', 'instruct', 'tired', 'chores', 'lounge' and 'cloth'.

Shared writing

Children remind themselves and each other of their planning ideas from Phase 2. Ask children to make suggestions for the opening lines of the conversation poem, revisiting 'Shut Your Mouth When You're Eating' as an example. Remind children to imagine real life conversations at school or home and the kinds of things that might be said between parent and child, teacher and child, siblings or friends.

Independent writing

The children can now write their own first section, applying the VGP focus on using a thesaurus to get the right words. Some children may benefit from guided group writing or peer-paired writing at this stage.

Plenary

At appropriate points throughout the lesson, invite children to share their writing with small groups, partners or the whole class. Ask the children questions about what they have created during that lesson, for example: 'How have your vocabulary choices created the intended impact on readers?' 'How authentic is the dialogue?' 'How do you expect the conversation to move on?' 'What advice do you have for your partner?'

Lesson 2

Starter (VGP focus) – Grammar: Synonyms and antonyms

Remind the children that synonyms are words with similar meanings and antonyms are words that have opposite meanings.

Write the word sets below on the board. Children must decide the odd word out for each set. Encourage children to use dictionaries and thesauruses to help. Discuss nuances and appropriate contexts of each word.

Word set one: water, irrigate, liquid, spray, drench, soak (The answer is 'liquid'.)

Word set two: comprehend, apprehend, understand, gather, fathom, perceive (The answer is 'apprehend'.)

Word set three: surprise, astonish, acknowledge, startle, stun, shock (The answer is 'acknowledge'.)

Shared writing

With the children's input, model writing the next part of the conversation which sets the scene further by describing the surroundings. Encourage children to think about what the characters want to achieve as this will affect the way they

Year 6, Sequence 5
Poetry: Free verse

speak and the details of what they say. Encourage the children to use the thesaurus to improve the vocabulary as you write.

Independent writing

The children can now write their own second section, applying the VGP focus on using a thesaurus to source new and interesting vocabulary. Some children may benefit from guided group writing or peer-paired writing at this stage.

Plenary

At the end of the lesson, ask the children questions to help them focus on their progress and what they have created during that lesson, for example: 'How have your vocabulary choices created the intended impact on readers?' 'How authentic is the dialogue?' 'How do you expect the conversation to move on?' 'What advice do you have for your partner?'

Lesson 3

Starter (VGP focus) – Grammar: modal verbs

In this sequence, the children are working on a conversation poem where somebody is telling somebody else what to do. This provides a good opportunity to model modal verbs in action.

Write the title 'Do your homework' on the board. Then read the children the following conversation. (You could invite a volunteer to read the responses for you.)

'Do your homework …'

'I would (but I'm not going to).'

'Go on then …'

'I might (or I may not).'

'You need to do it now …'

'I could (though I won't).'

'Come on, you can do it …'

'I can (but I don't feel like doing it right now).'

'I would', 'I might', 'I could' and 'I can' are all examples of modal verbs. Challenge the children to create a line containing a modal verb for the class conversation poem.

Shared writing

With the children's input, model writing the next part of the poem. Introduce another character or action and develop the speech to reflect the change. Check that the conversation is reasonably balanced between the characters and that it is flowing like natural speech. Apply modal verbs, as appropriate.

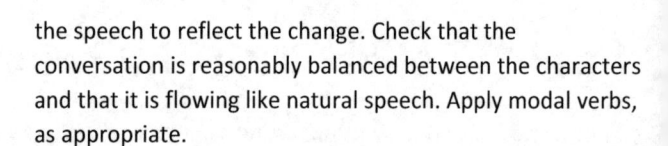

Independent writing

The children can now write their own third section, applying the VGP focus to include modal verb. Some children may benefit from guided group writing or peer-paired writing at this stage.

Plenary

At the end of the session, ask the children questions to help them focus on their progress and what they have created during that lesson, for example: 'How does your story so far compare with the original?' 'What modal verbs have you included?' 'Share your writing. What modal verbs has your partner used?' 'To what effect has your partner used modal verbs?'

Lesson 4

Starter (VGP focus) – Grammar: Modal verbs

Some modal verbs can also refer to people's duties or obligations to do something, for example: 'You **ought to** stop that.' 'You **should** stop that.' 'You **must** stop that.'

These are all examples of modal verb forms. Challenge children to create a line for the poem containing a modal verb form that refers to duties or obligations. Discuss the strength of the meaning of the words.

Shared writing

With the children's input, continue modelling how to write the ongoing dialogue between the characters. Remind the children of the funny ending in 'Shut Your Mouth When You're Eating' where the son catches the father being a hypocrite, because he eats with his mouth open. Discuss ideas with the children for including a humorous twist at the end of the poem. Include an example of a modal verb form as a duty or obligation.

Independent writing

The children can now write their own fourth section, applying the VGP focus on modal verb forms. Some children may benefit from guided group writing or peer-paired writing at this stage.

Year 6, Sequence 5
Poetry: Free verse

Plenary

At the end of the lesson, ask the children questions to help them focus on their progress and what they have created during that lesson, for example: 'How have your vocabulary choices created the intended impact on readers?' 'How authentic is the dialogue?' 'What modal verbs have you included?' 'Share your writing. What modal verbs has your partner used?' 'To what effect has your partner used modal verbs?'

Rehearsing and performing

Once the children have written their conversation poem, encourage them to read it out in pairs using intonation and pauses to help convey meaning or by creating a performance. Discuss how different or similar the class poem is to the original 'Shut Your Mouth When You're Eating' conversation poem and talk about what the children have learned from Rosen.

Review of the Big Picture

Once you have completed all the lessons for this phase, remind the children of this sequence's Big Picture. Reflect upon and discuss their learning so far.

Year 6, Sequence 5
Poetry: Free verse

Phase 4: Write independently

This final phase brings all the children's learning and writing skills together so that they can write their own independent conversation poem set at home or school, in which someone is told what to do. Through their writing, they will be able to utilise the different VGP focuses that they have been practising throughout previous phases.

> **Programmes of study: Year 6**
> - **Composition:** Select appropriate grammar and vocabulary, understanding how such choices can change and enhance meaning.
> - **Composition:** Use further organisational and presentational devices to structure text and to guide the reader.
> - **Composition:** Assess the effectiveness of their own and others' writing and suggest improvements.
> - **Composition:** Propose changes to grammar and vocabulary to enhance effects and clarify meaning.
> - **Composition:** Proofread for spelling and punctuation errors.
> - **Composition:** Perform their own compositions, using appropriate intonation, volume and movement so that meaning is clear.

Introduction

Introduce the phase by highlighting the overall Big Picture to the children. Recap on learning and progress through Phases 1–3 and explain that in Phase 4 they will be applying their learning to write their own conversation poem independently. Discuss and list examples of conversations that might take place at home, at school or somewhere else that is familiar, where someone is told what to do. For example, a parent could ask a child to tidy their bedroom, fold laundry, or do homework, or a teacher could ask a child to do school work, wash their hands, or blow their nose. Recap on the structure used in the class writing sessions in Phase 3.

Writing

Give each child a Poetry planner and instruct them to start planning and writing each section of their poem. Display the class writing structure and a copy of the model text, "Shut Your Mouth When You're Eating', for reference. All the children should be encouraged to try to write independently to the best of their ability. Ask open questions such as: 'How will you show how the character is reacting at this point?' Avoid telling children what to write. Some children may benefit from guided composition. Focus on perseverance and resilience in the independent application.

Proofreading and redrafting

Have the children proofread their work periodically as they write. Proofreading and improvement without support means that the writing may happen over a few lessons.

Offer the children the Editor's checklist or create your own checklist that includes the VGP focuses covered throughout this sequence. Highlight the importance of redrafting, linking their efforts to the overall Big Picture.

Self- and peer-assessment

Encourage the children to take time to self-assess their own writing as well as that of others in their group. Offer them a set of self-assessment questions such as: 'How does the writing convey the characters' reactions through speech?' 'How has the desired tone been achieved? 'What changes would improve the reader's experience?'

Rehearsing and performing

Once the children have written their independent conversation poem, encourage them to perform it either as performance poetry or acted out in role. Discuss how the children's poems are the same or different to the source texts. Encourage the children to feed back on one another's writing and performances.

Final review of the Big Picture

Individually or with partners, have children reflect on what they have learned from this sequence and what they will apply in their future writing.

Year 6, Sequence 6
Poetry: Descriptive techniques

Sequence 6
Poetry: Descriptive techniques

Approximate duration: Two weeks

Big Picture

Through this teaching sequence, children will explore the way in which poets use techniques such as personification, repetition and description. Understanding the techniques, styles and syntax used by poets will help children to use these techniques within their own writing. Children will be able to write descriptive poems based on the image of a scene.

Phase 1: Enjoy and immerse

Children analyse the stylistic features of the model text, 'Hiawatha's Childhood' by Henry Wadsworth Longfellow.

Phase 2: Capture and organise

Children begin to develop ideas for creating their own descriptive poem based on the image of a scene.

Phase 3: Collaborate and compose

Children undertake supported writing sessions to develop the content and features of their descriptive poem.

Phase 4: Write independently

Children write, edit and present their own descriptive poem that will engage and entertain readers.

Main source text

Treasure House Anthology Sequence 6 text. Treasure House Online, Year 6, Comprehension Unit 6: Poetry: 'The Song of Hiawatha'

Extra source texts

'Hiawatha's Fishing', *The Song of Hiawatha*, Henry Wadsworth Longfellow, There are multiple editions available, for example ISBN 978-0-14-054981-2, published by Puffin

Background knowledge

'The Song of Hiawatha' is part of an epic 22 chapter narrative poem called *The Song of Hiawatha*, written by Henry Longfellow in 1885. *The Song of Hiawatha* is fictional but is loosely based on the legends of the Ojibwe and other Native American people. 'The Song of Hiawatha' tells the tale of how Nokomis, Hiawatha's grandmother, taught him the ways of life, nature and the animals after his mother died in childbirth. Set in the stunning landscapes of Michigan, North America, Longfellow has used description, personification and repetition to create a strong example of blank verse with a clear rhythm.

Spoken outcome

To perform poems to an audience of peers or parents

Writing outcome

To write a descriptive poem based on the image of a scene, in the style of Henry Wadsworth Longfellow

Prior knowledge

Check children's knowledge and understanding of:
- poetry by Henry Wadsworth Longfellow
- personification in poetry
- repetition in poetry
- descriptive techniques in poetry.

Year 6, Sequence 6
Poetry: Descriptive techniques

Diagnostic assessment options

Before starting the sequence, you may want to conduct an initial diagnostic assessment of the children's understanding of the typical characteristics of a descriptive poem.

Ideas for initial diagnostic assessment options include:
- discussion about descriptive poems, their purpose and features
- a brief, unsupported writing activity creating a short descriptive text
- practising speaking and listening skills relating to a descriptive text
- a short reading comprehension activity / quiz on a descriptive text.

Cross-curricular links

KS2 Geography – Locational knowledge

Locate the world's countries, using maps to focus on Europe (including the location of Russia) and North and South America, concentrating on their environmental regions, key physical and human features, countries, and major cities.

KS2 Geography – Geographical skills and fieldwork

Use maps, atlases, globes and digital / computer mapping to locate countries.

Treasure House links

All digital and pupil book units have the same names and numbers, but different questions.

- Treasure House, Year 6, Comprehension Unit 6: Poetry: 'The Song of Hiawatha'
- Treasure House, Year 6, Composition Unit 4: Personification
- Treasure House, Year 5, Vocabulary Unit 1: Expanded noun phrases
- Treasure House, Year 6, Spelling Unit 7: The ee sound spelt ei after c
- Treasure House, Year 6, Punctuation Unit 2: Hyphens to avoid ambiguity

Resources

Atlas or globe to show North America; Source texts – see Anthologies; Poetry planner

Year 6, Sequence 6
Poetry: Descriptive techniques

Phase 1: Enjoy and immerse

In Phase 1, the children are introduced to a descriptive, narrative poem, 'The Song of Hiawatha'. 'The Song of Hiawatha' tells the tale of how Nokomis, Hiawatha's grandmother, taught him the ways of life, nature and the animals after his mother died in childbirth. Over several lessons, children are offered the opportunity to immerse themselves fully in the poem through comprehension and discussion activities, as well as exploring its characters and structure through drama, storytelling, writing and analysis of the text.

Programmes of study: Year 6

- **Comprehension:** Increase their familiarity with a wide range of books, including myths, legends and traditional stories, modern fiction, fiction from our literary heritage, and books from other cultures and traditions.
- **Comprehension:** Prepare poems and plays to read aloud and to perform, showing understanding through intonation, tone and volume so that the meaning is clear to an audience.
- **Comprehension:** Discuss and evaluate how authors use language, considering the impact on the reader.
- **Composition:** Identify the audience for and purpose of the writing, selecting the appropriate form and using other similar writing as models for their own.
- **Vocabulary, grammar and punctuation:** Use expanded noun phrases to convey complicated information concisely.
- **Spelling:** Use words with the /i:/ sound spelt ei after c.

Sparking interest

Introduce the sequence by highlighting the overall Big Picture to the children: they will be working towards writing their own descriptive poem based on an image of a scene using similar features to those used the 'The Song of Hiawatha' poem. Show children Michigan (Central North America) on the globe or in an atlas and explain that this was where the poem 'The Song of Hiawatha' was set.

Use opening questions such as: 'Why might a poet want to write a long descriptive, narrative poem?' 'Why not just write a descriptive story?'

Reading and discussion

Introduce the text, read it with the class and check their understanding of the language. Discuss children's understanding of the content of the poem.

Discuss the following with the children.
- Who are the characters in the poem?
- What happens in the poem?
- How does the poem make you feel?
- How does the poem make you feel about Hiawatha?
- Why do you think Longfellow wrote this poem?
- What patterns or features do you notice?
- Do you think Hiawatha enjoyed his childhood? Why?

Drama and storytelling

Use drama and storytelling activities to reinforce the children's understanding of the poem. Select the activities that would suit your class or fit in with your lesson timing. Encourage mixed-ability grouping for the chosen activities.

- **Hot-seating Hiawatha or Nokomis:** This activity can be done in pairs, small groups or as a class situation with different children representing Hiawatha and Nokomis. Questions from the audience could include: 'What it is like in winter where you live?' 'What do you like to do?' 'Which animals live in the forest?' 'What is Ishkoodah?'
- **Freeze-framing key moments:** Put the children into different scenes in the right story order. Use thought-tracking by asking each child in the freeze-frame what they're thinking at a particular moment.
- **Role-play:** Act out the story in the poem in small groups or as a whole class.
- **Storytelling:** Become a storyteller. Explain that storytellers would retell different traditional stories to people often sitting around them. The children could accompany your performance, either by using props for sound effects or by taking the roles of the characters.
- **Performance:** Encourage the children to rehearse and perform the poem in small groups, with one or two narrators.
- **Presentation:** Create a newsflash related to the story in the poem.

Year 6, Sequence 6
Poetry: Descriptive techniques

Incidental writing

A short writing activity would enhance the children's understanding of the text and characters. Select activities that you think appropriate for the abilities and interests of your class. Children could compose:

- a diary entry by Hiawatha describing a day in his life
- a newspaper article about Ishkoodah
- a letter to Nokomis from an old friend looking forward to seeing her, Hiawatha and the scenery.

Analysis

Show the text to the children and explain that, as a class, they are going to work with you to look more closely at how the poem's text is organised. With the children, count how many lines per verse and how many syllables per line. Provide children with individual copies of the poem so they can highlight, underline and make notes as they investigate the structure of the poem. Find and note examples of repetition through the poem, then examples of personification. Ask children: 'Why do you think Longfellow has used personification?' Discuss the progression of the story of Hiawatha's childhood through the poem. Challenge children to summarise what happens in each verse. Find and note examples of description of the setting. Ask children: 'Is there enough detailed description to help you form an image of the scene in your mind?' Discuss the use of action verbs (showing what the characters are doing) and make a list of them. Discuss what purpose they serve. Look for rhyming patterns and explore saying lines slowly to establish the rhythm.

Grammar: Expanded noun phrases

Tell children that we use expanded noun phrases to give more information about nouns. A noun can be expanded using adjectives before it and extra information (a prepositional phrase) after it. For example:

Noun: tree

Noun phrase: the tree

With adjectives: the tall, spindly tree

With a prepositional phrase: the tall, spindly tree with the spiky leaves.

Ask children to locate and note down examples of expanded noun phrases in the poem. To provide further support, you could ask children to first locate and underline nouns, then work with a partner to decide whether that noun has been expanded and how.

Phonics and spelling

Display the word 'seized' on the board. Underline the letters **ei** and explain that the word 'seized' contains a spelling pattern that we might call an exception to a rule. Ask if anybody knows the rule and can explain it to their partner or the class. Take suggestions.

Explain that we can use this rhyme '**i** before **e**, except after **c**' to help us spell the /ee/ sound. After **c**, the letters that make the /ee/ sound are the other way around: **e** comes before **i**. There are a small number of exceptions to the rule. Draw a chart on the board or on a large sheet of paper with three columns.

/ee/ i before e	/ee/ e before i after c	exceptions

Challenge children to say each word carefully and sort it into the correct column. You could extend the activity by asking children to put words into sentences.

ei / ie words: believe, either, priest, receipt, conceited, seize, chief, field, ceiling, brief, protein, caffeine, thief, piece, receive, deceive, conceive, weird, neither

Review of the Big Picture

Once you have completed this phase, remind the children (or have them remind each other) of the sequence's Big Picture: they are working towards independently writing their own descriptive poem based on an image of a scene.

Year 6, Sequence 6
Poetry: Descriptive techniques

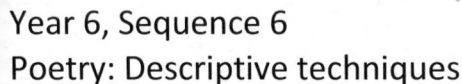

Phase 2: Capture and organise

During Phase 2, the children are able to use their knowledge from the previous lessons in Phase 1 to create their own class descriptive poem about a scene. The group and class discussions, as well as drama or short writing opportunities, offer chances for children of all abilities to contribute and use their skills towards designing a poem structure and developing features for their poem. Their ideas can be recorded in picture, diagram or note form with the help of the Poetry planner.

Programmes of study: Year 6

- **Comprehension:** Draw inferences such as inferring characters' feelings, thoughts and motives from their actions.
- **Comprehension:** Identify how language, structure and presentation contribute to meaning.
- **Comprehension:** Explain and discuss their understanding of what they have read, including through formal presentations and debates, maintaining a focus on the topic and using notes where necessary.
- **Composition:** Note and develop initial ideas, drawing on reading and research where necessary.
- **Composition:** In writing narratives, consider how authors have developed characters and settings in what children have read, listened to or seen performed.
- **Spelling:** Use words with the /i:/ sound spelt ei after c.

Introduction

Remind the children about the sequence's Big Picture. Reread 'The Song of Hiawatha' and discuss briefly why Longfellow may have written it: to share the culture of Native American Indians. With the children, recap how the poem structure is presented, for example, the content of the verse telling a story and progressing. Show the children the notes made from the structural analysis covered in Phase 1.

Introduce the idea that the children are going to work together to create their own class poem in a similar style to 'The Song of Hiawatha'. Read the extra source text to provide further examples and interest.

Discussing ideas

Find suitable scene images from magazines, newspapers, etc. and show them to the children. Ask for a hands-up vote to decide which image to base the class poem on. Discuss and decide on the main character for the poem. It could be Hiawatha or a completely new character.

Once the main two decisions have been made, put the children into mixed-ability groups and encourage them to discuss and come up with answers to the following questions. You may want to give them a selection of questions or just one question per group. Bring the groups together to listen and make decisions on the contents and structure.

- What is the place in the image like? Use your senses to imagine how it looks, feels, smells.
- Why is the character there? What is their story?
- How could the story develop and progress through the poem?
- Which poetic techniques do we need to include based on our analysis of 'The Song of Hiawatha'?
- What other characters could be in the poem and what are their roles?
- What can we keep from the original poem and what will we change?

Drama and storytelling

Use drama and storytelling activities to allow the children to explore the suggestions for their new characters, setting and poem plot. Select the activities that would suit your class or fit in with your lesson timing. Encourage mixed-ability grouping for the chosen activities.

- **Hot-seating the main character:** This activity can be done in pairs, small groups or as a class situation. Encourage the children to think and, if necessary, write down their questions before the hot-seat session starts. Discuss the character's responses.
- **Role-play explorers:** To encourage children to focus on describing the imaginary surroundings, ask children to imagine they are explorers and they have just discovered the setting in the poem. Encourage them to work in pairs or small groups to role-play looking around the setting and describing it as thoroughly as they can.

Year 6, Sequence 6
Poetry: Descriptive techniques

- **Poetry rehearsal:** Encourage the children to work in groups to develop some of the new poem ideas orally and then retell their oral compositions to the rest of the class. Discuss the differences between the different groups' poem ideas and which parts worked better than others.

Incidental writing

Before you select any incidental writing, make sure the children are able to orally articulate the main events of their class descriptive poem. Select activities that you think appropriate for the abilities and interests of your class. Children could compose:

- a diary entry of the character or an explorer
- a newspaper article about the discovery of the new setting
- a descriptive and persuasive holiday brochure to persuade people to visit the area
- a character profile
- a blog entry or email.

Organising the class descriptive poem into a structure

Once the children have thoroughly explored their ideas for their class poem, bring them together and use their final suggestions to model how to plot the new poem in picture, diagram or note form with the help of the Poetry planner. Once recorded, go through the frame and ask the children to evaluate the poem.

Phonics and spelling

Use these words spelt with the **ie** for /ee/ spelling pattern to practise.

Challenge children to use as many of the words as possible to create a short story or passage. Encourage children to use a dictionary to check the meanings of new or unknown words. Ask children to dictate their **ie** stories to each other and to assess the work of their peers.

ie words: shield, wield, field, yield, brief, achieve, believe, relieved, reprieve, grief, chief, belief, relief, mischief, retrieve, diesel, hygiene, niece, piece, tier, pier, cashier, siege, shriek, priest, fierce, pierce

Review of the Big Picture

Once you have completed all the lessons for this phase, remind the children of the sequence's Big Picture. Discuss what they have learned so far and recap on Phase 2.

Year 6, Sequence 6
Poetry: Descriptive techniques

Phase 3: Collaborate and compose

This phase focuses on the teaching and learning of how to write a descriptive poem, with one lesson per story part, so that the children are taken through the writing of the whole piece, learning new vocabulary, grammar and punctuation along the way. Children should have the planning framework from Phase 2 in front of them throughout, and should be able to revisit the original 'The Song of Hiawatha' poem.

Programmes of study: Year 6
- **Composition:** Identify the audience for and purpose of the writing, selecting the appropriate form and using other similar writing as a model for their own.
- **Composition:** Note and develop initial ideas, drawing on reading and research where necessary.
- **Composition:** Select appropriate grammar and vocabulary, understanding how such choices can change and enhance meaning.
- **Composition:** Use further organisational and presentational devices to structure text and to guide the reader.

Introduction

Remind the children about the Big Picture and recap on the learning in Phases 1 and 2. Explain that over several lessons, the children are going to start work on writing their class descriptive poem using the planning from the previous lessons.

Lesson 1

Starter (VGP focus) – Grammar: Create expanded noun phrases using prepositional phrases

Remind children that noun phrases are useful in helping us express ourselves more vividly. Tell children: 'You are visiting your poem's main character and all their family. You want to tell your friend about the people you have met and you wonder if your friend knows them already.' Ask children: 'How would you describe the people if you didn't know their names?' Explain that you could say 'I met a girl' but that isn't helpful or interesting. Explain that it might be better to say 'I met a girl with beautiful, long, red plaits in her hair.' Other examples could be: 'A man with a limp', 'The woman from down the lane', 'The twins with the cheeky grins'.

Ask the children to work with a partner to create six expanded noun phrases using prepositional phrases after the noun that could be used in their poems. To support them, you could provide ideas for the nouns: 'snake', 'girl', 'boy', 'man', 'woman', 'deer', 'fish', 'badger', 'eagle', 'tree' and 'stream'.

Shared writing

Children remind themselves and each other of their planning ideas from Phase 2. Ask children to make suggestions for the wording of the opening verse of the class poem, revisiting 'The Song of Hiawatha' as an example. Ideally this verse should focus on introducing the setting in a way that creates an impact on the reader, for example, how beautiful the place is. Include at least one example of an expanded noun phrase. Model writing the opening verse with the children's input, focusing on setting the scene.

Independent writing

The children can now write their own first section, applying the VGP focus on expanded noun phrases using prepositional phrases after the noun. Some children may benefit from guided group writing or peer-paired writing at this stage.

Plenary

At appropriate points throughout the lesson, invite children to share their writing with small groups, partners or the whole class. Ask the children questions to help them focus on their progress and what they have created during the lesson, for example: 'How have you described the setting so that it has an impact on the reader?' 'What prepositional phrases have you included?' 'What effect do the prepositional phrases have on the writing?'

Year 6, Sequence 6
Poetry: Descriptive techniques

Lesson 2

Starter (VGP focus) – Grammar: Create expanded noun phrases using words added before the noun

Remind children that expanded noun phrases are important if we are trying to explain something and we need to be specific to avoid confusion. Give children an example: 'Imagine giving someone directions for finding their way through the forest to a character's hut by the stream. You want to tell them to turn left at the tree. How will you accurately convey which tree it is? It would be better to say "the old, gnarly, brown oak tree"'.

Ask children to work with a partner to create a set of six specific directions to guide someone on an imaginary journey through a forest. They should then swap the set of directions with another pair to assess the work of their peers.

Shared writing

With the children's input, model writing the next part of the poem (one or two verses) which introduces the main character/s in the poem. Model using expanded noun phrases and focus on description of the characters personalities and actions as well as continuing to describe the setting in detail.

Independent writing

The children can now write their own second section, applying the VGP focus on expanded noun phrases. Remind children to use a thesaurus and / or dictionary to support them with new or tricky words. Some children may benefit from guided group writing or peer-paired writing at this stage.

Plenary

At the end of the lesson, invite children to share their writing with groups or the whole class. Ask the children questions to help them focus on their progress and what they have created during that lesson, for example: 'How easy is it to visualise the setting?' 'What expanded noun phrases have you included?' 'What effect do the expanded noun phrases have on your writing?'

Lesson 3

Starter (VGP focus) – Punctuation: Using hyphens to avoid ambiguity

Ask children to explain what a hyphen is and why we use them. Take suggestions. Explain that we can use a hyphen to join two or more words and make them into a compound adjective or noun. They are another tool to help us communicate with clarity. They make it clear which words 'work together'. Write on the board, and then say these words: 'A man eating shark; a man-eating shark.' Discuss how the intonation and meaning changes with the use of a hyphen.

Look through 'The Song of Hiawatha' with the children and highlight and discuss the use of hyphens. Ask children: 'How would this read differently without the hyphens?' 'Are there any other places hyphens could have been used?' In poetry it is common to see hyphens used to create new compound words for effect.

Ask children to work in pairs to create six new compound words using hyphens that could be used in their poems. To provide additional support, you could put a selection of words on the board for children to choose from: 'forest', 'sparkly', 'cold', 'warm', 'river', 'leaves', 'golden', 'emerald', 'dancing', 'singing', 'crisp', 'soft'.

Shared writing

With the children's input, model writing the next part of the poem (one or two verses) which moves the story forward, perhaps of the character growing up or any actions you have decided with the children during Phase 2. Continue to focus on description of setting as well as description of characters' actions. Refer back to 'The Song of Hiawatha' as a model. Consider including some simple dialogue. This would also be a good point at which to include personification of some features of the setting, such as the weather or plants.

Independent writing

The children can now write their own third section, applying the VGP focus on hyphens. They should also try to include at least one example of personification. Some children may benefit from guided group writing or peer-paired writing at this stage.

Plenary

At the end of the lesson, ask children to share their writing with groups or the whole class. Ask the children questions to help them focus on their progress and what they have created during that lesson, for example: 'Have you included any dialogue?' 'How have you developed description of the setting?' 'How have you used hyphens and for what effect?'

Year 6, Sequence 6
Poetry: Descriptive techniques

Lesson 4

Starter (VGP focus) – Punctuation: Using hyphens to avoid ambiguity

Provide the children, in pairs, with copies of the extra source text from the Anthologies, 'Hiawatha's Fishing'. Challenge each pair to find all the hyphenated words throughout and write them down. Tell the children to prepare a brief explanation for two of the examples they have found. They should state where in the poem the example was found and why they think Longfellow chose to use a hyphen there. They then present their findings to another pair or the class.

Shared writing

With the children's input, continue to model the final parts of the poem (one or two verses). Try to include content that concludes the action in the poem or shows the progression in plot from the beginning of the poem to this point. Perhaps the seasons have changed and the landscape needs new description, or a visitor has arrived or left, or the character is growing up (like Hiawatha). Refer to the original poem, 'The Song of Hiawatha', for reference. Ask for children's suggestions for dialogue and description, expanded noun phrases, personification, repetition and hyphenated words.

Independent writing

The children can now write their own fourth section, applying the punctuation focus on hyphenated words. Encourage the use of repetition and links to content or words used in earlier verses. Some children may benefit from guided group writing or peer-paired writing at this stage.

Plenary

At the end of the lesson, ask the children questions to help them focus on their progress and what they have created during that lesson, for example: 'How have you concluded the action of the poem?' 'How have you used dialogue, description, expanded noun phrases, personification, repetition and / or hyphenated words?' 'Share your writing. How has your partner used dialogue, description, expanded noun phrases, personification, repetition and / or hyphenated words?'

Rehearsing and performing

Once the children have written their poem, encourage them to retell it with audience awareness or by creating a performance. Discuss how different or similar the tale is to the original, 'The Song of Hiawatha'.

Review of the Big Picture

Once you have completed all the lessons for this phase, remind the children of the sequence's Big Picture. Discuss what they have learned so far in Phases 1–3.

Year 6, Sequence 6
Poetry: Descriptive techniques

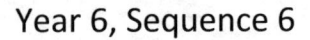

Phase 4: Write independently

This final phase brings all the children's learning and writing skills together so that they can write their own descriptive poem using some of the features they have observed in 'The Song of Hiawatha'. Through their writing, they will be able to utilise the different VGP focuses that they have been investigating and applying to their shared writing in the previous phases.

> **Programmes of study: Year 6**
> - **Composition:** Select appropriate grammar and vocabulary, understanding how such choices can change and enhance meaning.
> - **Composition:** Use further organisational and presentational devices to structure text and to guide the reader.
> - **Composition:** Assess the effectiveness of their own and others' writing and suggest improvements.
> - **Composition:** Propose changes to grammar and vocabulary to enhance effects and clarify meaning.
> - **Composition:** Proofread for spelling and punctuation errors.
> - **Composition:** Perform their own compositions, using appropriate intonation, volume and movement so that meaning is clear.

Introduction

Introduce this phase by highlighting the overall Big Picture to the children. Recap on learning and progress through Phases 1–3 and explain that in Phase 4 they will be applying their learning to write their own poem independently. Find suitable scene images from magazines, newspapers, etc. and show them to the children. Then discuss and list examples of content they could use. Examples could include a character who lives in the forest, someone taking a camping trip to the forest, an animal who lives in the forest, an explorer who has discovered a new place, travellers who stop to rest at an abandoned cabin. Recap on the structure and poetic features used in the class writing sessions in Phase 3.

Writing

Give each child a Poetry planner and encourage them to start planning and writing each section of their own poem. Display the class plan and a copy of both 'Hiawatha's Childhood' and 'Hiawatha's Fishing' for reference. All children should be encouraged to write independently to the best of their ability. Ask open questions such as: 'How will you show how stunning this landscape is?' Avoid telling the children what to write. Some children may benefit from guided composition. Focus on perseverance and resilience in their independent application.

Proofreading and redrafting

Have the children proofread their work periodically as they write. Proofreading and improvement without support means that the writing will happen over a few lessons. Offer the children the Editor's checklist or create your own checklist that includes the VGP and spelling focuses covered throughout this sequence. Highlight the importance of redrafting, linking their efforts to the overall Big Picture.

Self- and peer-assessment

Encourage the children to take time to self-assess their own writing as well as assess that of others in their group. Offer them a set of self-assessment questions, such as: 'Does the poem effectively show how striking the setting is?' 'Has personification been used and what effect does it create?' 'How clearly is the poem structured?' 'What makes this an engaging poem?' 'What changes would improve the reader's experience?'

Rehearsing and performing

Once the children have written their independent poem, encourage them to retell it with audience awareness or by creating a performance. Discuss how different or similar the tale is to the original poem, 'The Song of Hiawatha'. Encourage the children to feed back on one another's writing and performances.

Final review of the Big Picture

Individually or with partners, have children reflect on what they have learned from this sequence and what they will apply in their future writing.

Year 6, Sequence 7
Poetry: Narrative techniques

Sequence 7
Poetry: Narrative techniques

Approximate duration: Two weeks

Big Picture

Through this teaching sequence, children will explore the way in which some poets use a narrative style to engage and entertain readers. Understanding how a narrative style is created in poetry will help children to use narrative techniques within their own writing. Children will be able to write a narrative poem based on the theme 'Is Anybody There?'

Phase 1: Enjoy and immerse

Children analyse the stylistic features of the model text, 'The Listeners' by Walter de la Mare.

Phase 2: Capture and organise

Children begin to develop ideas for creating their own narrative poem based on the theme 'Is Anybody There?'

Phase 3: Collaborate and compose

Children undertake supported writing sessions to develop the content and features of their narrative poem.

Phase 4: Write independently

Children write, edit and present their own narrative poem that will engage and entertain readers.

Main source text

Treasure House Anthology Sequence 7 text. 'The Listeners', *The Listeners and Other Poems*, Walter de la Mare, ISBN 978-1-44-445745-2, pp.44–45

Extra source texts

Treasure House Online, Year 6, Comprehension Unit 7: Poetry: 'The Highwayman'

Background knowledge

'The Listeners' is a narrative poem written by Walter de la Mare and first published in London in 1912. It tells the tale of a traveller who arrives on horseback late at night and knocks on the door of a forest dwelling. Nobody answers the door but his calls are listened to by a group of spirits. The narrator presents the story in the third person and describes the action inside and outside of the house. The action takes place late on a moonlit evening and the tone is eerie and serious. When the traveller leaves, he calls out to the listeners, as if he somehow knew they were present.

Spoken outcome

To perform poems to an audience of peers or parents

Writing outcome

To write a short narrative poem based on the theme 'Is Anybody There?'

Prior knowledge

Check children's knowledge and understanding of:
- poetry by Walter de le Mare
- narrative poems
- poetic devices in general.

Diagnostic assessment options

Before starting the sequence, you may want to conduct an initial diagnostic assessment of the children's understanding of the typical characteristics of a narrative poem.

Ideas for initial diagnostic assessment options include:
- discussion about narrative poems, their purpose and form
- a brief, unsupported writing activity creating a short narrative poem or text
- practising speaking and listening skills relating to a well-known narrative poem
- a short reading comprehension activity / quiz on a narrative poem or text.

Year 6, Sequence 7
Poetry: Narrative techniques

Treasure House links

All digital and pupil book units have the same names and numbers, but different questions.

- Treasure House, Year 6, Comprehension Unit 7: Poetry: 'The Highwayman'
- Treasure House, Year 6, Composition, Unit 2: Summaries
- Treasure House, Year 6, Grammar Unit 3: Relative clauses
- Treasure House Year 6, Spelling Unit 10: Homophones and near-homophones (1)
- Treasure House, Year 6, Spelling Unit 14: Homophones and near-homophones (5)
- Treasure House, Year 3, Grammar Unit 10: Prepositions of place
- Treasure House, Year 4, Grammar Unit 4: Using pronouns to make your writing clear
- Treasure House, Year 4, Punctuation Unit 2: Apostrophes to show possession (1)
- Treasure House, Year 4, Punctuation Unit 3: Apostrophes to show possession (2)

Resources

Source texts – see Anthologies; Poetry planner; Editor's checklist

Year 6, Sequence 7
Poetry: Narrative techniques

Phase 1: Enjoy and immerse

In Phase 1, the children are introduced to the model text: a narrative poem called 'The Listeners' by Walter de la Mare. The poem tells the tale of a mysterious traveller, arriving on horseback, who knocks at the door of a house. There is no answer at the door but the reader is made aware of a group of spirits listening to the traveller. Over several lessons, the children are offered the opportunity to immerse themselves fully in the story through comprehension and discussion activities, as well as exploring its characters and structure through drama, storytelling, writing and analysis of the text.

> **Programmes of study: Year 6**
> - **Comprehension:** Continue to read and discuss an increasingly wide range of fiction, poetry, plays, non-fiction and reference books or textbooks.
> - **Comprehension:** Prepare poems and plays to read aloud and to perform, showing understanding through intonation, tone and volume so that the meaning is clear to an audience.
> - **Comprehension:** Draw inferences such as inferring characters' feelings, thoughts and motives from their actions.
> - **Composition:** Identify the audience for and purpose of the writing, selecting the appropriate form and using other similar writing as models for their own.
> - **Vocabulary, grammar and punctuation:** Use relative clauses beginning with who, which, where, when, whose, that or with an implied (i.e. omitted) relative pronoun.
> - **Spelling:** Continue to distinguish between homophones and other words which are often confused.

Sparking interest

Introduce the sequence by highlighting the overall Big Picture to the children: they will be working towards writing their own narrative poem in a similar style to 'The Listeners'.

Use an opening question such as: 'Why is the traveller knocking on the door of this seemingly abandoned house?'

Reading and discussion

Introduce the text, read it with the class and check their understanding of the language. Discuss children's understanding of the content of the poem as well as the poetic techniques used.

Discuss the following with the children.

- What is this poem about?
- Who do you think the traveller could be?
- Who do you think the traveller expects to find at the house?
- Where might the traveller have come from or be going to?
- Who do you think the phantom listeners are?
- Where do you think the owners of the house might be?
- How does the poem make you feel?
- What poetic techniques do you notice?
- Why does the traveller call out when he leaves, if no-one is there?

Drama and storytelling

Use drama and storytelling activities to reinforce the children's understanding of the poem. Select the activities that would suit your class or fit in with your lesson timing. Encourage mixed-ability grouping for the chosen activities.

- **Hot-seating the traveller:** This activity can be done in pairs, small groups or as a class situation with different children representing the traveller to gather a range of responses. Questions for the traveller could include: 'Who were you expecting to answer the door?' 'Where will you go now?' 'Will you go back to the house?' 'Where do you think the residents of the house are?'
- **Role-play:** Act out the poem and develop the story further. Encourage children to explore what they think will happen when the traveller returns to the house later and who they think the phantom listeners are.
- **Storytelling:** Become a storyteller. Explain that storytellers would retell different traditional stories and poems to people often sitting around them. The children could accompany your performance, either by using props for sound effects or by taking the roles of the characters.

Year 6, Sequence 7
Poetry: Narrative techniques

- **Performance:** Encourage the children to rehearse and perform the poem in small groups, with one or two narrators.
- **Presentation ideas:** Create a newsflash related to the story in the poem.

Incidental writing

A short writing activity would enhance the children's understanding of the text and characters. Select activities that you think appropriate for the abilities and interests of your class. Use the children's written outcomes to inform the emphases during the collaborative composition phase. Children could compose:

- a one-paragraph summary of the poem
- a newspaper article about the history of the house, perhaps explaining the mystery of the house being deserted, or about the traveller
- a letter from the traveller to the person he was looking for at the house.

Analysis

Show the text to the children and discuss and make notes about the characters, the setting and plot. Then discuss the structure and poetic techniques in the poem. Discuss the way that the poem starts with a question: 'Is anybody there?' Discuss how this question is the underlying theme throughout the poem. Discuss the reasons the poet may have written this poem, what he was trying to show, or what experience may have motivated him to write it. Talk about how much balance there is in the poem between description of characters, setting and action. With the children, count the lines and syllables in each line and discuss any instances of rhyming words, alliteration or personification. Discuss the atmosphere in the poem. Highlight any vocabulary that needs to be looked up or have its meaning clarified. Discuss how the poet advances the story and how important the use of dialogue is.

Grammar: Relative clauses

Remind the children that we use relative clauses to give more information about nouns. They can start with a relative pronoun ('that', 'which', 'who' or 'whose') or a relative adverb ('where' or 'when').

Ask the children to locate examples of relative clauses in the poem.

Ask children to work in pairs to create sentences using the following relative clauses (or your own examples).

'… where the wind blew bitterly.'

'… where the tower loomed over the forest.'

'… whose horse stood braying at the creek.'

'… who haunts the old cabin by the cave.'

Phonics and spelling

Display the words 'weary' and 'wary' on the board. Ask children if they know what they mean and, if not, ask children to look them up in the dictionary.

Ask children why people may get in a muddle when writing these words (they are near homophones).

Ask children to look up three of the following pairs of homophones and near-homophones in the dictionary and note down the definitions, then share their findings with groups or the class.

Homophone and near-homophone pairs: weary, wary; desert, dessert; affect, effect; compliment, complement; precede, proceed

Review of the Big Picture

Once you have completed this phase, remind the children (or have them remind each other) of the sequence's Big Picture: they are working towards writing their own narrative poem in a similar style to 'The Listeners'.

Year 6, Sequence 7
Poetry: Narrative techniques

Phase 2: Capture and organise

During Phase 2, the children start to develop ideas about new content and the poetic techniques needed to create a class narrative poem. The group and class discussions, as well as drama or short writing opportunities, offer chances for children of all abilities to contribute and use their skills towards designing a poem structure and developing characters and a storyline for the poem. Their ideas can be recorded in picture, diagram or note form with the help of the Poetry planner.

Programmes of study: Year 6
- **Comprehension:** Identify how language, structure and presentation contribute to meaning.
- **Comprehension:** Discuss and evaluate how authors use language, including figurative language, considering the impact on the reader.
- **Comprehension:** Explain and discuss their understanding of what they have read, including through formal presentations and debates, maintaining a focus on the topic and using notes where necessary.
- **Composition:** Note and develop initial ideas, drawing on reading and research where necessary.
- **Composition:** In writing narratives, consider how authors have developed characters and settings in what children have read, listened to or seen performed.
- **Spelling:** Continue to distinguish between homophones and other words which are often confused.

Introduction

Remind the children about the sequence's Big Picture. Reread the poem 'The Listeners' and recap on the analysis from Phase 1. Read the extra source text, 'The Highwayman', for a further example of a narrative poem. Briefly discuss the similarities and differences between the source texts.

Discussing ideas

As a class, encourage the children to decide where the setting for the new poem could be and what event or action it will focus on. Suggest that the new poem could be titled 'Is Anybody There?' and build on the theme of the main character looking for someone or calling out for someone.

Once the main two decisions have been made, put the children into mixed-ability groups and encourage them to discuss and come up with suggestions in answer to the following questions. Depending on your class, you may want to give them a selection of questions or just one question per group. Bring the groups together to listen and make decisions on the characters and story-structure.

- Who could the main character be?
- What could the main character's background story be?
- Who are they looking for and why?
- Where do they look and for how long?
- What other characters are in the poem and what are their roles?
- What ideas can we keep from the original poem?

Drama and storytelling

Use drama and oracy activities to allow the children to explore the suggestions for their new characters and conversation development. Select the activities that would suit your class or fit in with your lesson timing. Encourage mixed-ability grouping for the chosen activities.

- **Hot-seating the main characters:** This activity can be done in pairs, small groups or as a class. Encourage the children to think and, if necessary, write down their questions before the hot-seat session starts. Discuss the characters' responses.
- **Freeze-framing key moments:** Once the structure of the draft story for the poem is created, try out the different scenes in the right story order. Use thought-tracking by asking each child in the freeze-frame what they are thinking at a particular moment.
- **Poetry rehearsal:** Have the children work in pairs to retell the ideas for the poem and then retell it to the rest of the class. Discuss the differences between the different groups' conversations and which parts worked better than others. Try retelling it in the first person and in the third person and discuss how that changes the impact. Ask children which version they prefer.

Year 6, Sequence 7
Poetry: Narrative techniques

Incidental writing

Before you select any incidental writing, make sure the children are able to orally articulate the main events of their class narrative poem. Select activities that you think appropriate for the abilities and interests of your class. Children could compose:

- a diary entry
- further dialogue
- a character profile
- a blog entry or an email.

Organising the class narrative poem into a structure

Once the children have thoroughly explored their ideas for their class narrative poem, bring them together and use their final suggestions to model how to plot the new poem in picture, diagram or note form with the help of the Poetry planner. Once recorded, go through the frame and ask the children if they are happy with the tale.

Phonics and spelling

Homophone pairs: ascent, assent; morning, mourning; profit, prophet; steal, steel; who's, whose; father, farther; bridal, bridle

Following on from the Phase 1 activity to locate and record definitions for the homophone and near-homophone words, ask children to choose five of the above homophones to write in sentences. Discuss the meanings of the words. Then share sentences with groups or the class.

Explain that, when spelling (and reading) words that are homophones or near-homophones, the context of the sentence is vital as it tells the reader the meaning required.

Review of the Big Picture

Once you have completed all the lessons for this phase, remind the children of the sequence's Big Picture. Recap on the learning achieved in Phase 2.

Year 6, Sequence 7
Poetry: Narrative techniques

Phase 3: Collaborate and compose

This phase focuses in detail on supporting children to draft and write individual sections of their narrative poem. Children should have the planning framework from Phase 2 in front of them throughout, and should be able to revisit the original narrative poem, 'The Listeners'.

> **Programmes of study: Year 6**
> - **Composition:** Identify the audience for and purpose of the writing, selecting the appropriate form and using other similar writing as a model for their own.
> - **Composition:** Note and develop initial ideas, drawing on reading and research where necessary.
> - **Composition:** In writing narratives, consider how authors have developed characters and settings in what children have read, listened to or seen performed.
> - **Composition:** Select appropriate grammar and vocabulary, understanding how such choices can change and enhance meaning.
> - **Composition:** In narratives, describe settings, characters and atmosphere and integrate dialogue to convey character and advance the action.

Introduction

Remind the children about the Big Picture and recap on the learning in Phases 1 and 2. Explain to the children that through Phase 3 they will be learning how to write their own narrative poem called 'Is Anybody There?' Over several lessons, the children are going to start work on writing their class narrative poem using the planning ideas from the previous lessons.

Lesson 1

Starter (VGP focus) – Grammar: Revising word classes: Prepositions of place

Ask children to recall what a preposition is. Take suggestions. Remind the children that a preposition is a word that tells us how one thing is connected to another. Some prepositions tell the reader about locations or places.

Provide pairs of children with copies of 'The Listeners' to annotate. Ask children to highlight all of the prepositions that they can find in the poem. Compare answers with other children. Ask children to think of alternative prepositions and record suggestions to be displayed as a poster on the classroom wall. Remind children to refer to the poster when writing their poem to help them use a variety of vocabulary.

Prepositions could include: behind, inside, beneath, across, below, down, throughout, at, past, among, near, above, on, under, outside, toward, upon, over, through.

Shared writing

Children remind themselves and each other of their planning ideas from Phase 2. Ask the children to make suggestions for the wording of the opening section of the poem (approximately ten lines), revisiting 'The Listeners' as an example. With the children's input, model the first few lines, focusing on introducing the character, the setting and the action of calling out or looking for someone who isn't there. This part of the poem could convey that there was a person (the main character) who called out for someone and got no response. Discuss and include prepositions of place if appropriate.

Independent writing

The children can now write their own first section, applying the VGP focus on prepositions of place where appropriate. Some children may benefit from guided group writing or peer-paired writing at this stage.

Plenary

At appropriate points throughout the lesson, invite children to share their writing with small groups, partners or the whole class. Ask the children questions to help them focus on their progress and what they have created during that lesson, for example: 'How have you introduced the setting and the main character?' 'How have you established the scenario?' 'What prepositions of place have you included?'

Year 6, Sequence 7
Poetry: Narrative techniques

Lesson 2

Starter (VGP focus) – Grammar: Revising word classes: Pronouns

Ask children to recall what a pronoun is. Take suggestions. Remind the children that a pronoun is a word that takes the place of a noun to help us avoid repetition.

Provide children in pairs with the copies of 'The Listeners' to annotate from Lesson 1. Ask children to highlight all of the pronouns that they can find in the poem. Compare answers with other children.

Write this sentence on the board: 'Robert wanted to talk to Mr Beaumont, but **he** was too busy.' Ask children why the pronoun in this sentence is causing a problem. Establish that occasionally using too many pronouns can cause confusion. In the sentence we are not clear whether it is Robert or Mr Beaumont who is too busy to talk.

Shared writing

With the children's input, model writing the next part of the poem (approximately ten lines). In 'The Listeners' this part of the poem shows the traveller knocking and calling out for a second time. Some animals outside the house move but there is still no response from inside. The reader is introduced to the phantom listeners inside the house. You could introduce another character at this point and include further description of any noises and movements that contrast with the lack of response from the person your character is looking or calling for. Discuss the use of pronouns throughout where appropriate.

Independent writing

The children can now write their own second section, applying the VGP focus on pronouns where appropriate. Some children may benefit from guided group writing or peer-paired writing at this stage.

Plenary

At the end of the lesson, invite children to share their writing with groups or the whole class. Ask the children questions to help them focus on their progress and what they have created during that lesson, for example: 'How have you used dialogue and / or description to progress the story?' 'How have you created a sense of atmosphere in your poem?' 'Share your work. What pronouns has your partner used?'

Lesson 3

Starter (VGP focus) – Punctuation: Revision of apostrophes to show possession

Ask the children to recall how an apostrophe to show possession is used. Ask the children how the apostrophe to show possession is used when the noun is a plural already ending in 's'. Take suggestions. Remind the children that, to show possession, we use an apostrophe and the letter 's' at the end of a singular noun. At the end of a plural noun that already ends in 's', we add only the apostrophe.

Ask the children to find the examples of apostrophes used to show possession in 'The Listeners'. Ask children: 'Are there singular and plural examples?'

Write the following phrases on the board and ask children to copy them, adding in the apostrophe in the correct place.

'A mans house'

'The travellers horses tail'

'His three friends horses tails'

'The girls groups paintings'

Shared writing

With the children's input, model writing the next part of the poem (approximately ten lines). In 'The Listeners', this section of the poem focuses on the phantom listeners and the reader feels as if they are able to see inside the house. The poem then reverts back to focus on the traveller but with a powerful line showing that the traveller can sense the phantom listeners even though he / she cannot see them ('And he felt in his heart their strangeness'). Use this model if your poem is similar, or focus on the progression of the character starting to realise that the person they are searching for is not there, although perhaps they have a sense of not being alone. Perhaps in your poem the person being sought is there, but hiding and silent, unresponsive to the caller. Refer to the characters' feelings. If appropriate include the VGP focus on apostrophes to show possession.

Independent writing

The children can now write their own third section, applying the VGP focus on apostrophes to show possession if appropriate. Some children may benefit from guided group writing or peer-paired writing at this stage.

Year 6, Sequence 7
Poetry: Narrative techniques

Plenary

At the end of the lesson, invite children to share their writing with groups or the whole class. Ask the children questions to help them focus on their progress and what they have created during that lesson, for example: 'How have you created a sense of atmosphere in your poem?' 'What poetic techniques have you used?' 'Share your work. Has your partner used apostrophes to show possession correctly?'

Lesson 4

Starter (VGP focus) – Punctuation: Revision of apostrophes to show possession

Ask the children to recall the Lesson 3 starter on how an apostrophe to show possession is used. Ask the children how the apostrophe to show possession is used when the noun is a plural that does not end in 's'. Take suggestions. Remind the children that to show possession, we use an apostrophe and the letter 's' at the end of a singular noun. At the end of a plural noun that already ends in 's', we add only the apostrophe. To show possession with a plural noun that does not end in 's', we use an apostrophe and the letter 's', just like a singular noun.

Write the following phrases on the board and ask children to copy them, adding in the apostrophe in the correct place.

'The peoples choice'

'The childrens poems'

'The geeses nests'

Shared writing

With children's input, continue modelling how to write the narrative poem (the final ten lines, approximately). In the final part of 'The Listeners', the traveller speaks to the phantom listeners to leave a message for the house owners. He then leaves on horseback. In your poem, this section might include your characters' final attempts to call out and they might leave a message and go. In 'The Listeners' the reader is left feeling as if they have been left behind at the setting with the phantom listeners rather than leaving with the traveller. Discuss with the children how their reader will feel at the end of their poem. If appropriate, include an example of the VGP focus on apostrophes to show possession.

Independent writing

The children can now write their own fourth and final section, applying the VGP focus if appropriate. Some children may benefit from guided group writing or peer-paired writing at this stage.

Plenary

At the end of the lesson, invite children to share their writing with groups or the whole class. Ask the children questions to help them focus on their progress and what they have created during that lesson, for example: 'How have you concluded the action of your poem?' 'How should the reader feel at the end of your poem and how do you hope to achieve this?' 'Share your work. Has your partner used apostrophes to show possession correctly?'

Rehearsing and performing

Once the children have written their narrative poem, encourage them to retell it either as storytellers or by creating a performance. Discuss how different or similar the tale is to the source text, 'The Listeners'.

Review of the Big Picture

Once you have completed all the lessons for this phase, remind the children of the Big Picture for this sequence. Discuss what they have learned so far.

Year 6, Sequence 7
Poetry: Narrative techniques

Phase 4: Write independently

This final phase brings all the children's learning and writing skills together so that they can write their own independent narrative poem with the suggested title 'Is Anybody There?' based upon the poem, 'The Listeners'. Through their writing, they will be able to utilise the different VGP focuses that they have been practising throughout previous phases.

> **Programmes of study: Year 6**
> - **Composition:** Select appropriate grammar and vocabulary, understanding how such choices can change and enhance meaning.
> - **Composition:** In narratives, describe settings, characters and atmosphere and integrate dialogue to convey character and advance the action.
> - **Composition:** Assess the effectiveness of their own and others' writing.
> - **Composition:** Propose changes to vocabulary, grammar and punctuation to enhance effects and clarify meaning.
> - **Composition:** Proofread for spelling and punctuation errors.
> - **Composition:** Perform their own compositions, using appropriate intonation, volume and movement so that meaning is clear.

Introduction

Introduce this phase by highlighting the overall Big Picture to the children. Recap on learning and progress through Phases 1–3 and explain that in Phase 4 they will be applying their learning to write their own narrative poem independently. Discuss and list examples of situations where somebody might be looking for someone but cannot find them. Examples could include: somebody revisits a house they used to live in; somebody trying to track down a long lost relative; somebody looking for an elderly person that lives locally but hasn't been seen for a few weeks; somebody that has just moved in to a new village and is looking for their neighbour. Recap on the structure used in the class writing sessions in Phase 3.

Writing

Give each child a Poetry planner and instruct them to start planning and writing each section of their poem. Display the class writing structure and a copy of the model texts 'The Listeners' and 'The Highwayman' for reference. All the children should be encouraged to try to write independently to the best of their ability. Ask open questions such as: 'How will you portray the atmosphere to the readers?' Avoid telling children what to write. Some children may benefit from guided composition. Focus on perseverance and resilience in the independent application.

Proofreading and redrafting

Have the children proofread their work periodically as they write. Proofreading and improvement without support means that the writing may happen over a few lessons. Offer the children the Editor's checklist or create your own checklist that includes the VGP and spelling focuses covered throughout this sequence. Highlight the importance of redrafting, linking their efforts to the overall Big Picture.

Self- and peer-assessment

Encourage the children to take time to self-assess their own writing as well as that of others in their group. Offer them a set of self-assessment questions, such as: 'How does the writing convey the character's unsuccessful search?' 'How has the desired tone been achieved?' 'What changes would improve the reader's experience?'

Rehearsing and performing

Once the children have written their independent narrative poem, encourage them to perform it either as performance poetry or acted out in role. Discuss how the children's poems are the same or different to the source texts. Encourage the children to feed back on one another's writing and performances.

Final review of the Big Picture

Individually or with partners, have children reflect on what they have learned from this sequence and what they will apply in their future writing.

Year 6, Sequence 8
Non-fiction: Journalism

Sequence 8
Non-fiction: Journalism

Approximate duration: Two weeks

Big Picture

Through this teaching sequence, children will explore the way in which journalists present information in news reports. Understanding how journalists construct news reports will help children to use the conventions of report writing in their own work. Children will be able to write a newspaper article, using an impersonal form, which effectively conveys an information topic.

Phase 1: Enjoy and immerse

Children analyse the techniques used in the model text, a newspaper article about the topic of a fuel shortage.

Phase 2: Capture and organise

Children begin to develop ideas for creating their own newspaper article using report writing techniques.

Phase 3: Collaborate and compose

Children undertake supported writing sessions to develop the writing features of their newspaper article.

Phase 4: Write independently

Children write, edit and present their own newspaper article using an impersonal form.

Main source text

Treasure House Anthology Sequence 8 text. 'Warning: Oil supplies are running out fast', News report text taken from: http://www.independent.co.uk/news/science/warning-oil-supplies-are-running-out-fast-1766585.html

Extra source texts

Treasure House Online, Year 6, Comprehension Unit 8: Non-fiction (news report): Save it!

What if We Run Out of Oil?, Nick Hunter, ISBN 978-0-00-742834-2, pp.26–31

Background knowledge

Many scientists believe that at some point oil production will start to decline. The reduction in oil availability has a catalogue of consequences for human beings. Prices will rise but oil companies know that the law of supply and demand is not straightforward. With new technologies, the search is on to find and conquer new oil fields. In this sequence, children are given a purposeful investigation into news report writing as they explore the issue of fuel consumption across the world. Through a real news report, children observe news report writing features such as headlines, by-lines, summary introduction (who, what, when) and body text (how and why), quotes and captioned photographs.

Spoken outcome

To present an article as an oral performance to an audience of peers or parents

Writing outcome

To write a news report, using an impersonal form, which effectively conveys an information topic

Prior knowledge

Check children's knowledge and understanding of:
- characteristics common to report writing
- fuel production and shortages.

Year 6, Sequence 8
Non-fiction: Journalism

Diagnostic assessment options

Before starting the sequence, you may want to conduct an initial diagnostic assessment of the children's understanding of the typical characteristics of news reports.

Ideas for initial diagnostic assessment options include:

- discussion about news reports, their purpose and common characteristics
- a brief, unsupported writing activity creating a short news report
- practising speaking and listening skills relating to a news report
- a short reading comprehension activity / quiz on a news report.

Cross-curricular links

KS2 Geography – Human and physical geography

Describe and understand key aspects of human geography, including: types of settlement and land use, economic activity including trade links, and the distribution of natural resources including energy, food, minerals and water.

Treasure House links

All digital and pupil book units have the same names and numbers, but different questions.

- Treasure House, Year 6, Comprehension Unit 8: Non-fiction (news report): Save It!
- Treasure House, Year 6, Composition Unit 7: Journalism
- Treasure House, Year 6, Composition Unit 12: Paragraphs in non-fiction
- Treasure House, Year 6, Grammar Unit 2: Using the passive voice
- Treasure House, Year 4, Spelling Unit 2: The /i/ sound spelled y
- Treasure House, Year 6, Punctuation Unit 1: Using commas for clearer meaning
- Treasure House, Year 6, Punctuation Unit 3: Brackets, dashes and commas
- Treasure House, Year 6, Punctuation Unit 6: Punctuating bulleted lists

Resources

Source texts – see Anthologies; Non-fiction planner; Editor's checklist

Year 6, Sequence 8
Non-fiction: Journalism

Phase 1: Enjoy and immerse

In Phase 1, the children are introduced to a news report and information texts that inform readers about the problems caused by a potential shortage of fuel (oil). Over several lessons, they are offered the opportunity to immerse themselves fully in the article, information texts and topic through comprehension and discussion activities, as well as exploring the news report's structure and features through drama, writing and analysis of the text.

Programmes of study: Year 6
- **Comprehension:** Continue to read and discuss an increasingly wide range of fiction, poetry, plays, non-fiction and reference books or textbooks.
- **Comprehension:** Summarise the main ideas drawn from more than one paragraph, identifying key details that support the main idea.
- **Comprehension:** Distinguish between statements of fact and opinion.
- **Composition:** Identify the audience for and purpose of the writing, selecting the appropriate form and using other similar writing as models for their own.
- **Vocabulary, grammar and punctuation:** Use passive verbs to affect the presentation of information in a sentence.

Sparking interest

Introduce the sequence by highlighting the overall Big Picture to the children: they will be working towards writing their own news report, using an impersonal tone, to explore the suggested topic of fuel shortages, independently.

Reading and discussion

Introduce the main source text, read it with the class and check their understanding of the language. Discuss children's opinions of the contents of the news report as well as the structure and features.

Discuss the following with the children.
- What is this article about?
- Who is the intended audience?
- What is the style of the writing like in the article?
- What is the purpose of the article?
- Why would people want to know about potential oil shortages?
- Does the news report contain facts, opinions or both?
- How would you describe the language in the opening sentence of the article?
- Does the article contain all the features you might expect of a news report?

Drama and storytelling

Use drama and oracy activities to reinforce the children's understanding of the contents and structure of the news report. Select the activities that would suit your class or fit in with your lesson timing. Encourage mixed-ability grouping.

- **In the news:** In small groups, children pretend to be television news presenters and the people quoted in the article. Role-play interviewing the people quoted and present the information in the article as a television news item.
- **Role-play discussion:** In pairs or small groups, children assume the roles of different citizens (elderly, homemakers, business people, teenagers) who pretend to read the news report over breakfast in a café. In role, the characters then discuss their opinions about the article as they read through it.
- **Hot-seating the journalist:** This activity can be done in pairs, small groups or as a whole class situation with nominated children or the teacher assuming the role of the journalist. Questions and answers could be derived from the news report contents.

Incidental writing

A short writing activity would enhance the children's understanding of the content of the article. Select activities that you think appropriate for the abilities and interests of your class. Use the children's written outcomes to inform the emphases during the collaborative composition phase.

Year 6, Sequence 8
Non-fiction: Journalism

Children could compose:
- a diary entry by one of the experts quoted in the article
- a narrative story involving the oil crisis
- a fact-file about the oil crisis.

Analysis

Show the model text to the children and discuss the structure and features of the writing. Notice particularly how much of the article is attributed to comments made by experts. Discuss whether this makes the content primarily opinion rather than fact. Discuss what makes an expert respected and believed. Ask children whether being an expert necessarily makes somebody correct. Discuss what motives different experts might have. Look at the length of the article, the quantity of paragraphs, the sizes of paragraphs and the lengths of sentences. Ask children: 'How are the various sentences and paragraphs started to give variety?' 'How are the paragraphs linked cohesively?' 'Where in the article does the reader learn what, who, where, when, how and why?' 'How does the article keep readers engaged?' 'How important are direct quotes in the article?'

Grammar: Using the passive voice

Explain to the children that in active voice sentences the subject does the action. In passive voice sentences the subject receives the action. Although using the active voice is more common, there is an important role for the passive voice. We often use the passive voice when the action is more important than who or what did it.

Write the following active voice sentences on the board and ask children to turn them into passive voice sentences. Then ask children to discuss with a partner and feedback on whether they prefer the active or passive voice version of each sentence.

'A journalist wrote the article.'

'The scientist explained the situation.'

'The oil company released a statement.'

'An expert outlined the consequences.'

'The article provides lots of information.'

Phonics and spelling

Write the following passage on the board for the children to copy and fill in the gaps with the correct spelling: **i** or **y**. (Alternatively, use the passage as a dictation.)

It may be a m_th, but archaeologists in Eg_pt have reported a new discovery. They had been to the g_m for a workout before they entered the p_ramid. Down three flights of steps they discovered ox_gen in a lower cr_pt.

Children could use a dictionary to check spellings.

Review of the Big Picture

Once you have completed this phase, remind the children (or have them remind each other) of the sequence's Big Picture: they are working towards writing their own news report, independently.

Year 6, Sequence 8
Non-fiction: Journalism

Phase 2: Capture and organise

During Phase 2, children start to develop ideas about new content and the features needed to create a class news report about the oil shortage. Working collaboratively, children research and decide on the content, features and structure of the news report.

> **Programmes of study: Year 6**
> - **Comprehension:** Summarise the main ideas drawn from more than one paragraph, identifying key details that support the main idea.
> - **Comprehension:** Retrieve, record and present information from non-fiction.
> - **Comprehension:** Identify how language, structure and presentation contribute to meaning.
> - **Composition:** Identify the audience for and purpose of the writing, selecting the appropriate form and using other similar writing as models for their own.
> - **Composition:** Note and develop initial ideas, drawing on reading and research where necessary

Introduction

Remind the children of the Big Picture for the sequence and recap on the learning achieved through Phase 1. Read one or both of the additional source texts to provide ideas for the content about oil shortages.

Discussing ideas

As a class, discuss and make decisions to form the basis of the children's own news report.

- Who is the audience of the news report?
- What messages do we want the article to convey?
- What information will the readers want to learn?
- How should we organise the structure?
- What information do we need to research to enable us to write the article?
- What typical characteristics of news reports could we include?

Drama and storytelling

Use drama and oracy activities to encourage children to develop their ideas further. Select the activities that would suit your class or fit in with your lesson timing. Encourage mixed-ability grouping for the chosen activities.

- **Hot-seating an environmental expert:** After researching and gathering facts about the oil shortage issue, children can take turns to assume the role of an environmental expert or scientist who answers questions on the environmental issue from the hot-seat.

- **Improvised role-play:** Create and act out an improvised role-play situation in groups. Assume the roles: a newspaper boss who decides that the oil shortage is a topic to be investigated; some journalists in the newspaper office who discuss the issue; and various experts or professionals who might be asked about the oil shortage issue by the journalists.

- **News presenters:** In groups, children plan and present a television news item about the oil shortages. They could include interviews with civilians and / or experts.

Incidental writing

Before you select any incidental writing, make sure the children are able to orally articulate the main ideas for their news report on oil shortages. Select activities that you think appropriate for the abilities and interests of your class. Children could compose:

- a fact-file about oil production
- a story about someone who produces or uses lots of oil
- a letter of complaint to oil companies about price changes.

Organising the class news report into a structure

Once the children have thoroughly explored ideas for the contents of their news report, bring them together and use their final suggestions to model how to plot their news article in diagram or note form with the help of the Non-fiction planner. Once recorded, go through the frame and ask the children to evaluate the contents and organisation.

Year 6, Sequence 8
Non-fiction: Journalism

Review of the Big Picture

Once you have completed all the lessons for this phase, remind the children of the sequence's Big Picture. Recap on the learning achieved in Phase 2.

Phonics and spelling

Display the word 'oxygen' on the board. Discuss the **y** that represents the /i/ sound. Explain to children that the best way to remember which words are spelt in this way is to practise using them and to remember the word bank below. Use the word bank of words spelt with this pattern and put each word in a sentence. Challenge children to use the words in a brief news report or silly story to help them remember the words.

Words where **y** stands for /i/: gym, hymn, crypt, calypso, crystal, cygnet, gypsy, lyric, mystery, oxygen, physics, symbol, symptom, syrup, system, typical

Year 6, Sequence 8
Non-fiction: Journalism

Phase 3: Collaborate and compose

This phase focuses in detail on supporting children to write individual sections of the news report. Through four shared writing lessons, the children collaboratively compose a news report about oil shortages using the model article to refer to and extra source texts to provide content information.

> **Programmes of study: Year 6**
> - **Composition:** Identify the audience for and purpose of the writing, selecting the appropriate form and using other similar writing as a model for their own.
> - **Composition:** Note and develop initial ideas, drawing on reading and research where necessary.
> - **Composition:** Select appropriate grammar and vocabulary, understanding how such choices can change and enhance meaning.
> - **Composition:** Use a wide range of devices to build cohesion within and across paragraphs.
> - **Composition:** Use further organisational and presentational devices to structure text and to guide the reader.

Introduction

Remind the children about the Big Picture and recap on the learning in Phases 1 and 2. Explain to children that through Phase 3, they will be learning how to write their own news report about oil shortages, in an impersonal tone.

Lesson 1

Starter (VGP focus) – Grammar: Using the passive voice

Ask children to remind one another how the passive voice is used in sentences and why it might be used. Establish that we often use the passive voice when an action is more important than who or what did it. The subject of the sentence comes first, and has the action done to it.

Passive Quiz: Write the following sentences on the board.

'The oil prices are always checked by the companies on Mondays.'

'The crisis was discussed by the executives.'

'Mr Jones read the article with great interest.'

'The journalist interviewed the experts.'

Ask children to copy each one, noting whether it is active or passive. Suggest that children underline the subject of the sentence and circle the action. Then ask children to rewrite the active sentences using the passive voice.

Shared writing

Children remind themselves and each other of their planning ideas from Phase 2. Explain to children that in this writing session, you will be working as a team to write the first part of their news report. Ask the children to make suggestions for the heading of the article. The heading could use alliteration, a pun, or a rhetorical question, or be dramatic to interest readers. With the children's contributions, model writing an introductory paragraph for the article. This section should sum up the main point of the article. In the model article, exaggeration is used to shock and hook the readers' interest. Discuss the use of appropriate impersonal language throughout. In the model article, reported speech has been used to cleverly make opinion sound as if it is fact. Ask children to contribute ideas for content and wording as you model writing. Discuss the information children feel is relevant for this section (the details of where, what, when who).

Independent writing

The children can now write their own headline and opening paragraph/s for their article. Some children may benefit from guided group writing or peer-paired writing at this stage.

Plenary

At appropriate points throughout the lesson, invite children to share their writing with small groups, partners or the whole class. Ask the children questions to help them focus on their progress and what they have created during that lesson, for example: 'How well does your heading and opening paragraph communicate your ideas?' 'How have you grabbed the reader's attention?' 'Where have you used the passive voice and what effect has this had on your writing?'

Year 6, Sequence 8
Non-fiction: Journalism

Lesson 2

Starter (VGP focus) – Punctuation: Using commas for clearer meaning

Ask the children to suggest the reasons writers use commas. Collect and discuss ideas. Provide pairs of children with copies of the model text and ask them to find and highlight examples of commas being used. Children should then choose an example of a comma being used and discuss with their partner why it has been used and how the sentence would read differently without it. Pairs should then present their findings to a larger group or the class.

Shared writing

Remind the children of the heading and opening paragraphs they constructed in Lesson 1. Explain that this lesson will involve continuing the article. Together with the children, model how to write the next section of the article. The content could focus on developing the introduction by expanding on the information gathered from the expert and providing some factual content to explain or support what has been said. The tone of this section should be serious and highlight the crisis of the oil shortage, making the reader feel concerned and interested to read on further. Again, ensure discussion to highlight the use of impersonal language and the use of commas for clarity where appropriate.

Independent writing

The children can now write their second section of the news report, focusing on expanding and explaining the information included in their first section and maintaining a serious and shocking tone to hook the reader's interest. Some children may benefit from guided group writing or peer-paired writing at this stage.

Plenary

At the end of the lesson, invite children to share their writing with groups or the whole class. Ask the children questions to help them focus on their progress and what they have created during that lesson, for example: 'How have you developed and expanded on your opening paragraph?' 'Share your writing. Has your partner used commas to aid clarity effectively?' 'Should your partner add or remove any commas to make their writing clearer?'

Lesson 3

Starter (VGP focus) – Punctuation: Brackets, dashes and commas

Ask children to recall and explain the meaning of 'parenthesis'. Take suggestions, encouraging children to expand on their answers by giving examples. Establish that 'parenthesis' refers to the use of brackets, dashes and commas to separate words, phrases or clauses that add extra detail to a sentence. Provide pairs of children with copies of the source text and ask them to find and highlight examples of parentheses. Children should then discuss with their partner why the writer may have chosen to use brackets, dashes or commas in particular. Pairs then present their findings to a larger group or the class.

Shared writing

With the children's input, model writing the third section of the news report. In this section, include information which links the previous content of concerning facts and opinions to the readers' own lives. Ask children: 'How will the oil shortage impact on everyday lives?' 'How will the global or local environments be affected?' This section should explore the finer details of the oil shortage topic: who will be affected and how they will be affected. You could introduce a new expert to give their opinion or details of research.

Independent writing

The children can now write their own third section of the news report, focusing on the impact of the oil shortage on people's everyday lives and consequences for the environment. Some children may benefit from guided group writing or peer-paired writing at this stage.

Plenary

At the end of the lesson, invite children to share their writing with groups or the whole class. Ask the children questions to help them focus on their progress and what they have created during that lesson, for example: 'How have you made the topic of this article directly relevant to the reader?' 'What language choices have you made to ensure the right tone for the article?' 'Share your writing. Has your partner used brackets, dashes and / or commas to include extra information in parenthesis correctly?'

Year 6, Sequence 8
Non-fiction: Journalism

Lesson 4

Starter (VGP focus) – Punctuation: Punctuating bulleted lists

Ask children to suggest why we might use bulleted lists. Establish that we can use bullet points to make a list clearer and easier to read. Look at the bulleted lists in both of the extra source texts. Ask children to make a simple poster, to be displayed on the classroom wall, containing the following information.

Three main rules when using bullet points:

1) Use a colon after an introduction.

2) Start list items with bullet points.

3) Write items below each other.

There are also some further guidelines about punctuation, as follows. If items are full sentences, start them with capital letters and end them with full stops or semi-colons. End the last item with a full stop. If items are not full sentences, end them with no punctuation or commas, or semi-colons if any items already contain a comma. End the last item with nothing or a full stop.

Finally, ask children to review the bulleted lists in the extra source texts and decide which rules and guidelines have been applied.

Shared writing

With children's input, model writing the final section of the news report. In this section the drama of the shocking news about the oil shortages and potential impact on people's lives could now be calmed and counteracted by differing opinions or contrasting evidence / research. It could also take a practical approach to explain what, if anything, people can do to avoid the potential problem. In the source text, additional question and answer style information is provided to give clarity on the things mentioned earlier in the article. Include a bullet-pointed list if appropriate.

Independent writing

The children can now write their own final part of the news report, based on the shared writing session and model text. Encourage children to include a bulleted list. Some children may benefit from guided group or peer-paired writing at this stage.

Plenary

At the end of the lesson invite children to share their writing with groups or the whole class. Ask the children questions to help them focus on their progress and what they have created during that lesson, for example: 'How have you concluded your article?' 'What final impression do you want to leave the reader with and how do you intend to achieve this?' 'Have you presented information in a correctly punctuated bulleted list? If not, is there any information in your article that would be better presented as a bulleted list?'

Encourage reading-back to ensure consistency of impersonal tone.

Rehearsing and performing

Once the children have written all of their news reports, encourage the children to present them by reading them to an audience. Discuss the similarities and differences to the original source text. Discuss any interesting points arising from the oil shortage topic.

Review of the Big Picture

Once you have completed all the lessons for this phase, remind the children of the sequence's Big Picture. Discuss what they have learned during Phase 3.

Year 6, Sequence 8
Non-fiction: Journalism

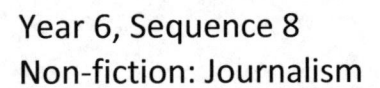

Phase 4: Write independently

This final phase brings all the children's learning and writing skills together so that they can write their own independent news report. Through their writing, they will be able to utilise the different VGP focuses that they have been practising throughout the previous phases.

> **Programmes of study: Year 6**
> - **Composition:** Select appropriate grammar and vocabulary, understanding how such choices can change and enhance meaning.
> - **Composition:** Use a wide range of devices to build cohesion within and across paragraphs.
> - **Composition:** Use further organisational and presentational devices to structure text and to guide the reader.
> - **Composition:** Assess the effectiveness of their own and others' writing and suggest improvements.
> - **Composition:** Propose changes to grammar and vocabulary to enhance effects and clarify meaning.
> - **Composition:** Proofread for spelling and punctuation errors.
> - **Composition:** Perform their own compositions, using appropriate intonation, volume and movement so that meaning is clear.

Introduction

Introduce this phase by highlighting the overall Big Picture to the children. Recap on learning and progress through Phases 1–3 and explain that in Phase 4 they will be applying their learning to write their own news report independently. Discuss and list examples of the possible contents of the news report related to the oil shortage topic. Recap on the typical characteristics of news reports.

Writing

Give each child a Non-fiction planner and instruct them to start planning and writing each section of their article. Display the class planning structure and a copy of the model text for reference. All children should be encouraged to try to write independently to the best of their ability. Ask open questions such as: 'How will you achieve the purpose of the article?' Avoid telling children what to write. Some children may benefit from guided composition. Focus on perseverance and resilience in their independent application.

Proofreading and redrafting

Have the children proofread their work periodically as they write. Proofreading and improvement without support means that the writing may happen over a few lessons. Offer the children the Editor's checklist or create your own checklist that includes the VGP and spelling focuses covered throughout this sequence. Highlight the importance of redrafting, linking their efforts to the overall Big Picture.

Self- and peer-assessment

Encourage the children to take time to self-assess their own writing as well as that of others in the group. Offer them a set of self-assessment questions, such as: 'Does the article convey all the information a reader would want to know?' 'How clearly is the writing structured?' 'What impact does the writing have?' 'Have the typical characteristics of news reports been used appropriately?' 'What changes would improve the reader's experience?' 'How have you used the VGP focuses?'

Rehearsing and performing

Once the children have written their independent news report, encourage them to perform in pairs, in role to one another and the whole class. Discuss how similar or different the article is to the original source text. Encourage the children to feed back on one another's writing and performances.

Final review of the Big Picture

Individually or with partners, have the children reflect on what they have learned from this sequence and what they will apply in their future writing.

Year 6, Sequence 9
Non-fiction: Reports

Sequence 9
Non-fiction: Reports

Approximate duration: Two weeks

Big Picture

Through this teaching sequence, children will explore how to compose explanation and information reports. Understanding how authors construct reports will help children to use the conventions of report writing in their own work. Children will be able to write an explanation or information text, on a current classroom topic.

Phase 1: Enjoy and immerse

Children analyse the techniques used in the model text, an explanation text about the heart.

Phase 2: Capture and organise

Children begin to develop ideas for creating their own explanation or information report using report writing techniques.

Phase 3: Collaborate and compose

Children undertake supported writing sessions to develop the writing features of their report.

Phase 4: Writing independently

Children write, edit and present their own explanation or information report based on a current classroom topic.

Main source text

Treasure House Anthology Sequence 9 text. *The Heart*, Simon Seymour, ISBN 978-0-06-087721-7, pp.4–9

Extra source texts

Treasure House Online, Year 6, Comprehension Unit 9: Non-fiction (information text): Deserts

Background knowledge

Simon Seymour, the author of the main source text, gives an insight into his style of writing explanation and information texts which is great to share with the children: 'I've written more than 250 books, and I've thought a lot about different ways to encourage interest in the natural world, as well as how to show the joys of non-fiction. When I write, I use comparisons to help explain unfamiliar ideas, complex concepts, and impossibly large numbers. I try to engage your senses and imagination to set the scene and to make science fun. For example, in *Penguins*, I emphasize the playful nature of these creatures on the very first page by mentioning how penguins excel at swimming and diving. I use strong verbs to enhance understanding. I make use of descriptive detail and ask questions that anticipate what you might be thinking.'

Spoken outcome

To present information orally to an audience of peers or parents

Writing outcome

To write an explanation or information report about a current classroom topic

Prior knowledge

Check children's knowledge and understanding of:
- characteristics common to explanation reports
- characteristics common to information reports.

Year 6, Sequence 9
Non-fiction: Reports

Diagnostic assessment options

Before starting the sequence, you may want to conduct an initial diagnostic assessment of the children's understanding of the typical characteristics of explanation or information reports.

Ideas for initial diagnostic assessment options include:
- discussion about what distinguishes explanation and information reports, making comparisons
- a brief, unsupported writing activity creating a short explanation or information report
- a brief oral explanation or report on a familiar topic
- a short quiz on an explanation or information report.

Cross-curricular links

KS2 Science – Animals including humans

Identify and name the main parts of the human circulatory system, and describe the functions of the heart, blood vessels and blood.

Treasure House links

All digital and pupil book units have the same names and numbers, but different questions.

- Treasure House, Year 6, Comprehension Unit 9: Non-fiction (information text): Deserts
- Treasure House, Year 6, Composition Unit 11: Explanations
- Treasure House, Year 6, Composition Unit 12: Paragraphs in non-fiction
- Treasure House, Year 6, Grammar Unit 4: Linking ideas in paragraphs
- Treasure House, Year 6, Spelling Unit 8: The letter-string ough
- Treasure House, Year 6, Grammar Unit 2: Using the passive voice
- Treasure House, Year 6, Punctuation Unit 2: Hyphens to avoid ambiguity
- Treasure House, Year 3, Punctuation Unit 1: Final punctuation

Resources

Source texts – see Anthologies; Non-fiction planner; Editor's checklist

Year 6, Sequence 9
Non-fiction: Reports

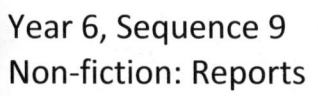

Phase 1: Enjoy and immerse

In Phase 1, the children are introduced to a non-fiction text written by an experienced non-fiction author, Simon Seymour. The topic of the text is the heart. Over several lessons, they are offered the opportunity to immerse themselves fully in the text through comprehension and discussion activities, as well as exploring its structure and features through drama, storytelling, writing and analysis of the text.

Programmes of study: Year 6

- **Comprehension:** Continue to read and discuss an increasingly wide range of fiction, poetry, plays, non-fiction and reference books or text books.
- **Comprehension:** Read books that are structured in different ways and read for a range of purposes.
- **Comprehension:** Summarise the main ideas drawn from more than one paragraph, identifying key details that support the main ideas.
- **Composition:** Identify the audience for and purpose of the writing, selecting the appropriate form and using other similar writing as models for their own.
- **Vocabulary, grammar and punctuation:** Link ideas in paragraphs.
- **Spelling:** Use words with the letter-string ough.

Sparking interest

Introduce the sequence by highlighting the overall Big Picture to the children: they will be working towards creating their own explanation or information text on a topic they are interested in or that is relevant to the current class topic.

Reading and discussion

Introduce the main source text, read it with the class and check the children's understanding of the language. Discuss children's understanding of the content and structure of the extract.

Discuss the following with the children.
- What is the text about?
- Why do you think this text has been written?
- What questions does the text answer?
- What else might a reader want to know?
- How would you describe the structure of the text?
- How would you describe the language used in the text?
- How does the text keep the reader interested?

Drama and storytelling

Use drama and oracy activities to reinforce the children's understanding of the contents and structure of the text. Select the activities that would suit your class or fit in with your lesson timing. Encourage mixed-ability grouping for the chosen activities.

- **In the news:** In small groups, children take the role of TV news presenters and present the information in the text as a TV news item, for example, 'Breaking news … just discovered by scientists … how the heart works.'
- **Presentation ideas:** In pairs or small groups, children use the model text to prepare a short talk about the heart. They could use flash cards or hold up posters to support their talk.
- **Hot-seating a scientist:** This activity can be done in pairs, small groups or as a whole-class situation with nominated children or the teacher assuming the role of the scientist. Questions and answers could be derived from the model text contents.

Incidental writing

A short writing activity would enhance the children's understanding of the text and characters. Select activities that you think appropriate for the abilities and interests of your class. Children could compose:

- a letter from one friend to another to tell them what they have learned about the heart
- a web-page for the British Heart Foundation, promoting heart-health
- a leaflet to promote caring for your heart.

Year 6, Sequence 9
Non-fiction: Reports

Analysis

Show the text to the children and discuss the contents, features and structure. Look at the way the reader is engaged straight away and given a comparison between their fist and the size of the heart that they can relate to. Look at the lengths and variety of sentence structures. Try to summarise in one or two words what each paragraph is about. Look at how the information flows and progresses. Look at how many facts are used. Notice how the information is explained in a very detailed way. Tell the children that many explanation and information texts use an impersonal tone but that this example uses a personal tone to help convey the information in a way that keeps the reader interested. Perhaps a personal tone was used because the text was written with children in mind. Look at the diagrams and labels. Ask children: 'What purpose do the diagrams and labels serve?' 'How do they enhance the readers' experience?' 'What questions are answered by the text?'

Grammar: Linking ideas in paragraphs

Tell children that we can organise our writing into paragraphs to make the different sets of ideas clear. We can link ideas across different paragraphs using repetition, synonyms and pronouns that refer back to what has been mentioned in previous paragraphs. We can also link ideas using connecting adverbials such as: 'Most people believe ...', 'However ...', 'As a result ...'

Provide pairs of children with copies of the model text and ask them to find and highlight examples of how the paragraphs are linked. They should then present their ideas to other groups or the whole class.

Phonics and spelling

Display the letter-string ough. Establish that this letter-string is tricky because it can be pronounced in multiple ways.

Ask children to say each of the words below and sort them into groups of the same sound. Then write each word in a sentence to show what it means.

ough words: dough, though, although, tough, cough, enough, plough, thought, fought, brought, nought, rough, through

Review of the Big Picture

Once you have completed this phase, remind the children (or have them remind each other) of the sequence's Big Picture: they are working towards writing their own explanation or information text about a current class topic (or topic of their choice).

Year 6, Sequence 9
Non-fiction: Reports

Phase 2: Capture and organise

During Phase 2, the children start to develop ideas about new content and features needed to create a class explanation or information report. The group and class discussions, as well as drama or short writing opportunities, offer chances for children of all abilities to contribute and use their skills towards designing a structure and planning features for the report. Their ideas can be recorded in picture, diagram or note form with the help of the Non-fiction planner.

Programmes of study: Year 6
- **Comprehension:** Identify how language, structure and presentation contribute to meaning.
- **Comprehension:** Retrieve, record and present information from non-fiction.
- **Comprehension:** Explain and discuss their understanding of what they have read, including through formal presentations and debates, maintaining a focus on the topic and using notes where necessary.
- **Composition:** Identify the audience for and purpose of the writing, selecting the appropriate form and using other similar writing as models for their own.
- **Composition:** Note and develop initial ideas, drawing on reading and research where necessary.
- **Spelling:** Use words with the letter-string ough.

Introduction

Remind the children of the Big Picture for the sequence and recap on the learning achieved through Phase 1. Read the extra source text about deserts to see further examples of typical characteristics of explanation and information reports.

Discussing ideas

As a class, encourage the children to decide on the topic for the class report. Ideally, choose something that links to your current class topic.

Once the main decision of the topic has been made, put the children into mixed-ability groups and encourage them to discuss and come up with suggestions in answer to the following questions. Depending on your class, you may want to give them a selection of questions or just one question per group. Bring the groups together to listen and make decisions on the structure and features to be used in the class report.

- What diagrams and flowcharts should be included?
- What headings and subheadings should be used?
- What photos or illustrations should be used?
- What is the purpose of the text?
- Who will be the readers of the report?
- How will the readers be hooked at the beginning of the report?
- How will readers remain engaged throughout the report?

Drama and storytelling

Use drama and oracy activities to allow the children to explore the suggestions for their new explanation or information report content. Select the activities that would suit your class or fit in with your lesson timing. Encourage mixed-ability grouping for the chosen activities.

- **Hot-seating the expert:** This activity can be done in pairs, small groups or as a class situation. Allow children to research the topic beforehand. Encourage the children to think and, if necessary, write down their questions before the hot-seat session starts. Discuss the (imaginary) expert's responses.
- **In the news:** Present the information for the new report as a news item with children assuming the roles of news presenters and guests to be interviewed.
- **Role-play discussion:** Children work in groups to imagine they are teams of authors about to create a new series of information books for children. In a role-play team meeting, children should brainstorm and discuss as many questions as they can about the topic.

Incidental writing

Before you select any incidental writing, make sure the children are able to orally articulate the main contents of their report. Select activities that you think appropriate for the abilities and interests of your class.

Year 6, Sequence 9
Non-fiction: Reports

Children could compose:
- a detailed flowchart or diagram
- a magazine article
- a letter to tell a friend about the topic
- an email to ask questions about the topic to an expert.

Organising the class explanation or information report into a structure

Once the children have thoroughly explored their ideas for their class report, bring them together and use their final suggestions to model how to plot the new report in picture, diagram or note form with the help of the Non-fiction planner. Once recorded, go through the frame and ask the children if they are happy with the plan for the contents and structure.

Phonics and spelling

Ask children: 'What do these ough words mean?' Tell children to look up the ough words in a dictionary to check their meanings; say them to a friend to check the pronunciation; find words that rhyme; then put all the words into a short silly story.

ough words: trough, bough, fought, plough, slough, thoughtfully, nought

Review of the Big Picture

Once you have completed all the lessons for this phase, remind the children of the sequence's Big Picture. Recap on the learning achieved in Phase 2.

Year 6, Sequence 9
Non-fiction: Reports

Phase 3: Collaborate and compose

This phase focuses on the teaching and learning of how to write an explanation or information report, with one lesson per section, so that the children are taken through the writing of the whole piece, learning new vocabulary, grammar and punctuation along the way. Children should have the planning framework from Phase 2 in front of them throughout, and should be able to revisit the original source text, *The Heart*.

> **Programmes of study: Year 6**
> - **Composition:** Identify the audience for and purpose of the writing, selecting the appropriate form and using other similar writing as a model for their own.
> - **Composition:** Note and develop initial ideas, drawing on reading and research where necessary.
> - **Composition:** Select appropriate grammar and vocabulary, understanding how such choices can change and enhance meaning.
> - **Composition:** Use a wide range of devices to build cohesion within and across paragraphs.
> - **Composition:** Use further organisational and presentational devices to structure text and to guide the reader.

Introduction

Remind the children about the Big Picture and recap on the learning in Phases 1 and 2. Explain to the children that through Phase 3 they will be learning how to write their own explanation or information text based on the planning and ideas in Phase 2.

Lesson 1

Starter (VGP focus) – Grammar: Linking ideas in and across paragraphs

Ask the children to explain why we use paragraphs in our writing. Take suggestions and establish that using paragraphs makes a longer piece of writing easier to read. A paragraph is a group of sentences about one idea or topic.

We often use adverbials, conjunctions and pronouns to help the reader understand the connections between ideas in a piece of writing. We can use linking words and phrases to help the reader see these connections between sentences and clauses in a paragraph, for example: 'First of all ...', 'After that ...', 'Finally ...', 'so ...', 'but ...', 'because ...' We can also use repetition of the topic vocabulary.

Provide pairs of children with copies of the extra source text about deserts. Ask the children to locate and highlight any examples they can find that demonstrate how the paragraphs are linked.

Shared writing

Children remind themselves and each other of their planning ideas from Phase 2. Ask the children to make suggestions for the wording of the introductory paragraph of the class explanation / information report, using the model text, *The Heart*, for reference. Ask the children: 'How will we hook the reader in?' 'How will we make it clear to the reader what this report is about without going into details straight away?' Model writing the opening paragraph with the children's input, focusing on writing an introduction that is interesting, 'catchy' and gives an overview of the report to come. Discuss how the topic can be made relevant to the reader by using a comparison, following the example of the model text where the size of the heart is compared to the reader's fist. Try to include explanatory conjunctions in the paragraph such as 'because' and 'so'. At the end of the introductory paragraph, discuss how the next section could be started with an adverbial phrase.

Independent writing

The children can now write their own first section, applying the VGP focus on linking words and thinking about how the reader will be hooked into reading more of the report. Some children may benefit from guided group writing or peer-paired writing at this stage.

Year 6, Sequence 9
Non-fiction: Reports

Plenary

At appropriate points throughout the lesson, invite children to share their writing with small groups, partners or the whole class. Ask the children questions to help them focus on their progress and what they have created during that lesson, for example: 'How does your introduction hook the reader?' 'How have you made the content relevant to the readers, for example, have you used a comparison?' 'What adverbials, conjunctions and / or pronouns have you used to connect the ideas in your writing?'

Lesson 2

Starter (VGP focus) – Grammar: Using the passive voice

Write these examples of the passive voice on the board:

'A diagram of a heart was drawn by the scientist.'

'The blood cells are pumped around by the heart.'

We often use the passive voice when an action is more important than who or what did it. Ask the children to identify the subject of the sentences (the diagram, the blood cells) and the action of the sentences ('was drawn', 'are pumped'). Provide pairs of children with copies of the model text, *The Heart*, and ask them to choose five sentences at random. Ask them to work out whether the sentences use the active or the passive voice. To support them, remind them to find the subject of the sentence and then check if the action is being done to the subject (passive) or if the subject is the one doing the action (active). Ask children to present their findings to the class.

Shared writing

With the children's input, model writing the next part of the explanation / information report. You may decide to use a series of subheadings to make the contents of the report clearer. Focus on linking back to the introduction but now being more specific about the area of the topic being explained: this is the body of the report. Experiment with putting the sentences into the active and passive voice and discuss the effect on the reader to make a decision about the best to use. Talk about the contents of each paragraph and, when reading them back, ask children to imagine they have no knowledge of the topic. Ask: 'Is the information explained clearly and in enough detail?' 'What questions might the reader want to ask?'

Independent writing

The children can now write their own second section, applying the VGP focus by thinking about whether they are using the active or passive voice and the impact on the reader. Some children may benefit from guided group writing or peer-paired writing at this stage.

Plenary

At the end of the lesson, invite children to share their writing with groups or the whole class. Ask the children questions to help them focus on their progress and what they have created during that lesson, for example: 'How have you made your report clear for the reader?' 'How have you made your report engaging as well as informative?' 'Does the order of content make logical sense?' 'Have you used the passive voice and, if so, to what effect?'

Lesson 3

Starter (VGP focus) – Punctuation: Using hyphens to avoid ambiguity

Tell children that one of the most important features of explanation and information texts is clarity. Write the following on the board and invite children to discuss the different meanings.

'Grass-chewing sheep' 'Grass chewing sheep'

'One-way valve' 'One way valve'

Write the following sentences on the board and ask children to work in pairs to copy them, adding in a hyphen to make the meaning clear. Share children's answers and talk about whether everybody agreed on the meaning of the sentences.

1. For Sale: little used boat
2. Beware of car chasing dog on motorway
3. Two weeks holiday to be won!

Shared writing

With the children's input, model drawing and labelling a diagram, flowchart or table for the class explanation / information report. Discuss why this feature would be helpful for readers, and also how it is helpful for the author to communicate their explanation clearly. Model the layout of the diagram on a page (using the board) to enable plenty of space to add labels and discuss the key role that these play. Remind children not to draw boxes and then fill in the label as inevitably the label will be squashed. Model writing the label first then drawing a box around it using a ruler. Model using an arrow to link the label to the relevant part of the diagram. You could discuss the use of other visual features such as bulleted lists, fact boxes, pie charts and bar graphs as visual ways to explain information to readers.

Year 6, Sequence 9
Non-fiction: Reports

Independent writing

The children can now write (and illustrate) their own third section, paying particular attention to accuracy and detail. Encourage children to be able to explain why the diagram they are using will help to communicate the ideas in the report and why the reader may find this visual presentation useful. Some children may benefit from guided group writing or peer-paired writing at this stage.

Plenary

At the end of the lesson, invite children to share their writing with groups or the whole class. Ask the children questions to help them focus on their progress and what they have created during that lesson, for example: 'What information does your diagram explain?' 'What purpose do the labels serve in communicating your information to readers?' 'How does your diagram help to explain the information more clearly?' 'Would your writing be any clearer if you adjusted the punctuation (such as hyphens, commas and so on)?'

Lesson 4

Starter (VGP focus) – Grammar: Revision of exclamations

Ask children to recap what exclamation marks are used for. Take suggestions and establish that we use exclamation marks to show that the sentence should be read with feeling or read loudly. They can show anger, frustration, shock, pain, surprise or excitement. Generally speaking, exclamation marks should not be used in formal writing. It is considered too informal.

Although not included in the model text extract, later in Simon Seymour's book, *The Heart*, he does use exclamation marks. Read this sentence to the children and ask them to consider why he chose to include an exclamation mark:

'Yet stacked one upon another in a single column, the red blood cells in our bodies would tower thirty thousand miles high!'

Because Simon Seymour's book, *The Heart*, is written with children in mind he uses a relatively informal style, addressing the reader directly and using exclamation marks. Ask children to think of one fact or sentence they could use in their own report that uses an exclamation mark.

Shared writing

With the children's input, model how to write the final section of the explanation / information report. Suggest that this section both concludes the information and tries to link it to the readers' own experience. Recap on the other sections and consider whether the reader would feel satisfied with all the information or whether anything is missing. If lots of technical vocabulary has been used, consider including a glossary.

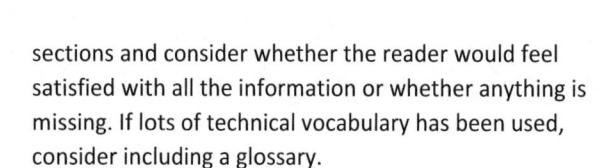

Independent writing

The children can now write their own fourth section, applying the VGP focus to use an exclamation.

Some children may benefit from guided group writing or peer-paired writing at this stage.

Plenary

At the end of the lesson, invite children to share their writing with groups or the whole class. Ask the children questions to help them focus on their progress and what they have created during that lesson, for example: 'Have you fully explained your topic's concept or processes?' 'Would the reader have any questions?' 'Have you linked the topic to the reader's own experience?' 'Could the effect of any particular sentence be enhanced by adding an exclamation mark?'

Rehearsing and performing

Once the children have written their explanation / information report, encourage them to present it to the class. Discuss how different or similar the report is to the original model text, *The Heart*.

Review of the Big Picture

Once you have completed all the lessons for this phase, remind the children of the sequence's Big Picture. Discuss what they have learned in Phase 3.

Year 6, Sequence 9
Non-fiction: Reports

Phase 4: Write independently

This final phase brings all the children's learning and writing skills together so that they can write their own explanation or information report about a current class topic or a topic of their own choice. Through their writing, they will be able to utilise the different VGP focuses that they have been investigating and applying to their shared writing in the previous phases.

> **Programmes of study: Year 6**
> - **Composition:** Select appropriate grammar and vocabulary, understanding how such choices can change and enhance meaning.
> - **Composition:** Use a wide range of devices to build cohesion within and across paragraphs.
> - **Composition:** Use further organisational and presentational devices to structure text and to guide the reader.
> - **Composition:** Assess the effectiveness of their own and others' writing and suggest improvements.
> - **Composition:** Propose changes to grammar and vocabulary to enhance effects and clarify meaning.
> - **Composition:** Proofread for spelling and punctuation errors.
> - **Composition:** Perform their own compositions, using appropriate intonation, volume and movement so that meaning is clear.

Introduction

Introduce this phase by highlighting the overall Big Picture to the children. Recap on learning and progress through Phases 1–3 and explain that in Phase 4 they will be applying their learning to write their own explanation or information report independently. Discuss and list examples of features that should be included in the report such as headings, subheadings, distinct but linked paragraphs and diagrams with labels. Discuss and list potential topics relevant to the children and their current classroom learning.

Writing

Give each child a Non-fiction planner and instruct them to start planning and writing each section of their own report. Display the class planning structure and a copy of the model text, *The Heart*, for reference. All the children should be encouraged to try to write independently to the best of their ability. Ask open questions such as: 'How will you relate the information to the readers' own experience?' 'How will you make the reader want to read more?' Avoid telling children what to write. Some children may benefit from guided composition. Focus on perseverance and resilience in their independent application.

Proofreading and redrafting

Have the children proofread their work periodically as they write. Proofreading and improvement without support means that the writing may happen over a few lessons. Offer the children the Editor's checklist or create your own checklist that includes the VGP and spelling focuses covered throughout the unit. Highlight the importance of redrafting, linking their efforts to the overall Big Picture.

Self- and peer-assessment

Encourage the children to take time to self-assess their own writing as well as assess that of others in their group. Offer them a set of self-assessment questions, such as: 'How does the report explain the information clearly to the reader?' 'Which features have worked particularly well and why?' 'What could be improved next time?' 'Which parts were challenging and what helped?'

Rehearsing and performing

Once the children have written their explanation or information report, encourage them to present it to the class. Discuss how different or similar the report is to the original model text, *The Heart*. Encourage the children to feed back on one another's writing and presentations.

Final review of the Big Picture

Individually or with partners, have children reflect on what they have learned from this sequence and what they will apply in their future writing.

Year 6, Sequence 10
Poetry: Contrasting perspectives

Sequence 10
Poetry: Contrasting perspectives

Approximate duration: Two weeks

Big Picture

Through this teaching sequence, children will explore the way in which poems that are written about the same topic can give contrasting perspectives. Understanding the techniques used by poets will help children to use these techniques within their own writing. Children will be able to write two poems about the same topic, providing contrasting perspectives.

Phase 1: Enjoy and immerse

Children analyse the perspectives portrayed in the model texts, 'Winter Morning' by Ogden Nash and 'Winter in a Wheelchair' by Emma Barnes.

Phase 2: Capture and organise

Children begin to develop ideas for creating their own poems with contrasting perspectives.

Phase 3: Collaborate and compose

Children undertake supported writing sessions to develop the content and features of their contrasting poems.

Phase 4: Writing independently

Children write, edit and present their own point-of-view poems with contrasting perspectives on a season of the year.

Main source text

Treasure House Anthology Sequence 10 text. Treasure House Online, Year 6, Comprehension Unit 10: Poetry: Views of winter

Extra source texts

'Christmas Landscape', Laurie Lee

'Snow and Snow', Ted Hughes

Both these poems can be found on the internet.

Background knowledge

'Winter Morning' by Ogden Nash is a positive, light-hearted reflection on the wonder and beauty of winter, summed up aptly by its first line 'Winter is the king of showmen'. 'Winter in a Wheelchair' by Emma Barnes is a poem that has many features in common with 'Winter Morning', including its seasonal theme. However, it provides a sombre and contrasting viewpoint which is particularly powerful when read immediately after 'Winter Morning'.

These poems provide a useful vehicle for teaching children about the connection between poet and poem as they see how the poets' thoughts and feelings are expressed through their writing.

Spoken outcome

To present poems to an audience of peers or parents

Writing outcome

To write two poems with contrasting perspectives on a season of the year

Prior knowledge

Check children's knowledge and understanding of:

- poetry by Ogden Nash and Emma Barnes
- forms of descriptive language used in poetry, including figurative language
- poems that portray point of view.

Year 6, Sequence 10
Poetry: Contrasting perspectives

Diagnostic assessment options

Before starting the sequence, you may want to conduct an initial diagnostic assessment of the children's understanding of the typical characteristics of poems with contrasting perspectives.

Ideas for initial diagnostic assessment options include:

- discussion about poems with viewpoints, their purpose and form
- a brief, unsupported writing activity to create a short perspective poem about a familiar topic
- practising speaking and listening skills relating to a poem that shows someone's perspective
- a short reading comprehension activity / quiz on a perspective poem.

Cross-curricular links

KS1 Science – Seasonal changes

Pupils should be taught to:

- observe changes across the 4 seasons
- observe and describe weather associated with the seasons and how day length varies.

Treasure House links

All digital and pupil book units have the same names and numbers, but different questions.

- Treasure House, Year 6, Comprehension Unit 10: Poetry: Views of winter
- Treasure House, Year 6, Composition Unit 9: Poems on similar themes
- Treasure House, Year 5, Vocabulary Unit 1: Expanded noun phrases
- Treasure House, Year 6, Spelling Unit 3: The suffixes -ant, -ance / -ancy, -ent and -ence / -ency
- Treasure House, Year 6, Spelling Unit 9: Words with 'silent' letters
- Treasure House, Year 6, Punctuation Unit 5: Colons and semi-colons in lists

Resources

Source texts – see Anthologies; Poetry planner; Editor's checklist

Year 6, Sequence 10
Poetry: Contrasting perspectives

Phase 1: Enjoy and immerse

In Phase 1, the children are introduced to two poems written on the same topic but portraying conflicting perspectives. 'Winter Morning' by Ogden Nash shows the season of winter in a positive light, whereas 'Winter in a Wheelchair' by Emma Barnes shows how the season can be a negative experience for some people. Over several sessions, children are offered the opportunity to immerse themselves fully in the poems through comprehension and discussion activities, as well as exploring the content and form through drama, writing and analysis of the text.

Programmes of study: Year 6

- **Comprehension:** Continue to read and discuss an increasingly wide range of fiction, poetry, plays, non-fiction and reference books or textbooks.
- **Comprehension:** Prepare poems and plays to read aloud and to perform, showing understanding through intonation, tone and volume so that the meaning is clear to an audience.
- **Comprehension:** Draw inferences such as inferring characters' feelings, thoughts and motives from their actions, and justifying inferences with evidence.
- **Composition:** Identify the audience for and purpose of the writing, selecting the appropriate form and using other similar writing as models for their own.
- **Vocabulary, grammar and punctuation:** Use expanded noun phrases to convey complicated information concisely.
- **Spelling:** Use words ending in -ance and -ence.

Sparking interest

Introduce the sequence by highlighting the overall Big Picture to the children: they will be working towards creating two of their own poems that show contrasting viewpoints about a season. Use an opening question such as: 'What influences the perspective shown by a poet in his work?'

Reading and discussion

Introduce both of the main source texts, read them with the class and check their understanding.

Discuss the following with the children.
- What are these poems about?
- Which poem do you prefer and why?
- Why do you think the poets wrote these poems?
- Who do you think they were written for?
- What atmosphere do the poems create?
- How do the poems make you feel?
- How did the poet make you feel things?
- How would you describe the rhythm?
- Are there any notable devices used in the poems?

Drama and storytelling

Use drama and oracy activities to reinforce the children's understanding of the poems. Select the activities that would suit your class or fit in with your lesson timing. Encourage mixed-ability grouping for the chosen activities.

- **Performance poetry:** Give children the stage and invite them to read the poems by themselves or with a friend in a style they think is appropriate for the styles of the poems. Encourage children to memorise one, or both, of the poems in preparation for performance.
- **Hot-seating the poet:** Research more about Ogden Nash and / or Emma Barnes. Then, imagine the poets have come to visit the class. Give children the opportunity, in pairs, groups or as a whole class, to ask the imaginary poets questions. The children and / or teacher playing the roles of the poets should improvise their answers.
- **Act it out:** Have children turn the poems into a series of freeze-frames. Use freeze-framing and thought-tracking to think about what the speakers in the poems are thinking. Compare freeze-frames for the two poems, drawing out the words, phrases and images that have evoked the tableaus created.

Year 6, Sequence 10
Poetry: Contrasting perspectives

Incidental writing

A short writing activity would enhance the children's understanding of the poem. Select activities that you think appropriate for the abilities and interests of your class.

Children could compose:

- a diary entry by the speakers of the poems
- an online article or blog entry about winter weather
- a letter of complaint from the speaker of Emma Barnes' poem to the council regarding icy pavements that prevent her from moving freely.

Analysis

Show the poems to the children and discuss the contents and the forms. Ask children: 'What are the similarities in the poems?' 'What are the differences?' Discuss the sentence lengths and presentation. Ask the children to decide whether there is a rhyming pattern. Ask the children to count the syllables in each line and see if there is a pattern. Ask children: 'How do the poems flow?' Practise reading them out to listen to the rhythms. Discuss how the structures and forms of the poems contribute to the messages the poet is conveying. Discuss how the poets ensure that the readers understand their perspective.

Grammar: Expanded noun phrases

Tell children that we use expanded noun phrases to give more information about nouns. A noun can be expanded using adjectives before it and extra information (a prepositional phrase) after it. For example:

Noun: snowman

Noun phrase: the snowman

With adjectives: the round, jolly snowman

With a prepositional phrase: the round, jolly snowman with the stripy scarf.

Ask children to locate and note down examples of expanded noun phrases in the poems. To provide further support, you could ask children to first locate and underline nouns, then work with a partner to decide whether that noun has been expanded and how.

Phonics and spelling

Ask the children to use a dictionary to find out whether the following words are spelt with -ance or -ence at the end of them, paying attention to definitions. Then children should write each word in a sentence, sharing sentences with a partner to check for sense.

resid_____; emerg_____; observ_____; confid_____;
innoc_____; extravag_____; neglig_____;
converg_____.

Review of the Big Picture

Once you have completed this phase, remind the children (or have them remind each other) of the sequence's Big Picture: they are working towards writing their own pair of poems portraying contrasting perspectives about a season.

Year 6, Sequence 10
Poetry: Contrasting perspectives

Phase 2: Capture and organise

During Phase 2, children start to develop ideas about new content and the literary features needed to create a pair of class poems portraying contrasting viewpoints about a season. Working collaboratively, children decide on the content, structure and form of the poems.

Programmes of study: Year 6
- **Comprehension:** Identify and discuss themes and conventions in and across a wide range of writing.
- **Comprehension:** Identify how language, structure and presentation contribute to meaning.
- **Comprehension:** Explain and discuss their understanding of what they have read, including through formal presentations and debates, maintaining a focus on the topic and using notes where necessary.
- **Composition:** Identify the audience for and purpose of the writing, selecting the appropriate form and using other similar writing as models for their own.
- **Composition:** Note and develop initial ideas, drawing on reading and research where necessary.
- **Spelling:** Use words with silent letters.

Introduction

Remind the children of the Big Picture for the sequence and recap on the learning achieved through Phase 1. Read the extra source texts to give further ideas.

Discussing ideas

As a class, discuss and make decisions to form the basis of their own seasonal poems.

- Which season should be used for the poems?
- What features of that season would people love?
- What features of that season might people hate?
- How can we portray the contrasting viewpoints?
- How should we structure the poems? Should they be similar or different in form?
- How do we want to make the readers feel upon reading each of the poems?

Drama and storytelling

Use drama and oracy activities to allow the children to explore the suggestions for their new poems and the viewpoints they will be trying to portray to readers. Select the activities that would suit your class or fit in with your lesson timing. Encourage mixed-ability grouping for the chosen activities.

- **Hot-seating the speaker in the poems:** This activity can be done in pairs, small groups or as a class. Encourage the children to think and, if necessary, write down their questions before the hot-seat session starts. Discuss the speakers' responses.

- **Freeze-framing key moments:** Once the structure of the poem is created, try out the different scenes in the right story order. Use thought-tracking by asking each child in the freeze-frame what they are thinking at a particular moment.

- **Poetry rehearsal:** Have the children work in pairs to retell the poems and then retell them to the rest of the class. Discuss the differences between the different groups' content and which parts worked better than others. Try retelling it in the first person and in the third person. Discuss how this changes the impact. Ask children which version they prefer.

Incidental writing

Before you select any incidental writing, make sure the children are able to orally articulate the main contents of their class season poems. Select activities that you think appropriate for the abilities and interests of your class. Children could compose:

- a diary entry written by the speaker in one of the poems
- further description of the season as a piece of prose text
- a character profile of the speaker in the poems
- a blog entry or personal email relating a perspective on a chosen season.

Year 6, Sequence 10
Poetry: Contrasting perspectives

Organising the class poems into a structure

Once the children have thoroughly explored ideas for their class season poems, bring them together and use their final suggestions to model how to plan their poems into a diagram or note form with the help of the Poetry planner. Once recorded, go through the frame and ask the children to evaluate the structure and organisation.

Phonics and spelling

Tell children that silent letters are the letters you cannot detect from the way a word is pronounced. They exist because the pronunciation of many words in the English language has changed over time. Some letters are no longer pronounced, even though they still exist in the spelling.

Ask children to add the missing silent letter to the following words. Remind them to use a dictionary if they aren't sure. Then put each word into a meaningful sentence.

Words with silent letters: w_ale; plum_er; ans_er; _naw; _nome; i_land; lim_; com_; _riter; _night.

Have the children generate other words using silent letters in a similar way, for example: 'island' – 'isle'; 'plumb' – 'thumb'.

Review of the Big Picture

Once you have completed all the lessons for this phase, remind the children of the sequence's Big Picture. Discuss what they have learned so far.

Year 6, Sequence 10
Poetry: Contrasting perspectives

Phase 3: Collaborate and compose

This phase focuses in detail on supporting children to draft and write individual sections of their contrasting season poems.

> **Programmes of study: Year 6**
> - **Composition:** Identify the audience for and purpose of the writing, selecting the appropriate form and using other similar writing as a model for their own.
> - **Composition:** Note and develop initial ideas, drawing on reading and research where necessary.
> - **Composition:** Select appropriate grammar and vocabulary, understanding how such choices can change and enhance meaning.
> - **Composition:** Use further organisational and presentational devices to structure text and to guide the reader.

Introduction

Remind the children about the Big Picture and recap on the learning in Phases 1 and 2. Explain to children that in Phase 3 they will be learning how to write their own contrasting perspective poems about a season, as discussed in Phase 2.

Lesson 1

Starter (VGP focus) – Grammar: Expanded noun phrases

Begin the lesson by asking the children to recap on the meaning and purpose of expanded noun phrases. Write the following nouns on the board (or tailor the list to fit the season you are writing about in the poems) and ask children to think of expanded noun phrases, adding two suitable adjectives before each noun, relevant to the nature of the poems and their perspectives. You could suggest the children work in pairs, presenting their top three to the class or a group.

Nouns: sun, pool, sunglasses, towel, flower, water, sandals, ice-cream, t-shirt, path, window, swing, ball

Shared writing

Children remind themselves and each other of their planning ideas from Phase 2. In this lesson and Lesson 2 they will be working on one poem and in Lessons 3 and 4 they will be working on the second poem with a different perspective. Ask children to make suggestions for the opening lines of the first seasonal poem, revisiting either of the model source poems as an example depending on whether you are working from a positive or negative viewpoint. Remind children to imagine they are in the mind of the speaker in the poem. They may not share the same viewpoint personally but they must try to make the poem convincing and authentic. Model writing the first half or one verse of the poem, using the source poem as a model.

Independent writing

The children can now write their own first part or first verse, applying the VGP focus on expanded noun phrases. Some children may benefit from guided group writing or peer-paired writing at this stage.

Plenary

At appropriate points throughout the lesson, invite children to share their writing with small groups, partners or the whole class. Ask the children questions to help them focus on their progress and what they have created during that lesson, for example: 'How does your poem so far compare with the original?' 'How have you expressed the speaker in the poem's viewpoint about the season?' 'How have you used expanded noun phrases?' 'How effectively have you chosen words and phrases to convey a particular mood?'

Lesson 2

Starter (VGP focus) – Grammar: Expanded noun phrases

Begin the lesson by asking the children to recap on the expanded noun phrases created in Lesson 1. Write the following same nouns on the board (or tailor the list to fit the season you are writing about in the poems). Ask children to come up with expanded noun phrases, this time by adding a preposition phrase after the noun, relevant to the nature of the poems and the mood to be conveyed. You could suggest that the children work in pairs and present their top three to the class or a group.

Year 6, Sequence 10
Poetry: Contrasting perspectives

Nouns: sun, pool, sunglasses, towel, flower, water, sandals, ice-cream, t-shirt, path, window, swing, ball

Shared writing

With the children's input, model writing the second part or second verse of the first poem. Remind children to think about how to authentically and clearly express the speaker in the poem's viewpoint about the season. Remind children to use the poetic techniques as discussed in the planning, this could include a set rhyming pattern, a particular rhythm, alliteration, personification, expanded noun phrases, rhetorical questions, a variety in sentence lengths for effect and / or an informal tone. Reread the model texts for inspiration. Ask children to close their eyes when reading the class poem back and ask them to visualise the scene that the poem describes. Have they referred to all the senses in the poem to help the reader imagine how the season looks, feels and smells?

Independent writing

The children can now write their own second verse or part of the first poem, applying the VGP focus. Some children may benefit from guided group writing or peer-paired writing at this stage.

Plenary

At the end of the lesson, invite children to share their writing with groups or the whole class. Ask the children questions to help them focus on their progress and what they have created during that lesson, for example: 'What poetic techniques have you used and to what effect?' 'How have you used expanded noun phrases?' 'How have you expressed the speaker's viewpoint about the season?'

Lesson 3

Starter (VGP focus) – Punctuation: Using a colon and semi-colons in lists

Explain to the children that we can use colons (:) to introduce a list. We can use semi-colons (;) between list items if any of the list items are phrases, particularly phrases containing other punctuation like commas. For example: 'We bought new furniture: nice, comfy beds; a large sofa; a wooden table; and chairs.'

Support the children to create their own lists using colons and semi-colons correctly. The theme of the lists could be things the children like about winter or changes that happen in winter.

Shared writing

With the children's input, model writing the first part or first verse of the second poem, showing a contrasting perspective on the season from the first poem. Remind the children to think about the reasons that the speaker in the poem might feel the way they do; what experiences they have had that contributed to their emotions and reactions. If the speaker in the poem feels strongly about their perspective, discuss how this might affect them physically. For example, they may have a racing heartbeat or sweaty palms for a negative response or a relaxed, slow heartbeat, or a warm tingly-all-over feeling for a positive response. Refer to earlier planning to include poetic features such as alliteration and rhyme.

Independent writing

The children can now write their own first part or first verse of their second poem, contrasting the speaker's perspective with the first poem, and applying the VGP focus. Some children may benefit from guided group writing or peer-paired writing at this stage.

Plenary

At the end of the lesson, invite children to share their writing with groups or the whole class. Ask the children questions to help them focus on their progress and what they have created during that lesson, for example: 'How have you communicated the speaker's perspective?' 'What poetic techniques have you used?' 'Is the meaning in your poem clearly understandable?' 'Could clarity be improved at any point by adjusting the punctuation (for example, adding / removing colons, semi-colons and / or commas)?'

Lesson 4

Starter (VGP focus) – Punctuation: Using commas for clearer meaning

Ask children to recall the uses for commas. Write the following sentences on the board and ask children to work in pairs to decide where commas should be placed to help make the sentences clearer.

'Autumn leaves shining crisp and golden carpet my journey along the pavement.'

'Autumn leaves trodden and squelching from the rain making the pathway slippery.'

Year 6, Sequence 10
Poetry: Contrasting perspectives

Shared writing

With the children's input, complete modelling the writing of the second poem. Model how to write with consistency and include any poetic features decided in the planning stage. If this poem is portraying the negative perspective of the season, discuss with the children whether the reader should be encouraged to agree, disagree, empathise or sympathise with the speaker's opinion. You may need to discuss the difference between empathy and sympathy.

Independent writing

The children can now complete writing the second poem applying the VGP focus. Some children may benefit from guided group writing or peer-paired writing at this stage.

Plenary

At the end of the lesson, invite children to share their writing with groups or the whole class. Ask the children questions to help them focus on their progress and what they have created during that lesson, for example: 'How does your poem make the reader feel?' 'How have you portrayed a contrasting perspective to the first poem?' 'Is meaning in your poem clearly understandable?' 'Could clarity be improved at any point by adding or removing commas?'

Rehearsing and performing

Once the children have written their contrasting poems, encourage them to read them out in pairs using intonation and pauses to help convey meaning or by creating a performance. Discuss how different or similar the poems are to the original winter-themed poems and what they have learned from the poets.

Review of the Big Picture

Once you have completed all the lessons for this phase, remind the children of the sequence's Big Picture. Reflect upon and discuss learning so far.

Year 6, Sequence 10
Poetry: Contrasting perspectives

Phase 4: Write independently

This final phase brings all the children's learning and writing skills together so that they can write their own independent contrasting perspective poems about a season (or topic of your choice). Through their writing, they will be able to utilise the different VGP focuses that they have been practising throughout previous phases.

> **Programmes of study: Year 6**
> - **Composition:** Select appropriate grammar and vocabulary, understanding how such choices can change and enhance meaning.
> - **Composition:** Use further organisational and presentational devices to structure text and to guide the reader.
> - **Composition:** Assess the effectiveness of their own and others' writing and suggest improvements.
> - **Composition:** Propose changes to grammar and vocabulary to enhance effects and clarify meaning.
> - **Composition:** Proofread for spelling and punctuation errors.
> - **Composition:** Perform their own compositions, using appropriate intonation, volume and movement so that meaning is clear.

Introduction

Introduce this phase by highlighting the overall Big Picture to the children. Recap on learning and progress through Phases 1–3 and explain that in Phase 4 they will be applying their learning to write their own contrasting perspective poems independently. Discuss and list examples of poetic techniques that might be used such as personification, alliteration, variety of sentence lengths, rhythm and rhymes. Recap on the structure used in the class writing sessions in Phase 3.

Writing

Give each child a Poetry planner and instruct them to start planning and writing each section of their contrasting perspective poems. Display the class writing structure and a copy of the model texts for reference. All children should be encouraged to try to write independently to the best of their ability. Ask open questions such as: 'How will you influence the way the reader is reacting at this point?' Avoid telling children what to write. Some children may benefit from guided composition. Focus on perseverance and resilience in the independent application.

Proofreading and redrafting

Have the children proofread their work periodically as they write. Proofreading and improvement without support means that the writing may happen over a few lessons. Offer the children the Editor's checklist or create your own checklist that includes the VGP and spelling focuses covered throughout this sequence.

Highlight the importance of redrafting, linking their efforts to the overall Big Picture.

Self- and peer-assessment

Encourage the children to take time to self-assess their own writing as well as that of others in their group. Offer them a set of self-assessment questions, such as: 'How does the writing convey the speaker's perspective?' 'How has the desired tone been achieved?' 'What changes would improve the reader's experience?'

Rehearsing and performing

Once the children have written their independent contrasting perspective poems, encourage them to perform them either as performance poetry to act them out in role. Discuss how children's poems are the same or different to the source texts. Encourage the children to feed back on one another's writing and performances.

Final review of the Big Picture

Working individually or with partners, have children reflect on what they have learned from this sequence and what they will apply in their future writing.

Year 6, Sequence 11
Fiction: Creating atmosphere

Sequence 11
Fiction: Creating atmosphere

Approximate duration: Two weeks

Big Picture

Through this teaching sequence, children will explore the way in which authors can create an atmosphere of mystery and intrigue between characters in a text, particularly through the characters' dialogue. Understanding the techniques used by real authors will help children to use these techniques within their own narrative writing. Children will be able to write text that has an impact on readers' responses.

Phase 1: Enjoy and immerse

Children analyse the dialogue and reactions of the characters in the model text, 'Nightmare' by Berlie Doherty.

Phase 2: Capture and organise

Children begin to develop ideas for creating their own scene containing an encounter with a fantastical being.

Phase 3: Collaborate and compose

Children undertake supported writing sessions to develop the writing features of their scene.

Phase 4: Write independently

Children write, edit and present their own narrative scene containing an encounter with a fantastical being.

Main source text

Treasure House Anthology Sequence 11 text. 'Nightmare', *Two Ghostly Tales*, Berlie Doherty, ISBN 978-0-00-730790-6, pp.2–26

Extra source texts

Treasure House Online, Year 6, Comprehension Unit 11: Fiction: 'The Phantom Tollbooth'

Alice in Wonderland, Lewis Carroll, ISBN 978-1-85-326002-5, pp.86–89

Background knowledge

'Nightmare' by Berlie Doherty is a dark, atmospheric story about a girl's unusual encounters with a traveller boy called Rab and a horse locked in ice. Written in the first person and set on the moors during winter, the reader is taken on a journey of discovery with the main character as she finds out where her friend has disappeared to and why she has been having nightmares about a big black horse.

Spoken outcome

To perform an oral story to an audience of peers or parents

Writing outcome

To write a story or scene that shows an encounter with a fantastical being, using dialogue and character reactions

Prior knowledge

Check children's knowledge and understanding of:

- stories with fantastical beings
- how dialogue is used in stories
- how authors portray characters' reactions.

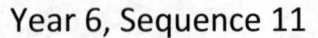

Year 6, Sequence 11
Fiction: Creating atmosphere

Diagnostic assessment options

Before starting the sequence, you may want to conduct an initial diagnostic assessment of the children's understanding of the typical characteristics of characters' encounters with mysterious beings.

Ideas for initial diagnostic assessment options include:

- discussion about characters and their encounters
- a brief, unsupported writing activity to create a short narrative text in which a character meets a strange being
- practising speaking and listening skills relating to a short piece of narrative containing a character encounter
- a short reading comprehension activity / quiz on a short story containing a character encounter.

Treasure House links

All digital and pupil book units have the same names and numbers, but different questions.

- Treasure House, Year 6, Comprehension Unit 11: Fiction: 'The Phantom Tollbooth'
- Treasure House, Year 6, Composition Unit 1: Story planning
- Treasure House, Year 6, Composition Unit 13: Paragraphs in fiction
- Treasure House, Year 6, Punctuation Unit 4: Boundaries between clauses
- Treasure House, Year 6, Spelling Unit 11: Homophones and near-homophones (2)
- Treasure House, Year 6, Spelling Unit 8: The letter-string ough
- Treasure House, Year 6, Grammar Unit 2: Using the passive voice
- Treasure House, Year 6, Vocabulary Unit 1: Using a thesaurus
- Treasure House, Year 4, Punctuation Unit 4: Punctuating direct speech (1)
- Treasure House, Year 4, Punctuation Unit 5: Punctuating direct speech (2)
- Treasure House, Year 6, Punctuation Unit 1: Using commas for clearer meaning

Resources

Source texts – see Anthologies; Story planner; Editor's checklist

Year 6, Sequence 11
Fiction: Creating atmosphere

Phase 1: Enjoy and immerse

In Phase 1, the children are introduced to 'Nightmare' by Berlie Doherty, which depicts the eerie story of a girl's friendship with Rab, a traveller boy, and her nightmare encounters with a large black horse. Over several sessions, children are offered the opportunity to immerse themselves fully in the story through comprehension and discussion activities, as well as exploring characters and structure through drama, storytelling, writing and analysis of the text.

Programmes of study: Year 6

- **Comprehension:** Continue to read and discuss an increasingly wide range of fiction, poetry, plays, non-fiction and reference books or textbooks.
- **Comprehension:** Draw inferences such as inferring characters' feelings, thoughts and motives from their actions.
- **Comprehension:** Discuss and evaluate how authors use language, considering the impact on the reader.
- **Composition:** Identify the audience for and purpose of the writing, selecting the appropriate form and using other similar writing as models for their own.
- **Vocabulary, grammar and punctuation:** Use semi-colons, colons or dashes to mark boundaries between independent clauses.
- **Spelling:** Use homophones and other words that are often confused.

Sparking interest

Introduce the sequence by highlighting the overall Big Picture to the children: they will be working towards writing their own story depicting a character's encounter with a fantastical being, including dialogue and description of characters' reactions.

Use an opening question such as: 'What nightmares can you remember, and how did they make you feel?'

Reading and discussion

Introduce the text, read it with the class (you may wish to read it in sections) and check their understanding. Discuss children's understanding of the content of the story.

Discuss the following with the children.

- Who are the characters in this extract?
- How do you think the speaker feels?
- Why does she feel that way?
- How would you explain the encounters with the black horse?
- Can you explain the story?
- How did the story make you feel?
- Why do you think Berlie Doherty chose to tell the story using the first person?

Drama and storytelling

Use drama and storytelling activities to reinforce the children's understanding of the atmosphere in the scene. Select the activities that would suit your class or fit in with your lesson timing. Encourage mixed-ability grouping for the chosen activities.

- **Hot-seating the speaker or Rab:** This activity can be done in pairs, small groups or as a class situation with different children representing the characters. Questions could include: 'How do you explain what happened?' 'How did you feel when …?' 'Will you ever visit Downpour Den again?'
- **Role-play discussion:** Have a discussion to debate whether the speaker should have gone out to Downpour Den. Encourage children to imagine how she felt.
- **Storytelling:** Become a storyteller. The children could accompany your or each other's performances, either by using props for sound effects or by taking the roles of the characters.
- **Performance:** Encourage the children to rehearse and perform the story in small groups, with one or two narrators.
- **Presentation ideas:** Create a newsflash related to a scene from the story.

Year 6, Sequence 11
Fiction: Creating atmosphere

Incidental writing

A short writing activity would enhance the children's understanding of the text and characters. Select activities that you think appropriate for the abilities and interests of your class. Use the children's written outcomes to inform the emphases during the collaborative composition phase. Children could compose:

- a diary entry by the narrator of the story
- a newspaper article about the accident
- a letter from Rab to the story's narrator, written before his accident.

Analysis

Show the text to the children and discuss the setting, characters and plot. Discuss the way the extract begins with the chapter title 'Stay with me!' Discuss the various things this phrase suggests to the reader. Discuss the opening sentence and how straight away we are given a description of Rab. With the children, try to summarise the plot into four parts. Discuss how the characters have been portrayed, what they are like, how they behave. Look at the language used and consider what figurative language the author has used to help the reader understand the story. Discuss how the author uses imagery to advance the story and provide insights into the characters. Look at what the characters are saying and how they are saying it.

Grammar: Boundaries between clauses

Remind children that we can use colons, semi-colons or dashes to separate main clauses, instead of full stops or conjunctions. Semi-colons show linked clauses that are equally important. Colons introduce reasons or examples. Dashes can be used instead, in informal writing. Provide pairs of children with copies of the story and ask them to find and highlight or note down examples of semi-colons, colons and dashes used to mark boundaries. Ask the children to choose one example to present to the class, explaining why that punctuation mark has been used.

Phonics and spelling

Ask children to recall what a homophone is. Take suggestions. Establish that homophones are words that sound the same, but they are spelt differently and have different meanings. You always need context to know how to spell homophones. Some homophone pairs can be told apart because one of the words is a past-tense verb.

Ask children to use a dictionary to check and discuss the meaning of each word, then write each word into a sentence to give it a meaningful context.

Homophones: guest, guessed; lead, led; heard, herd (verb), herd (noun); passed, past

Review of the Big Picture

Once you have completed this phase, remind the children (or have them remind each other) of the sequence's Big Picture: they are working towards writing a story (or extract) about an encounter with a strange being, independently.

Year 6, Sequence 11
Fiction: Creating atmosphere

Phase 2: Capture and organise

During Phase 2, children start to develop ideas about new content and the literary features needed to create a class short story portraying a character's encounter with a fantastical being. Working collaboratively, children decide on a setting, characters and plot ideas.

Programmes of study: Year 6

- **Comprehension:** Identify and discuss themes and conventions in and across a wide range of writing.
- **Comprehension:** Identify how language, structure and presentation contribute to meaning.
- **Comprehension:** Participate in discussions about books that are read to them and those they can read for themselves, building on their own and others' ideas and challenging views courteously.
- **Composition:** Note and develop initial ideas, drawing on reading and research where necessary.
- **Composition:** In writing narratives, consider how authors have developed characters and settings in what children have read, listened to or seen performed.
- **Spelling:** Use words with the letter-string ough.

Introduction

Remind the children of the Big Picture for the sequence and recap on the learning achieved through Phase 1. Read one or both of the additional texts to provide further examples of a character encountering an unusual being.

Discussing ideas

As a class, discuss and make decisions to form the basis of the children's own character encounter story.

- How should the reader feel during and after reading?
- Who should the main character be?
- Who will the fantastical being be?
- Will the encounter be positive or negative?
- Where will the setting be? Will it change throughout the story?
- What will the problem be?
- Will there be any other characters in the scene?
- How will the situation be resolved? Will it be resolved?

Drama and storytelling

Use drama and storytelling activities to allow the children to explore the suggestions for their new characters and story plot. Select the activities that would suit your class or fit in with your lesson timing. Encourage mixed-ability grouping for the chosen activities.

- **Hot-seating the main character:** This activity can be done in pairs, small groups or as a class situation. Encourage the children to think and, if necessary, write down their questions before the hot-seat session starts. Discuss the character's responses.
- **Freeze-framing key moments:** Once the structure of the story is created, try out the different scenes in the right story order. Use thought-tracking by asking each child in the freeze-frame what they're thinking at a particular moment.
- **Storytelling:** Encourage the children to work in groups to retell the story and then retell it to the rest of the class. Discuss the differences between the different groups' stories and which parts worked better than others.

Incidental writing

Before you select any incidental writing, make sure the children are able to orally articulate the main events of their character encounter story. Select activities that you think appropriate for the abilities and interests of your class. Children could compose:

- a diary entry
- a newspaper article
- a letter of complaint
- a character profile
- a blog entry or email.

Year 6, Sequence 11
Fiction: Creating atmosphere

Organising the class character encounter story into a structure

Once the children have thoroughly explored ideas for their class character encounter story, bring them together and use their final suggestions to model how to plot their new narrative in diagram or note form with the help of the Story planner Once recorded, go through the frame and ask the children to evaluate the structure and organisation.

Phonics and spelling

Tell children that the letter-string ough is one of the trickiest spellings in the English language. It can be used to spell a number of different sounds.

Ask children to discuss the meanings of these ough words. Encourage children to use a dictionary. Then use all of the words to make a short silly (perhaps ghostly) story.

ough words: bought, brought, thought, rough, cough, enough, though, tough

---

Review of the Big Picture

Once you have completed all the lessons for this phase, remind the children of the sequence's Big Picture. Recap on the learning achieved in Phase 2.

Year 6, Sequence 11
Fiction: Creating atmosphere

Phase 3: Collaborate and compose

This phase focuses in detail on supporting children to draft and write individual sections of their character encounter story. The four lessons guide the children through the suggested four-part structure of the introduction, the build up, the climax (their character meets the fantastical being) and the resolution. Additional sections could be added at your own discretion.

Programmes of study: Year 6
- **Composition:** Identify the audience for and purpose of the writing, selecting the appropriate form and using other similar writing as a model for their own.
- **Composition:** Note and develop initial ideas, drawing on reading and research where necessary.
- **Composition:** In writing narratives, consider how authors have developed characters and settings in what pupils have read, listened to or seen performed.
- **Composition:** Select appropriate grammar and vocabulary, understanding how such choices can change and enhance meaning.
- **Composition:** In narratives, describe settings, characters and atmosphere and integrate dialogue to convey character and advance the action.

Introduction

Remind the children about the Big Picture and recap on the learning in Phases 1 and 2. Explain to children that through Phase 3 they will be learning how to write their own story about a character's encounter with a fantastical being, using the characters' dialogue and actions.

Lesson 1

Starter (VGP focus) – Grammar: Using the passive voice

Explain to the children that in active voice sentences, the subject does the action. In passive voice sentences, the subject has the action done to it. Although using the active voice is more common, there is an important role for the passive voice. We often use the passive voice when the action is more important than who or what did it.

Write the following active voice sentences on the board and ask children to turn them into passive voice sentences. Ask children to consider how the passive voice affects how a reader receives the information and in which contexts the passive version might work best and why.

'I approached the stranger.'

'I assessed the situation.'

'The huge white owl caught a scrawny rat.'

'The mysterious creature stared at me.'

Shared writing

Children should remind themselves and each other of their planning ideas from Phase 2. Ask the children to make suggestions for the wording of the opening paragraph of the class narrative, revisiting the opening of 'Nightmare' as an example. Model writing the opening paragraph, with the children's input, focusing on setting the scene with the direct or indirect introduction of the main character, what they are doing and how they are feeling. The opening could set the scene by implying, through the main character's action, that they are bothered by something but may not reveal what the problem is yet. Discuss 'seeding' in a piece of detail that will be referred to later in the narrative to give cohesion through the whole story. This section should set the scene and lay the foundations of the story, enabling the reader to form a connection to the main character. Explain that this will help the reader feel more in-tune with the character's feelings later in the story. This section can be as long or as short as you would like, but consider that Lesson 2 will contain the build up to meeting the fantastical being.

Independent writing

The children can now write their own first section, applying the VGP focus on using the passive voice. Encourage children to experiment using the passive and active voice for some sentences in their work to explore the effect on the reader. Some children may benefit from guided group writing or peer-paired writing at this stage.

Year 6, Sequence 11
Fiction: Creating atmosphere

Plenary

At appropriate points throughout the lesson, invite children to share their writing with small groups, partners or the whole class. Ask the children questions to help them focus on their progress and what they have created during that lesson, for example: 'How does your opening paragraph compare with the original so far?' 'How does it make the reader feel?' 'Where have you included use of the passive voice?' 'What effect does it have on your writing?'

Lesson 2

Starter (VGP focus) – Vocabulary: Using a thesaurus

Remind the children that we can use a thesaurus to find words with similar meanings. It can help us to find new or better words for what we want to say. Ask children, in pairs, to choose one sentence from the 'Nightmare' story and alter it by replacing some of the words with alternatives found in the thesaurus. Share children's examples, checking that nuances of meaning are understood.

Shared writing

With the children's input, model writing the next part of the narrative, which describes the actions of the main character to build up the story in preparation for the encounter. The character could go somewhere or find something that will ultimately lead them to meet the fantastical being. Continue building the relationship between the main character and the reader. Ask children to consider what traits or habits the character could have that the reader will relate to. Encourage children to use the thesaurus to improve the vocabulary you are using as you write.

Independent writing

The children can now write their own second section, applying the VGP focus on using a thesaurus to source new or interesting vocabulary to improve their setting descriptions. This section should show the build up to the main character meeting the fantastical being and should either finish just before they meet or end on a cliff hanger of the character seeing the being but not yet speaking to them. Some children may benefit from guided group writing or peer-paired writing at this stage.

Plenary

At the end of the lesson, invite children to share their writing with groups or the whole class. Ask the children questions to help them focus on their progress and what they have created during that lesson, for example: 'How is the atmosphere developing for your reader?' 'How have you introduced the fantastical being?' 'What varied and effective vocabulary have you used?' 'Share your work. How effective is your partner's choice of vocabulary?'

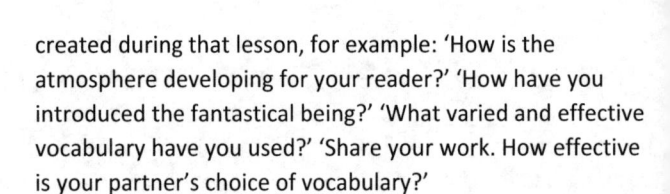

Lesson 3

Starter (VGP focus) – Punctuation: Revision of direct speech punctuation

Write a sentence of direct speech from the 'Nightmare' story on the board. Do not include any punctuation, for example: 'I wish you wouldn't go without telling me I say sometimes I hate that not saying goodbye and that' and invite children to correctly punctuate the sentence (adding all necessary punctuation marks). Remind children that if a statement in speech comes before an explanation, such as 'I say sometimes', the speech ends in a comma.

Shared writing

With the children's input, model writing the next part of the narrative. Introduce the fantastical being and the encounter with the main character. This part should be exciting and the reader should be gripped: try short, breathless sentences. Discuss with the children how the reader can be hooked in, with their heart racing and anticipating each sentence to see what will happen or be said between the characters. Features could include: narrative of the character's actions whilst speaking, for example, describing body language to show tension or anxiety; interrupted or informal speech; ellipses and exclamation marks used for effect. Throughout, reinforce the correct use of punctuation for direct speech.

Independent writing

The children can now write their own third section, applying the VGP focus on using correct punctuation for direct speech. Some children may benefit from guided group writing or peer-paired writing at this stage.

Plenary

At the end of the lesson, ask the children questions to help them focus on their progress and what they have created during that lesson, for example: 'How have you made this part of the story exciting?' 'How have you used speech to develop the story?' 'Share your writing. Has your partner punctuated direct speech correctly?'

Year 6, Sequence 11
Fiction: Creating atmosphere

Lesson 4

Starter (VGP focus) – Punctuation: Using commas for clearer meaning

Remind the children that commas can be useful for making the meaning of sentences clearer. Provide children with copies of the 'Nightmare' story and ask them to work in pairs to find examples of commas used within sentences. Have them use mini whiteboards to create sentences of similar structure, using the new content. As individuals, they can read their sentences aloud and have the class make notes of correct punctuation (capital letter(s), comma(s) and a full stop) as they listen.

Shared writing

With children's input, continue modelling how to write the ongoing dialogue between the characters, interspersed with narrative to help move the story along. Explain that sometimes when we write dialogue we can be caught up in the characters' conversation and forget to progress the story. Use techniques such as interrupting speech with narrative or describing the main character's thoughts as an aside. Include some reported speech to enhance narrative flow. Show, rather than tell, how the main character feels. At the end of the section, the story behind the fantastical being and the encounter should be resolved. Explain how the characters came to meet (it could be fate, a nightmare, or perhaps there is a twist). Be sure to include at least one example of using commas to aid clarity within a sentence.

Independent writing

The children can now write their own fourth and final section, applying the VGP focus on using commas to provide clarity. Some children may benefit from guided group writing or peer-paired writing at this stage.

Plenary

At the end of the lesson, invite children to share their writing with groups or the whole class. Ask the children questions to help them focus on their progress and what they have created during that lesson, for example: 'How have you concluded the story?' 'What is the story ending's intended effect on the reader and how is this achieved?' 'Could the clarity of your writing be improved by adding or removing commas?'

Rehearsing and performing

Once the children have written their story, encourage them to retell it either as narrators or by creating a performance. Discuss how different or similar the story is to the 'Nightmare' story or the additional texts.

Review of the Big Picture

Once you have completed all the lessons for this phase, remind the children of the sequence's Big Picture. Discuss what they have learned during Phase 3.

Year 6, Sequence 11
Fiction: Creating atmosphere

Phase 4: Write independently

This final phase brings all the children's learning and writing skills together so that they can write their own independent story depicting an encounter between the main character and a fantastical being, using dialogue and the description of behaviours. Through their writing, they will be able to utilise the different VGP focuses that they have been practising throughout previous phases.

> **Programmes of study: Year 6**
> - **Composition:** Select appropriate grammar and vocabulary, understanding how such choices can change and enhance meaning.
> - **Composition:** In narratives, describe settings, characters and atmosphere and integrate dialogue to convey character and advance the action.
> - **Composition:** Assess the effectiveness of their own and others' writing.
> - **Composition:** Propose changes to vocabulary, grammar and punctuation to enhance effects and clarify meaning.
> - **Composition:** Proofread for spelling and punctuation errors.
> - **Composition:** Perform their own compositions, using appropriate intonation, volume and movement so that meaning is clear.

Introduction

Introduce this phase by highlighting the overall Big Picture to the children. Recap on learning and progress through Phases 1–3 and explain that in Phase 4 they will be applying their learning to write their own story independently. Discuss and list examples of possible encounters between a character and a fantastical being. Examples could include a chance encounter in a mysterious forest, a nightmare, a mysterious being in an old haunted house, a peculiar child met in a park or the garden. Recap on the structure used in the class writing sessions in Phase 3.

Writing

Give each child a Story planner and instruct them to start planning and writing each section of their own story. Display the class story-structure and a copy of the 'Nightmare' story for reference. All the children should be encouraged to try to write independently to the best of their ability. Ask open questions such as: 'How will you show how the character is feeling at this point?' Avoid telling children what to write. Some children may benefit from guided composition. Focus on perseverance and resilience in their independent application.

Proofreading and redrafting

Have the children proofread their work periodically as they write. Proofreading and improvement without support means that the writing may happen over a few lessons. Offer the children the Editor's checklist or create your own checklist that includes the VGP and spelling focuses covered throughout this sequence. Highlight the importance of redrafting, linking their efforts to the overall Big Picture.

Self- and peer-assessment

Encourage the children to take time to self-assess their own writing as well as that of others in their group. Offer them a set of self-assessment questions such as: 'How does the writing convey the atmosphere between the characters?' 'How clearly is the writing structured?' 'Has correctly punctuated direct speech been used?' 'What impact does the writing have?' 'What changes would improve the reader's experience?'

Rehearsing and performing

Once the children have written their independent story, encourage them to retell it either as narrators or by creating a performance. Discuss how similar or different the scene is from the 'Nightmare' story. Encourage the children to feedback on one another's writing and performances.

Final review of the Big Picture

Individually or with partners, have children reflect on what they have learned from this sequence and what they will apply in their future writing.

Year 6, Sequence 12
Fiction: Plotting problems

Sequence 12
Fiction: Plotting problems

Approximate duration: Two weeks

Big Picture

Through this teaching sequence, children will explore the way in which authors plot problems and obstacles for their characters to overcome. The children will write their own story that involves bad news and a false accusation. Understanding the techniques used by authors will help children to use these techniques within their own narrative writing.

Phase 1: Enjoy and immerse

Children analyse the dialogue and reactions of the characters in the model text, *The Railway Children*.

Phase 2: Capture and organise

Children begin to develop ideas for creating their own short story involving a false accusation.

Phase 3: Collaborate and compose

Children undertake supported writing sessions to develop the writing characteristics of their story.

Phase 4: Writing independently

Children write, edit and present their own short story containing a false accusation being made.

Main source text

Treasure House Anthology Sequence 12 text. Treasure House Online, Year 6, Comprehension Unit 12: Fiction (classic): 'The Railway Children'

Extra source texts

The Railway Children, E. Nesbit, ISBN 978-1-85-326107-7, pp.154–156

Background knowledge

The Railway Children is a children's book by Edith Nesbit (1858–1924), originally serialised in *The London Magazine* during 1905 and first published in book form in 1906. It tells the story of three children whose lives are shattered when their father goes away with two strangers one evening. Roberta, Peter, Phyllis and their mother have to move from their comfortable London home to go and live in a simple country cottage, where Mother writes books to make ends meet. They soon come to love the railway that runs near their cottage, and they make a habit of waving every day to the Old Gentleman who rides on it. They befriend the porter, Perks, and have many adventures.

Spoken outcome

To perform a story to an audience of peers or parents

Writing outcome

To write a short story involving a false accusation being made

Prior knowledge

Check children's knowledge and understanding of:
- *The Railway Children* by E. Nesbit
- stories involving false accusations.

Year 6, Sequence 12
Fiction: Plotting problems

Diagnostic assessment options

Before starting the sequence, you may want to conduct an initial diagnostic assessment of the children's understanding of the common characteristics of a traditional narrative.

Ideas for initial diagnostic assessment options include:
- discussion about traditional narrative texts and their purpose
- a brief, unsupported writing activity to create a short traditional narrative text
- practising speaking and listening skills relating to a well-known short narrative text
- a short reading comprehension activity / quiz on a traditional narrative text.

Cross-curricular links

KS2 PSHE – Relationships

Treasure House links

All digital and pupil book units have the same names and numbers, but different questions.
- Treasure House, Year 6, Comprehension Unit 12: Fiction (classic): 'The Railway Children'
- Treasure House, Year 6, Composition Unit 10: Extended stories
- Treasure House, Year 6, Composition Unit 13: Paragraphs in fiction
- Treasure House, Year 6, Grammar Unit 3: Relative clauses
- Treasure House, Year 6, Spelling Unit 9: Words with 'silent' letters
- Treasure House, Year 6, Punctuation Unit 4: Boundaries between clauses
- Treasure House, Year 6, Punctuation Unit 1: Using commas for clearer meaning
- Treasure House, Year 6, Punctuation Unit 3: Brackets, dashes and commas
- Treasure House, Year 3, Unit 5: The present perfect tense

Resources

Source texts – see Anthologies; Story planner; Editor's checklist

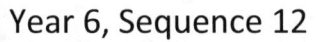

Year 6, Sequence 12
Fiction: Plotting problems

Phase 1: Enjoy and immerse

In Phase 1, the children are introduced to a classic children's story, *The Railway Children* by E. Nesbit, first published in 1906. Over several lessons, they are offered the opportunity to immerse themselves fully in the story through comprehension and discussion activities, as well as exploring its characters and structure through drama, storytelling, writing and analysis of the text.

Programmes of study: Year 6

- **Comprehension:** Increase their familiarity with a wide range of books, including myths, legends and traditional stories, modern fiction, fiction from our literary heritage, and books from other cultures and traditions.
- **Comprehension:** Check that the book makes sense to them, discussing their understanding and exploring the meaning of words in context.
- **Comprehension:** Draw inferences such as inferring characters' feelings, thoughts and motives from their actions.
- **Composition:** Identify the audience for and purpose of the writing, selecting the appropriate form and using other similar writing as models for their own.
- **Vocabulary, grammar and punctuation:** Use relative clauses beginning with who, which, where, when, whose, that, or with an implied relative pronoun .
- **Spelling:** Use words with silent letters.

Sparking interest

Introduce the sequence by highlighting the overall Big Picture to the children: they will be working towards writing their own story that involves a family member breaking bad news, with the theme of a false accusation being made. Use an opening question such as: 'What would you do if you were accused of doing something bad that you had not done?'

Reading and discussion

Introduce the main source text, *The Railway Children*, read it with the class and check their understanding.

Discuss the following with the children.

- What has happened in this part of the story?
- Why wouldn't Mother tell the children what was going on?
- How do you think the children felt?
- Was there anything they could do about the situation? Why or why not?
- Does the reader know more, less or the same amount of information as the characters?
- How do you feel as the reader?

Drama and storytelling

Use drama and storytelling activities to reinforce the children's understanding of the extract.

Select the activities that would suit your class or fit in with your lesson timing. Encourage mixed-ability grouping for the chosen activities.

- **Storytelling:** Become a storyteller. The children could accompany your performance, either by using props for sound effects or by taking the roles of the characters.
- **Hot-seating the characters:** This activity can be done in pairs, small groups or as a whole-class situation with different children representing the characters. Questions could include: 'How much information do you know about Father's situation?' 'How do you feel about it?' 'What can you do to help?' 'What do you think will happen next?'
- **Freeze-frame with thought-tapping:** Either in small groups or as a whole class, the children create a moment that shows the action in a narrative frozen in time, as if the pause button has been pressed. The teacher (or a child) gently taps a character on the shoulder to 'unfreeze' them. That child then voices their thoughts in character. This activity encourages children to engage with the actions and thoughts of the characters.
- **Presentation ideas:** Pairs role-play two neighbours, discussing what they have heard of the situation.

Year 6, Sequence 12
Fiction: Plotting problems

Incidental writing

A short writing activity would enhance the children's understanding of the text and characters. Select activities that you think appropriate for the abilities and interests of your class. Use the children's written outcomes to inform the emphases during the collaborative composition phase. Children could:

- rewrite part of *The Railway Children* from the perspective of a different character, for example, one of the other house maids, or Mother
- turn part of the tale into a playscript with stage directions
- write a diary entry by one of the older children, Roberta or Peter.

Analysis

Show the text to the children and discuss the following typical narrative characteristics, either by pointing them out, asking children to find them or prompting children to discover them.

- Dialogue between characters
- An opening that quickly establishes setting, characters or action
- Narrative description of characters' actions to move the story along
- Narrative description and dialogue that shows the reader how characters are feeling without explicitly stating it

Grammar: Relative clauses

Explain to children that we use relative clauses to give more information about nouns. They can start with a relative pronoun ('that', 'which', 'who' or 'whose') or a relative adverb ('where' or 'when').

We use a comma before a relative clause if the information is not vital to the meaning of the noun it describes. If it is vital, do not use a comma. We never use a comma before 'that', and always before 'which'.

Provide children with a copy of the model text and challenge them to find and highlight examples of relative clauses.

On pieces of A4 paper or card, write a selection of simple sentences (one per sheet). Then write a selection of relative pronouns and adverbs (one per sheet). Shuffle up the sentence sheets and hand them out to the children. Challenge the children to find a partner whose sentence could be joined to theirs by using a relative pronoun or adverb. The pair should then find the correct relative pronoun or adverb and hold up the cards to show the class their new sentence.

Phonics and spelling

Display the word 'government' on the board.

Ask children to explain what makes 'government' a tricky word to spell (the silent letter). Tell children that silent letters are letters you cannot detect from the way a word is pronounced. They exist because the English language has been developing for hundreds of years, and over that time, the pronunciation of many words has changed. Some letters are no longer pronounced even though they still exist in the spellings.

Read through the words below with the children and check that they understand what they mean.

Ask children to write each of these words in a sentence then underline the silent letter. The sentences could be linked to the theme of *The Railway Children*.

Words with silent letters: government, solemn, wrestle, aplomb, succumb, knowledge, knuckle, bristle, silhouette, cologne, campaign

Review of the Big Picture

Once you have completed this phase, remind the children (or have them remind one another) of the sequence's Big Picture: they are working towards independently writing their own story involving bad news and a false accusation.

Year 6, Sequence 12
Fiction: Plotting problems

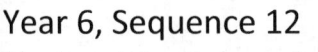

Phase 2: Capture and organise

During Phase 2, the children are able to use their knowledge from the previous lessons in Phase 1 to create their own class story, using the same theme as *The Railway Children* (bad news and a false accusation). The group and class discussions, as well as drama or short writing opportunities, offer chances for children of all abilities to contribute and use their skills towards designing a structure and developing characters for their story. Their ideas can be recorded in picture, diagram or note form with the help of the Story planner.

Programmes of study: Year 6
- **Comprehension:** Identify and discuss themes and conventions in and across a wide range of writing.
- **Comprehension:** Identify how language, structure and presentation contribute to meaning.
- **Comprehension:** Participate in discussions about books that are read to them and those they can read for themselves, building on their own and others' ideas and challenging views courteously.
- **Composition:** Note and developing initial ideas, drawing on reading and research where necessary.
- **Composition:** In writing narratives, consider how authors have developed characters and settings in what children have read, listened to or seen performed.
- **Spelling:** Use words with silent letters.

Introduction

Remind the children of the Big Picture for the sequence and recap on the learning achieved through Phase 1. Read the additional text for the sequence, an extract from *The Railway Children* taken from later in the story, and discuss how the story has progressed from the content of the first extract.

Discussing ideas

As a class, discuss and make decisions to form the basis of their own class story. Suggest that the class story could be a tale with a similar family to *The Railway Children*, or a more modern depiction of a family with one parent or fewer children. The storyline could involve one of the children being wrongly accused of doing something bad at school. Perhaps they often have unsettled behaviour so the teacher doesn't believe them when they protest their innocence, and now they are in big trouble.

- What should the accusation be?
- Who should the main character be?
- What will the setting be?
- What will the problem be?
- What other characters are in the tale and what are their roles?
- What can we keep from the original story?

Drama and storytelling

Use drama and storytelling activities to allow the children to explore the suggestions for their new characters and story plot. Select the activities that would suit your class or fit in with your lesson timing. Encourage mixed-ability grouping for the chosen activities.

- **Hot-seating the main character:** This activity can be done in pairs, small groups or as a class situation. Encourage the children to think and, if necessary, write down their questions before the hot-seat session starts. Discuss the character's responses.
- **Freeze-framing key moments:** Once the structure of the story is created, try out the different scenes in the right story order. Use thought-tracking by asking each child in the freeze-frame what they are thinking at a particular moment.
- **Storytelling:** Encourage the children to work in groups to orally compose the story and then retell it to the rest of the class. Discuss the differences between the different groups' stories and which parts worked better than others.

Incidental writing

Before you select any incidental writing, make sure the children are able to orally articulate the main events of their class story. Select activities that you think appropriate for the abilities and interests of your class.

Year 6, Sequence 12
Fiction: Plotting problems

Children could compose:
- a diary entry
- a newspaper article
- a letter to inform the parents about the incident (an accusation)
- a character profile
- a blog entry or email.

Organising the class story into a structure

Once the children have thoroughly explored their ideas for their class story, bring them together and use their final suggestions to model how to plot the new story in picture, diagram or note form with the help of the Story planner. Once recorded, go through the frame and ask the children if they are happy with the structure.

Phonics and spelling

Display the word 'guitar' on the board.

Ask children to explain what makes 'guitar' a tricky word to spell (the silent letter). Tell children that silent letters are letters you cannot detect from the way a word is pronounced. They exist because the English language has been developing for hundreds of years, and over that time, the pronunciation of many words has changed. Some letters are no longer pronounced even though they still exist in the spellings.

Read through the words below with the children and check that they understand what they mean.

Ask children to write each of these words in a sentence then underline the silent letter. The sentences could be linked to the theme of *The Railway Children* or the new class story.

Words with silent letters: guitar, biscuit, guide, disguise, rogue, fasten, listen, whistle, foreign, feign, subtle

Review of the Big Picture

Once you have completed all the lessons for this phase, remind the children of the sequence's Big Picture. Recap on the learning achieved in Phase 2.

Year 6, Sequence 12
Fiction: Plotting problems

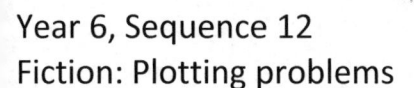

Phase 3: Collaborate and compose

This phase focuses on how to write a story, with one lesson per story part, so that the children are taken through writing the whole piece, learning new vocabulary, grammar and punctuation along the way. Children should have the planning framework from Phase 2 in front of them throughout, and should be able to revisit the original model text, *The Railway Children*.

Within each lesson, the children will also be able to work interactively on vocabulary, spelling and punctuation focuses. The children will then be able to apply their learned VGP focus during their independent writing.

Programmes of study: Year 6
- **Composition:** Identify the audience for and purpose of the writing, selecting the appropriate form and using other similar writing as a model for their own.
- **Composition:** Note and develop initial ideas, drawing on reading and research where necessary.
- **Composition:** In writing narratives, consider how authors have developed characters and settings in what children have read, listened to or seen performed.
- **Composition:** Select appropriate grammar and vocabulary, understanding how such choices can change and enhance meaning.
- **Composition:** In narratives, describe settings, characters and atmosphere and integrate dialogue to convey character and advance the action.

Introduction

Remind the children about the Big Picture and recap on the learning in Phases 1 and 2. Explain to children that through Phase 3 they will be learning how to write their own story based on the model text, *The Railway Children*. The new story will involve a family member breaking bad news, with the theme of a false accusation.

Lesson 1

Starter (VGP focus) – Punctuation: Boundaries between clauses

Explain to the children that we can use colons, semi-colons or dashes to separate main clauses. Semi-colons show linked clauses that are equally important, colons introduce reasons or examples and dashes can be used instead, in informal writing. Display on a screen or provide children with copies of the extracts from *The Railway Children*. Ask children to identify the examples of different punctuation used between clauses.

Shared writing

Children remind themselves and each other of their planning ideas from Phase 2. Ask the children to make suggestions for the wording of the opening paragraph of the class story, revisiting the opening of *The Railway Children* extract as an example. Explain to the children that, although the extract does not come from the very beginning of the book, nor the beginning of a chapter, it makes an effective opening. Ask the children to make suggestions about why the opening is effective. Establish that it starts with action straight away and uses dialogue which draws in readers and makes them want to know more. Model writing the opening paragraph, with the children's input, focusing on the introduction of the setting and the main character: what they are doing and how they are feeling. Apply the VGP focus on punctuating boundaries between clauses. Decide with the class whether you will start the action straight away, with the bad news being broken almost immediately, or whether you will set the scene and provide a build-up first.

Independent writing

The children can now write their own first section, applying the VGP focus on punctuating boundaries between clauses. Some children may benefit from guided group writing or peer-paired writing at this stage.

Plenary

At appropriate points throughout the lesson, invite children to share their writing with small groups, partners or the whole class. Ask the children questions to help them focus on their progress and what they have created during that

Year 6, Sequence 12
Fiction: Plotting problems

lesson, for example: 'How have you tried to draw the reader in?' 'How have you introduced the setting and / or the main character?' 'Share your writing. Has your partner used correct and effective clause demarcation?'

Lesson 2

Starter (VGP focus) – Punctuation: Using commas for clearer meaning

Remind the children that commas can be useful for making the meaning of sentences clearer. Provide children with copies of *The Railway Children* extract and ask them, in pairs, to find examples of commas used within sentences. Have them use mini whiteboards to create sentences of similar structure, using the new content. As individuals, they can read their sentences aloud and have the class make notes of correct punctuation (capital letter(s), comma(s) and a full stop) as they listen.

Shared writing

With the children's input, model writing the next part of the narrative, which either tackles the delivery of the bad news – if you didn't introduce that in Lesson 1 – or provides more detail about the bad news such as the characters' reactions and behaviour. Ask children: 'How can you show the way the characters are feeling without stating it directly?' Encourage children to suggest the use of commas to improve the clarity of the sentences as you write.

Independent writing

The children can now write their own second section, applying the VGP focus on using commas to improve their clarity. Some children may benefit from guided group writing or peer-paired writing at this stage.

Plenary

At the end of the lesson, invite children to share their writing with groups or the whole class. Ask the children questions to help them focus on their progress and what they have created during that lesson, for example: 'How have you shown how your characters feel without stating it directly?' 'How have you used dialogue and / or description to progress the story?' 'How appropriately have you used commas?'

Lesson 3

Starter (VGP focus) – Punctuation: Brackets, dashes and commas

Begin the lesson by writing the following sentence from the model text on the board: 'Ruth brushed the girls' hair and helped them to undress. (Mother almost always did this herself.)' Ask the children to explain why they think brackets have been used. Take suggestions and establish that brackets, dashes and commas can be used to separate words, phrases or clauses that add extra detail to a sentence. This is called 'parenthesis'. Sometimes, as in this case, the extra detail is known loosely as an 'aside' (a way of speaking directly to the reader).

Ask the children to think of a sentence that could be used in the class story that uses brackets to include an aside or extra information.

Shared writing

With the children's input, model writing the next part of the narrative. Introduce more content on the frustration of the accusation: perhaps clues are emerging that suggest it was a false accusation, but cannot yet be proven. Use direct speech between the characters to progress the story. Features could include: narrative of the characters' actions between speech, for example, body language to show feelings; interrupted or informal speech; use of exclamation marks; an example of parenthesis using brackets.

Independent writing

The children can now write their own third section, applying the VGP focus on using brackets (but ensure they are not over-used: one example is probably enough). Some children may benefit from guided group writing or peer-paired writing at this stage.

Plenary

At the end of the lesson, invite children to share their writing with groups or the whole class. Ask the children questions to help them focus on their progress and what they have created during that lesson, for example: 'How have you presented the false accusation?' 'What is the intended effect on the reader and how have you achieved it?' 'How appropriately have you or your partner used brackets?'

Year 6, Sequence 12
Fiction: Plotting problems

Lesson 4

Starter (VGP focus) – Grammar: Perfect form of verbs

Explain to the children that the 'perfect form' is the verb tense used to indicate a completed or 'perfected' action or condition. Verbs can appear in any one of three perfect tenses: present perfect, past perfect and future perfect. Verbs in the perfect form use a form of 'have' or 'had' followed by the past participle.

Present perfect: I have finished reading already.

Past perfect: He had read the book for an hour before tea.

Future perfect: She will have finished reading by the time her parents return.

Look at this example of the perfect verb form used in *The Railway Children*:

'When she had turned down the gas and left them she found Peter, still dressed, waiting on the stairs.'

Provide pairs of children with copies of the main source text extract and the extra source text extract and ask them to look for and highlight any further examples of the perfect form of verbs.

Shared writing

With children's input, continue modelling how to write and complete the ongoing dialogue between the characters, interspersed with narrative to help move the story along. Encourage the children to practise the application of the perfect form of verbs, as appropriate. Work towards resolving the misunderstanding of the false accusation, considering how the plot will unfold. You could tie up loose ends and ensure that the ending is a classic, happy one with no unresolved issues. Ask the children to try to think of any questions the reader might have and address them in the story. Ask the children how we want the reader to feel after completing the story.

Independent writing

The children can now write their own fourth section, applying the VGP focus on using the perfect form of verbs. Some children may benefit from guided group writing or peer-paired writing at this stage.

Plenary

At the end of the lesson, invite children to share their writing with groups or the whole class. Ask the children questions to help them focus on their progress and what they have created during that lesson, for example: 'How does your ending compare with the original?' 'What feeling do you want to leave the reader with?' 'How effectively have you used the perfect form?'

Rehearsing and performing

Once the children have written their scene, encourage them to retell it either as narrators or by creating a performance. Discuss how different or similar the scene is to *The Railway Children* extract or the additional source text.

Review of the Big Picture

Once you have completed all the lessons for this phase, remind the children of the sequence's Big Picture. Discuss what they have learned during Phase 3.

Year 6, Sequence 12
Fiction: Plotting problems

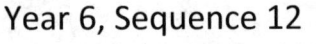

Phase 4: Write independently

This final phase brings all the children's learning and writing skills together so that they can write their own independent story depicting a family member breaking bad news, with the theme of a false accusation. Through their writing, they will be able to utilise the different VGP focuses that they have been practising throughout previous phases.

> **Programmes of study: Year 6**
> - **Composition:** Select appropriate grammar and vocabulary, understanding how such choices can change and enhance meaning.
> - **Composition:** In narratives, describe settings, characters and atmosphere and integrate dialogue to convey character and advance the action.
> - **Composition:** Assess the effectiveness of their own and others' writing.
> - **Composition:** Propose changes to vocabulary, grammar and punctuation to enhance effects and clarify meaning.
> - **Composition:** Proofread for spelling and punctuation errors.
> - **Composition:** Perform their own compositions, using appropriate intonation, volume and movement so that meaning is clear.

Introduction

Introduce this phase by highlighting the overall Big Picture to the children. Recap on learning and progress through Phases 1–3 and explain that in Phase 4 they will be applying their learning to write their own story independently. Discuss and list examples of situations that might be the cause of bad news and a false accusation. Examples could include a child being accused of stealing something, bullying someone or cheating in a test. Recap on the structure used in the class writing sessions in Phase 3.

Writing

Give each child a Story planner and instruct them to start planning and writing each section of their own story. Display the class story-structure and a copy of the extract from *The Railway Children* for reference. All the children should be encouraged to try to write independently to the best of their ability. Ask open questions such as: 'How will you show how the character is feeling at this point?' Avoid telling children what to write. Some children may benefit from guided composition. Focus on perseverance and resilience in their independent application.

Proofreading and redrafting

Have the children proofread their work periodically as they write. Proofreading and improvement without support means that the writing may happen over a few lessons. Offer the children Editor's checklist or create your own checklist that includes the VGP and spelling focuses covered throughout this sequence.

Highlight the importance of redrafting, linking their efforts to the overall Big Picture.

Self- and peer-assessment

Encourage the children to take time to self-assess their own writing as well as that of others in their group. Offer them a set of self-assessment questions such as: 'How does the writing convey atmosphere between the characters?' 'How clearly is the writing structured?' 'Has the false accusation been resolved?' 'What impact does the writing have?' 'What changes would improve the reader's experience?'

Rehearsing and performing

Once the children have written their independent story, encourage them to retell it either as narrators or by creating a performance. Discuss how similar or different the scene is from *The Railway Children* extract. Encourage the children to feed back on one another's writing and performances.

Final review of the Big Picture

Individually or with partners, have children reflect on what they have learned from this sequence and what they will apply in their future writing.

Year 6, Sequence 13
Fiction: Alternative perspectives

Sequence 13
Fiction: Alternative perspectives

Approximate duration: Two weeks

Big Picture

Through this teaching sequence, children will explore writing from different perspectives. Children will rewrite a scene from *Gulliver's Travels* from the point of view of a Lilliputian character. Understanding the techniques used by authors will help children to use these techniques within their own narrative writing.

Phase 1: Enjoy and immerse

Children analyse the actions, dialogue and reactions of the characters in the model text, *Gulliver's Travels*.

Phase 2: Capture and organise

Children begin to develop ideas for creating their own version of the model extract written from a different perspective.

Phase 3: Collaborate and compose

Children undertake supported writing sessions to develop the writing features of their story.

Phase 4: Write independently

Children write, edit and present their own version of the model extract written from a Lilliputian point of view.

Main source text

Treasure House Anthology Sequence 13 text. Treasure House Online, Year 6, Comprehension Unit 13: Fiction (classic): 'Gulliver's Travels'

Extra source texts

Gulliver's Travels, Jonathan Swift, ISBN 978-1-85-326027-8, pp.26–28

Background knowledge

Gulliver's Travels is a classic English novel written by Jonathan Swift in the early 1700s. It tells of the adventures of Lemuel Gulliver as he travels to the far reaches of the world. In the model text extract Gulliver's ship has been wrecked in a storm and he awakes to find himself on the island of Lilliput. He has been captured by Lilliputians, small people approximately six inches tall. Gulliver helps the Lilliputians with some of their problems, including the conflict they have with their enemy, the Blefescu. The story is presented in the first person, in the form of Gulliver's travel journal.

Spoken outcome

To tell a story to an audience of peers or parents

Writing outcome

To rewrite and extend the model text from a Lilliputian point of view

Prior knowledge

Check children's knowledge and understanding of:

- the story of *Gulliver's Travels*
- writing from a different character's point of view.

Year 6, Sequence 13
Fiction: Alternative perspectives

Diagnostic assessment options

Before starting the sequence, you may want to conduct an initial diagnostic assessment of the children's understanding of the typical characteristics of a narrative written in the first person.

Ideas for initial diagnostic assessment options include:

- discussion about the typical characteristics of first-person narrative
- a brief, unsupported writing activity to create a short first-person narrative
- practising speaking and listening skills relating to a well-known short first-person narrative
- a short reading comprehension activity / quiz on a first-person narrative

Treasure House links

All digital and pupil book units have the same names and numbers, but different questions.

- Treasure House, Year 6, Comprehension Unit 13: Fiction (classic): 'Gulliver's Travels'
- Treasure House, Year 6, Composition Unit 1: Story planning
- Treasure House, Year 6, Composition Unit 13: Paragraphs in fiction
- Treasure House, Year 6, Grammar Unit 2: Using the passive voice
- Treasure House, Year 6, Spelling Unit 1: The suffixes -cious and -tious
- Treasure House, Year 6, Spelling Unit 3: The suffixes -ant, -ance / -ancy, -ent and -ence / -ency
- Treasure House, Year 3, Unit 5: The present perfect tense
- Treasure House, Year 6, Vocabulary Unit 1: Using a thesaurus
- Treasure House, Year 6, Punctuation Unit 1: Using commas for clearer meaning
- Treasure House, Year 4, Grammar Unit 6: Fronted adverbials

Resources

Source texts – see Anthologies; Story planner; Editor's checklist

Year 6, Sequence 13
Fiction: Alternative perspectives

Phase 1: Enjoy and immerse

In Phase 1, the children are introduced to an extract from *Gulliver's Travels* which depicts a scene where Gulliver has woken up on an unknown beach after surviving a shipwreck and falling into a deep sleep. He encounters the Lilliputians, little people who are just six inches tall. Over several sessions, children are offered the opportunity to immerse themselves fully in the scene through comprehension and discussion activities, as well as exploring characters and structure through drama, storytelling, writing and analysis of the text.

Programmes of study: Year 6

- **Comprehension:** Increase their familiarity with a wide range of books, including myths, legends and traditional stories, modern fiction, fiction from our literary heritage, and books from other cultures and traditions.
- **Comprehension:** Draw inferences such as inferring characters' feelings, thoughts and motives from their actions.
- **Comprehension:** Discuss and evaluate how authors use language, considering the impact on the reader.
- **Composition:** Identify the audience for and purpose of the writing, selecting the appropriate form and using other similar writing as models for their own.
- **Vocabulary, grammar and punctuation:** Use passive verbs.
- **Spelling:** Use words with endings which sound like /shus/ spelt cious and tious.

Sparking interest

Introduce the sequence by highlighting the overall Big Picture to the children: they will be working towards rewriting the scene from the point of view of a Lilliputian character.

Use an opening question such as: 'What would you think if a giant person was found washed up on the beach one day?'

Reading and discussion

Introduce the main source text, read it with the class and check the children's understanding of the language. Discuss children's understanding of the content of the extract.

Discuss the following with the children.

- Who are the characters in this extract?
- How do you think Gulliver feels?
- How do you think the Lilliputians feel?
- Why doesn't Gulliver use his size and strength to break free and escape?
- What do you think the Lilliputian's are saying to Gulliver?
- What do you think might happen next?
- How did Gulliver end up asleep on the beach?
- Why do you think the Lilliputian's feed Gulliver?

Drama and storytelling

Use drama and storytelling activities to reinforce the children's understanding of the atmosphere in the scene. Select the activities that would suit your class or fit in with your lesson timing. Encourage mixed-ability grouping for the chosen activities.

- **Hot-seating Gulliver or the leader of the Lilliputians:** This activity can be done in pairs, small groups or as a class situation with different children representing the characters. Questions could include: 'What were you thinking when you saw the Lilliputians / Gulliver?' 'How do you feel?' 'What are your plans for the future?'
- **Role-play discussion:** Have a discussion to debate what Gulliver should do next and / or what the Lilliputians should do with Gulliver. Encourage children to imagine how the characters would be feeling.
- **Storytelling:** Become a storyteller. The children could accompany your performance, either by using props for sound effects or by taking the roles of the characters.
- **Performance:** Encourage the children to rehearse and perform the scene in pairs: one Gulliver, one narrator and imaginary Lilliputians.
- **Presentation ideas:** Create a newsflash related to the scene.

Year 6, Sequence 13
Fiction: Alternative perspectives

Incidental writing

A short writing activity would enhance the children's understanding of the text and characters. Select activities that you think appropriate for the abilities and interests of your class. Use the children's written outcomes to inform the emphases during the collaborative composition phase. Children could compose:

- a diary entry by Gulliver or a Lilliputian
- a Lilliputian newspaper article about Gulliver being found on the beach
- a letter to be thrown out to sea in a bottle from Gulliver to his family back home.

Analyse

Show the text to the children and discuss the setting, characters and plot. Discuss the way the extract is written in the first person from Gulliver's point of view. Ask: 'What is the effect of this style?' Discuss the opening sentence where Gulliver is describing the surroundings and the situation he finds himself in. Ask the children which words tell the reader how Gulliver is feeling. Look at the words and phrases used to start each paragraph. They provide variety, whilst linking the paragraphs and progressing the story. Look briefly at the variety of sentence structures and the short lengths of the paragraphs. Read the extra source text extract, also from *Gulliver's Travels*, and discuss how the story has progressed.

Grammar: Passive verbs

Explain to the children that in active voice sentences the subject does the action. In passive voice sentences the subject has the action done to it. Although using the active voice is more common, there is an important role for the passive voice. We often use the passive voice when the action is more important than who or what did it.

Provide pairs of children with copies of the source text and ask them to look for and highlight examples of passive verbs. Then share the examples with a larger group or the whole class. Discuss the effect created by the passive verb examples.

Phonics and spelling

Tell children that, because -cious and -tious both spell the sound /shus/, it is sometimes difficult to remember whether to spell the ending -cious or -tious.

For the following list of -cious / -tious words, ask the children to discuss the meaning of each word, then look it up in a dictionary to check. Then write each word in a short sentence. You could link the sentences to the theme of the model text, *Gulliver's Travels*.

-cious / -tious words: conscious, suspicious, delicious, subconscious, ferocious, conscientious, contentious, facetious, fictitious, scrumptious

Review of the Big Picture

Once you have completed this phase, remind the children (or have them remind each other) of the sequence's Big Picture: they are working towards rewriting the extract from a Lilliputian's point of view.

Year 6, Sequence 13
Fiction: Alternative perspectives

Phase 2: Capture and organise

During Phase 2, children start to develop ideas about new content and the literary features needed to create a new class version of the *Gulliver's Travels* extract, from a Lilliputian's point of view.

> **Programmes of study: Year 6**
> - **Comprehension:** Draw inferences such as inferring characters' feelings, thoughts and motives from their actions.
> - **Comprehension:** Identify how language, structure and presentation contribute to meaning.
> - **Comprehension:** Participate in discussions about books that are read to them and those they can read for themselves, building on their own and others' ideas and challenging views courteously.
> - **Composition:** Note and develop initial ideas, drawing on reading and research where necessary.
> - **Composition:** In writing narratives, consider how authors have developed characters and settings in what pupils have read, listened to or seen performed.
> - **Spelling:** Use words ending in -ant and -ent.

Introduction

Remind the children of the Big Picture for the sequence and recap on the learning achieved through Phase 1. Reread the main and extra source text extracts from *Gulliver's Travels*.

Discussing ideas

As a class, discuss and make decisions to form the basis of their own version of the extract.

- Which Lilliputian character should they tell the story through? (It could be a made up Lilliputian.)
- Put yourself in the shoes of a Lilliputian. How would they feel? What would their thoughts and opinions be?
- What would Lilliputians say to one another about Gulliver?
- Would all Lilliputians have the same opinions? What sorts of differing opinions might they have?
- What action could we add to the extract to extend its length?
- What other characters are in the scene and what are their roles?

Drama and storytelling

Use drama and storytelling activities to encourage children to develop their ideas further, especially their ideas relating to the viewpoint and perspective of the Lilliputian characters.

- **Hot-seating the new main character (the Lilliputian):** This activity will help the children to get to know their new characters as they must think carefully about the questions to ask and the answers to give.
- **Freeze-framing key moments:** Once there are sufficient ideas to start developing a scene, encourage children to act out their ideas either by improvising or scripting a brief scene. Children could work in small groups. At regular intervals, ask the children to freeze and use thought-tracking to develop their ideas about their characters' feelings, thoughts and actions.
- **Storytelling from a Lilliputian perspective:** Ask children to work together in pairs or small groups to develop their ideas, then present them to a larger group using storytelling techniques. The class could sit in a large circle or use props, puppets or music to help them tell their stories.

Incidental writing

Before you select any incidental writing, make sure the children are able to orally articulate the main events of their class story. Select activities that you think appropriate for the abilities and interests of your class. Children could compose:

- a diary entry by the Lilliputian character
- a newspaper article about life in Lilliput before or after Gulliver's arrival
- a letter of complaint from a Lilliputian about Gulliver causing a problem
- a character profile for the Lilliputian character.

Year 6, Sequence 13
Fiction: Alternative perspectives

Organising the class version of the scene into a structure

Once the children have thoroughly explored ideas for their class version of the scene, bring them together and use their final suggestions to model how to plot their new narrative in diagram or note form with the help of the Story planner. Once recorded, go through the frame and ask the children to evaluate the structure and organisation.

Phonics and spelling

Write the following words on the board, including the missing letter space.

Is the missing letter **a** or **e**? Or could it depend on the meaning of the word?

pati_nt; toler_nt; expect_nt; confid_nt; appar_nt; import_nt; evid_nt; obedi_nt; assist_nt; observ_nt; independ_nt; intellig_nt; innoc_nt

Challenge the children to use dictionaries to find the missing letter needed to spell each word correctly. Try 'beat the clock' and team-race strategies to encourage fun focus.

Review of the Big Picture

Once you have completed all the lessons for this phase, remind the children of the sequence's Big Picture. Recap on the learning achieved in Phase 2.

Year 6, Sequence 13
Fiction: Alternative perspectives

Phase 3: Collaborate and compose

This phase focuses in detail on supporting children to draft and write individual sections of their version, and an extension of the extract. The first two lessons focus on using the main source text and rewriting it in the first person but from the perspective of a Lilliputian. The third and fourth lessons encourage children to continue the writing, using their imaginations to develop and extend the extract.

Programmes of study: Year 6
- **Composition:** Identify the audience for and purpose of the writing, selecting the appropriate form and using other similar writing as a model for their own.
- **Composition:** Note and develop initial ideas, drawing on reading and research where necessary.
- **Composition:** In writing narratives, consider how authors have developed characters and settings in what pupils have read, listened to or seen performed.
- **Composition:** Select appropriate grammar and vocabulary, understanding how such choices can change and enhance meaning.
- **Composition:** In narratives, describe settings, characters and atmosphere and integrate dialogue to convey character and advance the action.

Introduction

Remind the children about the Big Picture and recap on the learning in Phases 1 and 2. Explain to children that through Phase 3 they will be learning how to rewrite the main source text extract from the perspective of a Lilliputian and then continue and extend the extract using their own ideas for the content and plot.

Lesson 1

Starter (VGP focus) – Grammar: Perfect form of verbs

Explain to the children that the 'perfect form' is the verb tense used to indicate a completed or 'perfected' action or condition. Verbs can appear in any one of three perfect tenses: present perfect, past perfect and future perfect. Verbs in the perfect form use a form of 'have' or 'had' followed by the past participle.

Present perfect example: 'I have finished reading already.'

Past perfect example: 'He had read the book for an hour before tea.'

Future perfect example: 'She will have finished reading by the time her parents return.'

Show children this example of the perfect form of a verb used in the extract from *Gulliver's Travels*:

'I must have slept for a long time ...'

Provide pairs of children with copies of the main source text extract and the extra source text extract. Ask them to choose three sentences, then rewrite them using the perfect form of the verbs, for example: 'I tried to stand up but found to my astonishment that I could not move.' This becomes: 'I **had** tried to stand up but found to my astonishment that I could not move.'

Shared writing

Children remind themselves and each other of their planning ideas from Phase 2. Ask the children to make suggestions for the wording of the opening paragraph of the class version, revisiting the main source text as an example and remembering that the extract must be retold through the eyes of the Lilliputian character. Model rewriting the first half of the extract with the children's input. Discuss the opening with the children. Ask: 'When was the first time the Lilliputian character saw Gulliver?' 'How can the opening sentences portray the shock or fear that the Lilliputian character felt?' Suggest that the children add extra details and tell them that they should not feel restricted to rewriting the extract too exactly. Include one or two perfect verb sentences or experiment with creating one to decide whether it would be appropriate to include.

Year 6, Sequence 13
Fiction: Alternative perspectives

Independent writing

The children can now write their own first section, applying the VGP focus on the perfect form of verbs. Some children may benefit from guided group writing or peer-paired writing at this stage.

Plenary

At appropriate points throughout the lesson, invite children to share their writing with small groups, partners or the whole class. Ask the children questions to help them focus on their progress and what they have created during that lesson, for example: 'How does your opening paragraph compare with the original so far?' 'Where have you applied the perfect form, and what does it contribute to the writing?' 'How effectively has it been applied by your partner?'

Lesson 2

Starter (VGP focus) – Vocabulary: Using a thesaurus

Remind the children that we can use a thesaurus to find words with similar meanings. It can help us to find new or better words for what we want to say. Ask children, in pairs, to choose one sentence from the *Gulliver's Travels* extract and alter it by replacing some of the words with alternatives found in the thesaurus. Share children's examples, checking that nuances of meaning are understood.

Shared writing

With the children's input, model rewriting the next part of the extract. Encourage children to use the thesaurus to improve the vocabulary you are using as you write. Encourage the children to add extra details and remind them that they should not feel restricted to rewriting the extract too exactly. Also remind them that you are thinking and writing as the Lilliputian character. Ask: 'How does the character feel?' 'Why does the character think the way they do?' 'What will the character do next?'

Independent writing

The children can now write their own second section, applying the VGP focus on using a thesaurus to source new or interesting vocabulary to improve their setting descriptions. Some children may benefit from guided group writing or peer-paired writing at this stage.

Plenary

At the end of the lesson, invite children to share their writing with groups or the whole class. Ask the children questions to help them focus on their progress and what they have created during that lesson, for example: 'How does your version compare with the original?' 'How have you shown a different point of view?' 'What synonyms have you used, and how do they help the story?'

Lesson 3

Starter (VGP focus) – Punctuation: Using commas for clearer meaning

Remind the children that commas can be useful for making the meaning of sentences clearer. Provide children with copies of the *Gulliver's Travels* extract and ask them to work in pairs to find examples of commas used within sentences. Have them use mini whiteboards to create sentences of similar structure, using the new content. As individuals, they can read their sentences aloud and have the class make notes of correct punctuation (capital letter(s), comma(s) and a full stop) as they listen.

Shared writing

With children's input, continue to model how to extend the writing beyond the content of the main source text extract. Use the ideas from the earlier planning phase to write about an event or occurrence and continue writing as the Lilliputian, in the first person. Remind children that the writing should be descriptive, as if it is the Lilliputian's journal. Be sure to include examples of using commas to aid clarity within a sentence.

Independent writing

The children can now write their own third section, extending the extract to use their own content but staying in the style of writing as the Lilliputian character. They can apply their knowledge of using commas within sentences. Some children may benefit from guided group writing or peer-paired writing at this stage.

Plenary

At the end of the lesson, invite children to share their writing with groups or the whole class. Ask the children questions to help them focus on their progress and what they have created during that lesson, for example: 'How have you moved the story on and developed the point of view?' 'Where have you used commas to aid clarity?'

Year 6, Sequence 13
Fiction: Alternative perspectives

Lesson 4

Starter (VGP focus) – Grammar: Revision of fronted adverbials

Ask the children to recall the meaning and purpose of fronted adverbials. Take suggestions. Establish that an adverbial is a word, phrase or clause that adds meaning to a verb. Adverbials can tell you how, when or where the verb was happening. If we put the adverbial at the front of the sentence, it is called a fronted adverbial. Fronted adverbials can make a sentence more atmospheric. For example: 'That night, something happened.'

Provide pairs of children with copies of the main source text (and / or the extra source text) extract from *Gulliver's Travels*. Ask the children to find and highlight any fronted adverbials.

Shared writing

With children's input, continue modelling how to write the rest of their extended piece as the Lilliputian character, writing about Gulliver and events related to Gulliver's arrival on Lilliput. Include fronted adverbials suggested by the children, demarcating them with a comma each time. Discuss with the children whether the ending of the piece of writing will be a cliff hanger (perhaps using an ellipsis to suggest that something is about to happen, or the Lilliputian got cut off from his journal writing) or whether the ending will be a resolved one, rounding off and concluding events.

Independent writing

The children can now write their own fourth and final section, applying the VGP focus using fronted adverbials. Some children may benefit from guided group writing or peer-paired writing at this stage.

Plenary

At the end of the lesson, invite children to share their writing with groups or the whole class. Ask the children questions to help them focus on their progress and what they have created during that lesson, for example: 'How have you developed the story?' 'What adverbials have you used and what effect to they have?'

Rehearsing and performing

Once the children have written their scene, encourage them to retell it either as narrators or by creating a performance. Discuss how different or similar the scene is to the extracts from *Gulliver's Travels*.

Review of the Big Picture

Once you have completed all the lessons for this phase, remind the children of the sequence's Big Picture. Discuss what they have learned during Phase 3.

Year 6, Sequence 13
Fiction: Alternative perspectives

Phase 4: Write independently

This final phase brings all the children's learning and writing skills together so that they can write their own independent text as a Lilliputian character to retell events about Gulliver's arrival and stay on Lilliput (using the text and their imaginations). Through their writing, they will be able to utilise the different VGP focuses that they have been practising throughout previous phases.

> **Programmes of study: Year 6**
> - **Composition:** Select appropriate grammar and vocabulary, understanding how such choices can change and enhance meaning.
> - **Composition:** In narratives, describe settings, characters and atmosphere and integrate dialogue to convey character and advance the action.
> - **Composition:** Assess the effectiveness of their own and others' writing.
> - **Composition:** Propose changes to vocabulary, grammar and punctuation to enhance effects and clarify meaning.
> - **Composition:** Proofread for spelling and punctuation errors.
> - **Composition:** Perform their own compositions, using appropriate intonation, volume and movement so that meaning is clear.

Introduction

Introduce this phase by highlighting the overall Big Picture to the children. Recap on learning and progress through Phases 1–3 and explain that in Phase 4 they will be applying their learning to write their own scene independently. Discuss and list examples of situations that did or could have happened with Gulliver in Lilliput. Examples could include Gulliver helping the Lilliputians with some building work, attending a party or playing with children. Also discuss which Lilliputian character the children could assume (someone from the extracts or someone they imagine). Recap on the structure used in the class writing sessions in Phase 3.

Writing

Give each child a Story planner and instruct them to start planning and writing each section of their own scene. Display the class writing plans and a copy of the extract from *Gulliver's Travels* for reference. All the children should be encouraged to try to write independently to the best of their ability. Ask open questions such as: 'How will you show how the character is feeling at this point?' Avoid telling children what to write. Some children may benefit from guided composition. Focus on perseverance and resilience in their independent application.

Proofreading and redrafting

Have the children proofread their work periodically as they write. Proofreading and improvement without support means that the writing may happen over a few lessons. Offer the children the Editor's checklist or create your own checklist that includes the VGP and spelling focuses covered throughout this sequence. Highlight the importance of redrafting, linking their efforts to the overall Big Picture.

Self- and peer-assessment

Encourage the children to take time to self-assess their own writing as well as that of others in their group. Offer them a set of self-assessment questions, such as: 'How does the writing convey the Lilliputian character's thoughts and feelings?' 'How clearly is the writing structured?' 'Have you used the correct punctuation?' 'What impact does the writing have?' 'What changes would improve the reader's experience?'

Rehearsing and performing

Once the children have written their independent scene, encourage them to retell it either as narrators or by creating a performance. Discuss how similar or different the scene is from the *Gulliver's Travels* extracts. Encourage the children to feed back on one another's writing and performances.

Final review of the Big Picture

Individually or with partners, have children reflect on what they have learned from this sequence and what they will apply in their future writing.

Year 6, Sequence 14
Fiction: Comparing forms

Sequence 14
Fiction: Comparing forms

Approximate duration: Two weeks

Big Picture

Through this teaching sequence, children will explore the differences between playscript and prose versions of the same text, *Macbeth* by William Shakespeare. By comparing playscript and prose versions of *Macbeth*, children will gain an understanding of the effect each form of presentation has on the audience. Children will be able to write a playscript text that has an impact on readers' responses.

Phase 1: Enjoy and immerse

Children analyse the content and features of the model text, a prose version of an extract from the play *Macbeth*.

Phase 2: Capture and organise

Children begin to develop ideas for creating a playscript version of the *Macbeth* prose model text.

Phase 3: Collaborate and compose

Children undertake supported writing sessions to develop the features and content of their playscript.

Phase 4: Write independently

Children write, edit and present their own version of the model extract written in the form of a playscript.

Main source text

Treasure House Anthology Sequence 14 text. *Macbeth*, Jon Mayhew and Adrian Stone, ISBN 978-0-00-753013-7, pp.7–11

Extra source texts

Macbeth, Act 1 Scene 3, William Shakespeare, ISBN 978-0-19-832400-3, pp.4–8

Treasure House Online, Year 6, Comprehension Unit 14: Playscript: 'Compere Lapin and Compere Tig'

Background knowledge

Macbeth is William Shakespeare's shortest tragedy. Written in 1606, it reflected the political and literary context of the times. *Macbeth* is a play about the perils of ambition. Macbeth, encouraged by his wife, attempts to remove the obstacles preventing him from being king. These obstacles are the other characters in the play. He accepts the prophecy of witches as a guide for what will be, and misjudges what they tell him. In the end, his complacency leads to his own death: he believes he cannot be harmed when, really, he is mortal like everyone else.

Spoken outcome

To perform a playscript of the witches' scene from *Macbeth* to an audience of peers or parents

Writing outcome

To rewrite the prose version of *Macbeth* as a playscript

Prior knowledge

Check children's knowledge and understanding of:
- typical characteristics of playscripts
- common characteristics of prose
- William Shakespeare
- *Macbeth* by William Shakespeare.

Year 6, Sequence 14
Fiction: Comparing forms

Diagnostic assessment options

Before starting the sequence, you may want to conduct an initial diagnostic assessment of the children's understanding of the typical characteristics of a playscript.

Ideas for initial diagnostic assessment options include:
- discussion about playscripts, their purpose and form
- a brief, unsupported writing activity to create a short playscript
- practising speaking and listening skills relating to a well-known short playscript
- a short reading comprehension activity / quiz on a playscript.

Treasure House links

All digital and pupil book units have the same names and numbers, but different questions.

- Treasure House, Year 6, Comprehension Unit 14: Playscript: 'Compere Lapin and Compere Tig'
- Treasure House, Year 6, Composition Unit 3: Adapting stories for plays
- Treasure House, Year 5, Grammar Unit 2: Adverbs and modal verbs showing possibility
- Treasure House, Year 6, Spelling Unit 4: The suffixes -able, -ible, -ably and -ibly
- Treasure House, Year 6, Spelling Unit 8: The letter-string ough
- Treasure House, Year 6, Punctuation Unit 1: Using commas for clearer meaning

Resources

Source texts – see Anthologies; Story planner; Editor's checklist

Year 6, Sequence 14
Fiction: Comparing forms

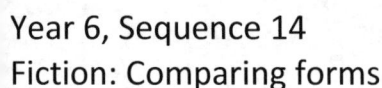

Phase 1: Enjoy and immerse

In Phase 1, the children are introduced to a prose narrative version of Shakespeare's play, *Macbeth*. In the main source text extract Macbeth and Banquo meet three weird women who predict that Macbeth will one day become king. Over several lessons, children are offered the opportunity to immerse themselves fully in the story through comprehension and discussion activities, as well as exploring its characters and structure through drama, storytelling, writing and analysis of the text.

> **Programmes of study: Year 6**
> - **Comprehension:** Read books that are structured in different ways and read for a range of purposes.
> - **Comprehension:** Draw inferences such as inferring characters' feelings, thoughts and motives from their actions.
> - **Comprehension:** Discuss and evaluate how authors use language, considering the impact on the reader.
> - **Composition:** Identify the audience for and purpose of the writing, selecting the appropriate form and using other similar writing as models for their own.
> - **Vocabulary, grammar and punctuation:** Use relative clauses beginning with who, which, where, when, whose, that, or with an implied relative pronoun.
> - **Spelling:** Use words ending in -able and -ible.

Sparking interest

Introduce the sequence by highlighting the overall Big Picture to the children: they will be working towards turning the prose version of the *Macbeth* extract into a playscript.

Use an opening question such as: 'If Shakespeare's *Macbeth* was originally written as a play, why might a prose version have been written in modern times?'

Reading and discussion

Introduce the text, read it with the class and check the children's understanding of the language. Discuss children's understanding of the content of the extract.

Discuss the following with the children.
- Who are the characters in the scene?
- Where had Macbeth and Banquo been prior to meeting the weird women?
- What happens in the scene?
- What do you think will happen next?
- Who do you think the weird women are?
- How does the scene make you feel?
- How does the scene make you feel about Macbeth?
- What questions does it make you want to ask?
- How does the extract make you want to read on?

Drama and storytelling

Use drama and storytelling activities to reinforce the children's understanding of the prose version. Select the activities that would suit your class or fit in with your lesson timing. Encourage mixed-ability grouping for the chosen activities.

- **Hot-seating Macbeth, Banquo or a weird woman:** This activity can be done in pairs, small groups or as a class situation with different children representing the characters. Questions from the audience could include: 'What were your thoughts when you met [the other character]?' 'Why were you in the woods?' 'Banquo, do you believe the weird women?' 'Macbeth, do you want to be king?'
- **Freeze-framing key moments:** Organise the children to re-enact the scene. Use thought-tracking by asking each child in the freeze-frame what they're thinking at a particular moment.
- **Storytelling:** Become a storyteller. Explain that storytellers would retell different stories to people often sitting around them. The children could accompany your performance, either by using props for sound effects or by taking the roles of the characters.
- **Performance:** Encourage the children to rehearse and perform the extract in small groups, with one or two narrators.
- **Presentation ideas:** Create a newsflash related to the story.

Year 6, Sequence 14
Fiction: Comparing forms

Incidental writing

A short writing activity would enhance the children's understanding of the text and characters. Select activities that you think appropriate for the abilities and interests of your class. Children could compose:

- a diary entry by Macbeth or Banquo reflecting on the encounter with the weird women
- a newspaper article about sightings of the weird women in the local area
- a letter from Macbeth to a friend or relative telling them about the strange encounter.

Analysis

Show the text to the children and explain that, as a class, they are going to work with you to look more closely at how the text is organised. With the children, look at the content of each paragraph. Discuss how much description, narration and dialogue there is, and at what points characters are introduced to the scene. Discuss how the scene is set and the setting described. Ask children if they think the reader is easily able to build a mental image of the scene. Notice the use of techniques such as similes: 'They looked like two specks of black on a scrubby brown hillside.' Point out that the extract is written in the first person and discuss who the speaker is. Note the points at which the reader is told how the speaker is feeling: 'My scalp prickled.' Ask children: 'How is a sense of atmosphere created?' 'How does the author keep the story progressing?'

Grammar: Adverbs and modal verbs showing possibility

Remind children that adverbs and modal verbs can show how likely the action of a verb is.

Adverbs: perhaps, maybe, possibly, probably, definitely, certainly, surely, often, seldom, never

Modal verbs: can, could, may, might, shall, should, will, would, will, ought (to)

Put the adverbs and modal verbs onto cards or sheets of A4 paper (one word per card). Each child takes one word. Challenge the children to organise themselves so they are standing in a line holding up their word cards in order of likelihood.

Provide children with a copy of the *Macbeth* extract and challenge them in pairs to find and highlight as many examples of adverbs and modal verbs showing possibility as they can.

Provide the sentence: 'You _____ tidy your bedroom.' Have children try different modals in the space, acting and expressing them appropriately.

Phonics and spelling

Write the following passage on the board for the children to copy and fill in the gaps with the correct spelling, -ible or -able. Alternatively, use the passage as a dictation.

Macbeth and his depend____ friend Banquo walked through the woods. They were having an enjoy____ walk and were engaged in sens____ conversation when they saw an unbeliev____ sight. In front of them were three horr____ looking women. Were they approach____, they wondered? The women told Macbeth and Banquo imposs____ information. Was it reli____?

Children could use a dictionary to check spellings.

Review of the Big Picture

Once you have completed this phase, remind the children (or have them remind each other) of the sequence's Big Picture: they are working towards turning the prose version of the *Macbeth* extract into a playscript, independently.

Year 6, Sequence 14
Fiction: Comparing forms

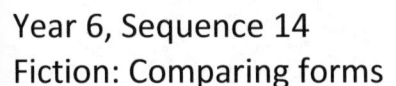

Phase 2: Capture and organise

During Phase 2, the children are able to use their knowledge from the previous lessons in Phase 1 to create their own class playscript. The group and class discussions, as well as drama or short writing opportunities, offer chances for children of all abilities to contribute and use their skills towards designing a structure and developing features for their playscript. Their ideas can be recorded in picture, diagram or note form onto the Story planner.

Programmes of study: Year 6
- **Comprehension:** Summarise the main ideas drawn from more than one paragraph, identifying key details that support the main idea.
- **Comprehension:** Make comparisons within and across books.
- **Comprehension:** Participate in discussions about books that are read to them and those they can read for themselves, building on their own and others' ideas and challenging views courteously.
- **Composition:** Note and developing initial ideas, drawing on reading and research where necessary.
- **Composition:** In writing narratives, consider how authors have developed characters and settings in what children have read, listened to or seen performed.
- **Spelling:** Use words with the letter-string ough.

Introduction

Remind the children about the sequence's Big Picture. Reread the prose extract of *Macbeth* and discuss briefly why it was written (to help younger audiences understand the stories written by Shakespeare). With the children, recap how the structure of the text is presented, for example, the combination of first-person narrative with some dialogue. Show the children the notes made from the structural analysis covered in Phase 1.

Introduce the idea that the children are going to work together to create their own class playscript of the prose extract.

Look at the extra source texts and discuss the typical characteristics of playscripts. What are the differences and similarities between prose and playscripts?

Discussing ideas

Show the children the prose extract and establish the characters needed in the playscript (Macbeth, Banquo, the three weird women and the speaker / narrator). Also decide on the setting, for example, whether they are in or near a woodland area or in an open field. Once the main two decisions have been made, put the children into mixed-ability groups and encourage them to discuss and come up with suggestions in answer to the following questions. You may want to give them a selection of questions or just one question per group. Bring the groups together to listen and make decisions on the contents and structure.

- What is the setting like? (Use your senses to imagine how it looks, feels, smells.)
- Why are the characters there? What is their story?
- What might the stage directions need to include?
- Which writing features will we need to include when writing the playscript?
- What other characters could be in the playscript and what are their roles?
- What can we keep from the original prose version and what will we change?

Drama and storytelling

Use drama and storytelling activities to allow the children to explore the suggestions for their new characters and story plot. Select the activities that would suit your class or fit in with your lesson timing. Encourage mixed-ability grouping for the chosen activities.

- **Hot-seating the main characters:** This activity can be done in pairs, small groups or as a class situation. Encourage the children to think and, if necessary, write down their questions before the session starts. Discuss the characters' responses.

Year 6, Sequence 14
Fiction: Comparing forms

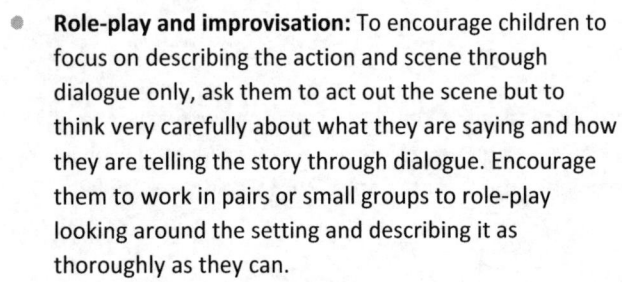

- **Role-play and improvisation:** To encourage children to focus on describing the action and scene through dialogue only, ask them to act out the scene but to think very carefully about what they are saying and how they are telling the story through dialogue. Encourage them to work in pairs or small groups to role-play looking around the setting and describing it as thoroughly as they can.
- **Play rehearsal:** Ask the children to work in groups and allocate roles of play directors and actors. The directors should take the lead in instructing and guiding the group through the scene. The children should make notes about positions, stage directions, facial expressions, intonation and body movements needed. The focus is on exploring the logistics of the play rather than just the dialogue.

Incidental writing

Before you select any incidental writing, make sure the children are able to orally articulate the main events of their class playscript. Select activities that you think appropriate for the abilities and interests of your class. Children could compose:

- a diary entry by one of the characters
- a newspaper article about the battle Macbeth and Banquo were involved in
- a poem about the scene
- a short story about what might happen next
- a character profile
- a blog entry or email.

Organising the class playscript into a structure

Once the children have thoroughly explored their ideas for their class playscript, bring them together and use their final suggestions to model how to plot the new playscript in picture, diagram or note form with the help of the Story planner. Once recorded, go through the frame and ask the children if they are happy with the plans.

Phonics and spelling

Display the letter-string ough. Establish that this letter-string is tricky because it can be pronounced in multiple ways.

Ask children to say each of the words below and sort them into groups of the same sound. Then write each word in a sentence to show what it means.

ough words: afterthought, borough, breakthrough, clough, drought, hiccough, roughage, sought, thoroughbred, wrought

Review of the Big Picture

Once you have completed all the lessons for this phase, remind the children of the sequence's Big Picture. Discuss what they have learned so far and recap on Phase 2.

Year 6, Sequence 14
Fiction: Comparing forms

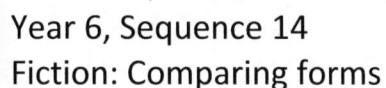

Phase 3: Collaborate and compose

This phase focuses on the teaching and learning of how to write a playscript using the prose version of the text, with one lesson per section, so that the children are taken through the writing of the whole piece, learning new vocabulary, grammar and punctuation along the way. Children should have the planning framework from Phase 2 in front of them throughout, and should be able to revisit the original source text, *Macbeth*.

> **Programmes of study: Year 6**
> - **Composition:** Identify the audience for and purpose of the writing, selecting the appropriate form and using other similar writing as a model for their own.
> - **Composition:** Note and develop initial ideas, drawing on reading and research where necessary.
> - **Composition:** In writing narratives, consider how authors have developed characters and settings in what children have read, listened to or seen performed.
> - **Composition:** Select appropriate grammar and vocabulary, understanding how such choices can change and enhance meaning.
> - **Composition:** In narratives, describe settings, characters and atmosphere and integrate dialogue to convey character and advance the action.

Introduction

Remind the children about the Big Picture and recap on the learning in Phases 1 and 2. Explain to the children that through Phase 3 they will be learning how to write their own playscript based on the planning and ideas in Phase 2.

Lesson 1

Starter (VGP focus) – Punctuation: Conventions of playscripts

Ask the children if they can recall the conventions of punctuating playscripts. Ask how colons and brackets are used. Take suggestions. Use the extra source texts to show the children how playscripts are laid out and punctuated. Ask children, in small groups, to use copies of the extra source texts to create a list of features that they notice. Feed back to the whole class and compare findings. Collate their findings into a class poster to display on the classroom wall.

Ideas could include:
- no speech marks when characters are speaking
- stage directions shown in brackets
- a colon used after the speaker's name
- a new line for every speaker
- capitals or italics used to emphasise words
- ellipses to show interruption
- present tense
- characters' names written on the left.

Shared writing

Children remind themselves and each other of their planning ideas from Phase 2. Ask the children to make suggestions for the wording of the opening paragraph of the playscript: the director's notes that set the scene by describing it. Discuss with the children how to take each sentence, consider the information in it and then decide whether to present that information through stage directions or through dialogue. For example, in the prose version it reads: 'The wet grass was slippery underfoot.' In the playscript this could be turned into speech, as follows.

Macbeth: Banquo! Take care! I nearly slipped on the wet grass underfoot.

Also model how the children can add in their own dialogue whilst maintaining the storyline. For example:

Banquo: Yes, it has been raining heavily, this field is pure mud. My shoes are soaked.

Guide the children to discuss the section from the director's note that sets the scene to the point at which the scene focuses in on the three women huddled around the fire. Model enough writing to get children going but do not model the entire section.

Year 6, Sequence 14
Fiction: Comparing forms

Independent writing

The children can now write their own first section, applying the VGP focus of the conventions of punctuating playscript writing. Some children may benefit from guided group writing or peer-paired writing at this stage.

Plenary

At the end of the daily writing session, invite children to share their writing with groups or the whole class. Ask the children questions to help them focus on their progress and what they have created during that lesson, for example: 'How does the beginning of your playscript compare with the prose version?' 'What setting details have you included in the opening paragraph?' 'Have you used correct playscript punctuation?'

Lesson 2

Starter (VGP focus) – Punctuation: Using commas for clearer meaning

Remind the children that commas can be useful for making the meaning of sentences clearer. Provide children with copies of the *Macbeth* prose extract and ask them, in pairs, to find examples of commas used within sentences. Have them use mini whiteboards to create sentences of similar structure, using the new content. As individuals read their sentences aloud, have the class make notes of correct punctuation (capital letter(s), comma(s) and a full stop) as they listen. Point out to the children that when actors learn a script it is particularly important that they can interpret the meaning of the text easily and clearly.

Shared writing

With the children's input, model translating the next section of the prose extract into a playscript version. Focus on the part of the scene where the three weird women are described and then approached by Macbeth and Banquo, and when the women begin to tell Macbeth about his future. Ask the children to suggest how the women can be described through dialogue, for example:

Macbeth: *(with a puzzled expression)* What do you think they are saying to one another whilst they are huddled round the fire, Banquo?

Banquo: *(screwing his face up)* I don't know, but look how haggard they are. Their thin, lank hair clings to their yellow scalps.

Independent writing

The children can now write their own second section, applying the VGP focus on using commas for clarity. Some children may benefit from guided group writing or peer-paired writing at this stage.

Plenary

At the end of the daily writing session, invite children to share their writing with groups or the whole class. Ask the children questions to help them focus on their progress and what they have created during that lesson, for example: 'How does your playscript so far compare with the prose version?' 'How have you used commas to aid clarity?' 'How have you used speech to describe characters?'

Lesson 3

Starter (VGP focus) – Grammar: Adverbs showing possibility

Remind children that adverbs of possibility can show how likely the action of a verb in a sentence is. Write the following adverbs of possibility on the board.

Adverbs of possibility: certainly, definitely, maybe, possibly, clearly, obviously, perhaps, probably

Ask children to write each word on a small strip of paper then work with a partner to order the words from the least to the most certain. As an extension, ask children to write each word in a sentence to show how it could be used within the *Macbeth* playscript.

Shared writing

With the children's input, model writing the next part of the playscript. Focus on the ongoing dialogue between the three women and Macbeth and Banquo. Ask the children to make suggestions about making the stage directions explicit for actors to understand. Include an example of the VGP focus, for example:

Macbeth: You are *clearly* talking rubbish!

First woman: No, I *certainly* am not! I know all about your future Macbeth.

Independent writing

The children can now write their own third section, applying the VGP focus on adverbs showing possibility. Some children may benefit from guided group writing or peer-paired writing at this stage.

Year 6, Sequence 14
Fiction: Comparing forms

Plenary

At the end of the lesson, ask children to share their writing with groups or the whole class. Ask the children questions to help them focus on their progress and what they have created during that lesson, for example: 'How have you used adverbs of possibility to enhance the script?' 'Are the stage directions clear?'

Lesson 4

Starter (VGP focus) – Grammar: Modal verbs showing possibility

Remind children that modal verbs of possibility can show how likely the action of a verb in a sentence is. Write the following modal verbs of possibility on the board.

Modal verbs of possibility: can, could, may, might, shall, should, will, would

Write the following sentence beginnings on the board.

Sentence beginnings: 'I can help you if ...'; 'You should have ...'; 'We might go ...'; 'I wouldn't do ...'; 'You ought to eat ...'; 'She will be late ...'

Ask children to complete the sentences with their own endings or make up three of their own sentences using modal verbs to show how likely something is. Discuss the nuances of modal verb choice, for example, whether they are tentative or, perhaps, bossy.

Shared writing

With the children's input, model translating the final part of the prose version of the *Macbeth* extract. You could elaborate and extend the conversation between Macbeth and Banquo as they analyse the encounter with the three women. Remind children to include information through the stage directions and dialogue that shows how the characters are feeling.

Independent writing

The children can now write their own final section, applying the VGP focus on modal verbs. Some children may benefit from guided group writing or peer-paired writing at this stage.

Plenary

At the end of the lesson, ask children to share their writing with groups or the whole class. Ask the children questions to help them focus on their progress and what they have created during that lesson, for example: 'How does your playscript compare with the original *Macbeth* playscript?' 'How have you used modal verbs to enhance your writing?'

Rehearsing and performing

Once the children have written their playscript, encourage them to retell it with audience awareness or by creating a performance. Discuss how different or similar the tale is to the original prose and playscript versions of Macbeth.

Review of the Big Picture

Once you have completed all the lessons for this phase, remind the children of the sequence's Big Picture. Discuss what they have learned so far in Phases 1–3.

Year 6, Sequence 14
Fiction: Comparing forms

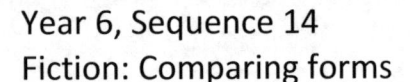

Phase 4: Write independently

This final phase brings all the children's learning and writing skills together so that they can write their own playscript, or extend the playscript they have been translating from the prose extract, using some of the features they have observed through Phase 3. Through their writing, they will be able to utilise the different VGP focuses that they have been investigating in the previous phases.

> **Programmes of study: Year 6**
> - **Composition:** Select appropriate grammar and vocabulary, understanding how such choices can change and enhance meaning.
> - **Composition:** In narratives, describe settings, characters and atmosphere and integrate dialogue to convey character and advance the action.
> - **Composition:** Assess the effectiveness of their own and others' writing.
> - **Composition:** Propose changes to vocabulary, grammar and punctuation to enhance effects and clarify meaning.
> - **Composition:** Proofread for spelling and punctuation errors.
> - **Composition:** Perform their own compositions, using appropriate intonation, volume and movement so that meaning is clear.

Introduction

Introduce this phase by highlighting the overall Big Picture to the children. Recap on learning and progress through Phases 1–3 and explain that in Phase 4 they will be applying their learning to write their own playscript scene independently. The children could rewrite the prose extract used in Phase 3 for support or could extend the playscript scene from Phase 3 to include their own content. Recap on the structure and typical playscript writing characteristics used in the class writing sessions in Phase 3.

Writing

Give each child a Story planner and encourage them to start planning and writing each section of their own playscript scene. Display the class planner and a copy of both the main and extra source texts for reference. All children should be encouraged to write independently to the best of their ability. Ask open questions such as: 'How will you show how the characters are feeling?' Avoid telling the children what to write. Some children may benefit from guided composition. Focus on perseverance and resilience in their independent application.

Proofreading and redrafting

Have the children proofread their work periodically as they write. Proofreading and improvement without support means that the writing may happen over a few lessons. Offer the children the Editor's checklist or create your own checklist that includes the VGP and spelling focuses covered throughout this sequence. Highlight the importance of redrafting, linking their efforts to the overall Big Picture.

Self- and peer-assessment

Encourage the children to take time to self-assess their own writing, as well as assess that of others in their group. Offer them a set of self-assessment questions such as: 'How will the actors know how to behave from the script?' 'Have playscript punctuation conventions been used correctly?' 'How clearly is the scene structured?' 'What makes this an engaging script?' 'What changes would improve the reader's experience?'

Rehearsing and performing

Once the children have written their independent playscript scene, encourage them to retell it with audience awareness or by creating a performance. Discuss how different or similar the tale is to the original playscript, *Macbeth*. Encourage the children to feed back on one another's writing and performances.

Final review of the Big Picture

Individually or with partners, have children reflect on what they have learned from this sequence and what they will apply in their future writing.

Year 6, Sequence 15
Non-fiction: Biographies

Sequence 15
Non-fiction: Biographies

Approximate duration: Two weeks

Big Picture

Through this teaching sequence, children will explore the purpose and typical characteristics of biographies and autobiographies. By exploring biographies and autobiographies, children will gain an understanding of the effect each form of text has on readers. Children will be able to write a biographical text about an inspirational figure that has an impact on readers' responses.

Phase 1: Enjoy and immerse

Children analyse the purpose and features of the model text, *Virginia Hall WWII Spy* (a biography).

Phase 2: Capture and organise

Children begin to develop ideas for creating a biographical text about an inspirational figure.

Phase 3: Collaborate and compose

Children undertake supported writing sessions to develop the features and content of their biographical text.

Phase 4: Writing independently

Children write, edit and present their own biographical text on an inspirational figure they have chosen and researched.

Main source text

Treasure House Anthology Sequence 15 text. *Virginia Hall WWII Spy*, Adrian Bradbury, ISBN 978-0-00-742836-6, pp.6–10

Extra source texts

Treasure House Online, Year 6, Comprehension Unit 15: Non-fiction (autobiography): 'Wild Swans'

Background knowledge

The main source text, *Virginia Hall WWII Spy*, is the biography of one of the bravest and most successful spies for the Allies during World War Two. She was born in 1906 to a rich family in Baltimore, America. The extract shows Virginia Hall's childhood and early life in chronological order. The extra source text, *Wild Swans*, is an autobiographical extract by Jung Chang. In the extract, Chang remembers being six years old and living in a regime under Chairman Mao who had ordered the people of China to produce vast quantities of steel. Both of the source texts provide motivating examples of biographical and autobiographical texts for children to evaluate.

Spoken outcome

To present a biography orally to an audience of peers or parents

Writing outcome

To write a biographical text on a chosen inspirational figure, researched independently

Prior knowledge

Check children's knowledge and understanding of:
- biographies
- autobiographies
- Virginia Hall.

Year 6, Sequence 15
Non-fiction: Biographies

Diagnostic assessment options

Before starting the sequence, you may want to conduct an initial diagnostic assessment of the children's understanding of the typical characteristics of biographies and autobiographies.

Ideas for initial diagnostic assessment options include:

- discussion about biographies / autobiographies, their purpose and form
- a brief, unsupported writing activity creating a short biography or autobiography
- practising speaking and listening skills relating to a well-known biography or autobiography
- a short reading comprehension activity / quiz on a biography or autobiography.

Cross-curricular links

KS2 Geography – Locational knowledge

Locate the world's countries, using maps to focus on Europe (including the location of Russia) and North and South America, concentrating on their environmental regions, key physical and human features, countries, and major cities.

KS2 Geography – Geographical skills and fieldwork

Use maps, atlases, globes and digital / computer mapping to locate countries.

Treasure House links

All digital and pupil book units have the same names and numbers, but different questions.

- Treasure House, Year 6, Comprehension Unit 15: Non-fiction (autobiography): 'Wild Swans'
- Treasure House, Year 6, Composition Unit 5: Biography
- Treasure House, Year 6, Composition Unit 12: Paragraphs in non-fiction
- Treasure House, Year 6, Punctuation Unit 5: Colons and semi-colons in lists
- Treasure House, Year 6, Spelling Unit 2: The suffixes -cial and -tial
- Treasure House, Year 6, Spelling Unit 12: Homophones and near-homophones (3)
- Treasure House, Year 6, Grammar Unit 3: Relative clauses
- Treasure House, Year 6, Vocabulary Unit 2: Synonyms and antonyms
- Treasure House, Year 6, Grammar Unit 2: Using the passive voice

Resources

Source texts – see Anthologies; Non-fiction planner; Editor's checklist

Year 6, Sequence 15
Non-fiction: Biographies

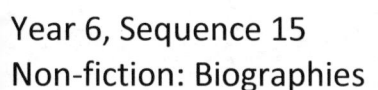

Phase 1: Enjoy and immerse

In Phase 1, the children are introduced to a biographical text about a heroic female spy in World War Two and a famous autobiographical text by the writer Jung Chang. Over several lessons, they are offered the opportunity to immerse themselves fully in the texts through comprehension and discussion activities, as well as exploring their structure and features through drama, storytelling, writing and analysis of the text.

Programmes of study: Year 6

- **Comprehension:** Continue to read and discuss an increasingly wide range of fiction, poetry, plays, non-fiction and reference books or textbooks.
- **Comprehension:** Make comparisons within and across books.
- **Comprehension:** Identify how language, structure and presentation contribute to meaning.
- **Composition:** Identify the audience for and purpose of the writing, selecting the appropriate form and using other similar writing as models for their own.
- **Vocabulary, grammar and punctuation:** Use the colon to introduce a list and semi-colons within lists.
- **Spelling:** Use words with endings which sound like /shul/ spelt -tial and -cial.

Sparking interest

Introduce the sequence by highlighting the overall Big Picture to the children: they will be working towards creating their own biographical text based on an inspirational figure, to be chosen and researched independently.

Reading and discussion

Introduce the main source text (a biography), read it with the class and check the children's understanding of the language. Discuss children's understanding of the content and structure of the extract. Then read, discuss and compare the extra source text (an autobiography) and note the similarities and differences.

Discuss the following with the children.

- Who is the text about?
- Why do you think this text has been written?
- What questions does the text answer?
- What else might a reader want to know?
- How would you describe the structure of the text?
- Is the text is a particular order?
- How would you describe the language used in the text?
- How does the text keep the reader interested?

Drama and storytelling

Use drama and oracy activities to reinforce the children's understanding of the contents and structure of the text.

Select the activities that would suit your class or fit in with your lesson timing. Encourage mixed-ability grouping for the chosen activities.

- **In the news:** In small groups, children take the role of television news presenters and present the information in the text as a television news item, for example: 'Breaking news ... Virginia Hall has died ... we look back at her life.'
- **Presentation ideas:** In pairs or small groups, children use the model text to prepare a short talk about Virginia Hall's life. They could use flash cards or hold up posters to support their talk.
- **Hot-seating Virginia Hall's friend or relative:** This activity can be done in pairs, small groups or as a whole-class situation. Nominated children or the teacher assume the role of the person who pretends they knew Virginia Hall. Questions and answers should be derived from the model text contents.

Incidental writing

A short writing activity would enhance the children's understanding of the text and characters. Select activities that you think appropriate for the abilities and interests of your class. Children could compose:

- a letter from Virginia Hall to a friend telling them about an incident from the source text
- a web-page about Virginia Hall's life
- a leaflet to promote a museum celebrating Virginia Hall's life.

Year 6, Sequence 15
Non-fiction: Biographies

Analysis

Show the Virginia Hall text to the children and discuss the contents, features and structure. Explore the following questions.

- Does the information make you want to read on and find out more? Can you explain why?
- Which tense is used? Is the text written in the first person or the third person?
- How many facts can you find?
- Is the information all factual or is there evidence of opinions given?
- How do we learn about the feelings or emotions of Virginia Hall, rather than the author?
- Can you find examples of any particularly well-chosen words?
- How are the paragraphs linked?
- Is the text in chronological order? How do you know?

Grammar: Colons and semi-colons in lists

Explain to the children that we can use colons (:) to introduce a list. We can use semi-colons (;) between list items if any of the list items are phrases, particularly phrases containing other punctuation like commas. For example: 'We bought new furniture: nice, comfy beds; a large sofa; a wooden table; and chairs.'

Support the children to create their own lists using colons and semi-colons correctly. The theme of the lists could be the achievements of Virginia Hall, or things the children have achieved in their own lives.

Phonics and spelling

Some words end in the suffixes -cial and -tial. They can be tricky to spell because they both spell the sound /shul/.

After a vowel, we usually use the ending -cial, for example, 'special'. After a consonant, we usually use the ending -tial, for example, 'torrential'.

For the following list of words, ask the children to underline the letter that comes before the -cial or -tial ending and say whether it is a vowel or consonant letter. Discuss the meaning of each word, then look it up in a dictionary to check. Then write each word in a short sentence. You could try to link the sentences to the theme of the model text, Virginia Hall's biography.

Words ending -cial / -tial: artificial, essential, confidential, crucial, beneficial, partial, confidential, facial, superficial, antisocial, potential

Review of the Big Picture

Once you have completed this phase, remind the children (or have them remind each other) of the sequence's Big Picture: they are working towards writing their own biographical text about an inspirational person of their own choosing.

Year 6, Sequence 15
Non-fiction: Biographies

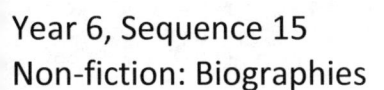

Phase 2: Capture and organise

During Phase 2, the children start to develop ideas about new content and features needed to create a class biographical text. The group and class discussions, as well as drama or short writing opportunities, offer chances for children of all abilities to contribute and use their skills towards designing a structure and planning features for the report. Their ideas can be recorded in picture, diagram or note form onto the Non-fiction planner.

Programmes of study: Year 6
- **Comprehension:** Summarise the main ideas drawn from more than one paragraph, identifying key details that support the main idea.
- **Comprehension:** Retrieve, record and present information from non-fiction.
- **Comprehension:** Participate in discussions about books that are read to them and those they can read for themselves, building on their own and others' ideas and challenging views courteously.
- **Composition:** Identify the audience for and purpose of the writing, selecting the appropriate form and using other similar writing as models for their own.
- **Composition:** Note and develop initial ideas, drawing on reading and research where necessary.
- **Spelling:** Use homophones and other words that are often confused.

Introduction

Remind the children of the Big Picture for the sequence and recap on the learning achieved through Phase 1. Recap on the typical characteristics of biographies and autobiographies as discovered in Phase 1 and reread the main source text: an extract from Virginia Hall's biography.

Discussing ideas

As a class, encourage the children to decide on the inspirational person you will use for the class biography. Children's authors or sports personalities would make a good choice as there is plenty of researchable information available about them in books or on the internet.

Once the main decision on which inspirational person to write about has been made, put the children into mixed-ability groups and encourage them to discuss and come up with suggestions in answer to the following questions. Depending on your class, you may want to give them a selection of questions or just one question per group. Bring the groups together to listen and make decisions on the structure and features to be used in the class biography.

- What information should be included in the biography?
- How will we find out the information we need?
- What photos or illustrations should be used?
- What is the purpose of the text?
- Who will be the readers of the biography? What will they want to learn?
- How will the readers be hooked at the beginning of the biography?

Drama and storytelling

Use drama and oracy activities to allow the children to explore the suggestions for their new biography. Select the activities that would suit your class or fit in with your lesson timing. Encourage mixed-ability grouping for the chosen activities.

- **Hot-seating the friend or relative of the inspirational person:** This activity can be done in pairs, small groups or as a class situation. Allow children to research the inspirational person beforehand. Encourage the children to think and, if necessary, write down their questions before the hot-seat session starts. Discuss the (imaginary) friend or relative's responses.
- **In the news:** Present the information for the new biography as a news item with children assuming the roles of news presenters and guests to be interviewed.
- **Role-play discussion:** Children work in groups to imagine they are teams of authors about to create a new series of biographical books for children. In a role-play team meeting, children should discuss as many questions as they can about biographies.

Year 6, Sequence 15
Non-fiction: Biographies

Incidental writing

Before you select any incidental writing, make sure the children are able to orally articulate the main contents of their biography. Select activities that you think appropriate for the abilities and interests of your class. Children could compose:

- a timeline of the inspirational person's life
- a magazine article
- a letter to tell a friend about the inspirational person
- an email to ask questions about the inspirational person to somebody who knew them.

Organising the class biographical text into a structure

Once the children have thoroughly explored their ideas for their class biographical text, bring them together and use their final suggestions to model how to plot the new biography in picture, diagram or note form with the help of the Non-fiction planner. Once recorded, go through the frame and ask the children if they are happy with the plan for the contents and structure. If you have not already done so, provide time for the children to conduct research on their inspirational person. They could research when and where they were born; their family; their childhood; the major events in their life; how these events affected them; how they are remembered now or what they do now; and any other important bits of information.

Phonics and spelling

Homophones are words that sound the same, but are spelt differently and have different meanings. Some homophone pairs can be told apart because one of the words is a verb and the other is a noun. For example, practice (with a **c**) is a noun meaning 'a custom or procedure' such as in the sentence: 'Prayer is a practice observed by many religions.' Practise (with an **s**) is a verb and means: 'to repeat something in order to improve' as in the sentence: 'Carl practises the piano every day.'

Ask children to look up the following pairs of homophones in the dictionary, note down the definitions, note whether they are verbs or nouns and then share their findings with groups or the class.

Homophone pairs: advice, advise; license, licence; device, devise; prophecy, prophesy

Review of the Big Picture

Once you have completed all the lessons for this phase, remind the children of the sequence's Big Picture. Recap on the learning achieved in Phase 2.

Year 6, Sequence 15
Non-fiction: Biographies

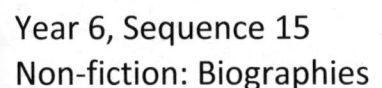

Phase 3: Collaborate and compose

This phase focuses on the teaching and learning of how to write a biographical text, with one lesson per section, so that the children are taken through the writing of the whole piece, learning new vocabulary, grammar and punctuation along the way. Children should have the planning framework from Phase 2 in front of them throughout, and should be able to revisit the original source text, the extract from Virginia Hall's biography.

> **Programmes of study: Year 6**
> - **Composition:** Identify the audience for and purpose of the writing, selecting the appropriate form and using other similar writing as a model for their own.
> - **Composition:** Note and develop initial ideas, drawing on reading and research where necessary.
> - **Composition:** Select appropriate grammar and vocabulary, understanding how such choices can change and enhance meaning.
> - **Composition:** Use a wide range of devices to build cohesion within and across paragraphs.
> - **Composition:** Use further organisational and presentational devices to structure text and to guide the reader.

Introduction

Remind the children about the Big Picture and recap on the learning in Phases 1 and 2. Explain to the children that through Phase 3 they will be learning how to write their own biographical text based on the planning and ideas in Phase 2. Discuss how the four writing lessons will be used: Lesson 1 for the inspirational person's childhood or early days; Lesson 2 to write about something that happened to the inspirational person early in their adult life or career; Lesson 3 for something that happened to them later in their life; and Lesson 4 to write about where that person is now or what they are doing now.

Lesson 1

Starter (VGP focus) – Grammar: Relative clauses

Tell children that we use relative clauses to give more information about nouns. They can start with a relative pronoun ('that', 'which', 'who' or 'whose') or a relative adverb ('where' or 'when').

Explain that we use a comma before a relative clause if the information is not vital to the meaning of the noun it describes. If it is vital, do not use a comma. We never use a comma before 'that', and always before 'which'.

Provide pairs of children with a copy of the model text and challenge them to find and highlight examples of relative clauses or relative adverbs.

Shared writing

With the children's input, model writing the first part of the biography. You may decide to use a series of sub-headings to make the contents of the biography clearer. Focus on introducing the inspirational person by writing about their birth place and date, and their very early childhood. Ask and write answers to questions such as: 'Who did they live with?' 'Which school did they attend?' 'Were they happy as a child?' 'Did anything interesting happen to them?' 'Did they have any siblings?' Discuss the contents of each paragraph and, when reading them back, ask children to imagine they have no knowledge of the person. Ask: 'Is the information explained clearly and in enough detail?' 'What questions might the reader want to ask?' The content of the biography may depend on the information available when conducting research. Discuss which pictures you might include. Use an example of a relative clause and highlight this to the children.

Independent writing

The children can now write their own first section, applying the VGP focus by including a relative clause. Some children may benefit from guided group writing or peer-paired writing at this stage.

Plenary

At the end of the lesson, invite children to share their writing with groups or the whole class. Ask the children questions to help them focus on their progress and what they have created during that lesson, for example: 'How have you made your information clear for the reader?' 'How have you

Year 6, Sequence 15
Non-fiction: Biographies

made your biography engaging as well as informative?' 'Does the order of content make logical sense?'

Lesson 2

Starter (VGP focus) – Punctuation: Using commas for clearer meaning

Remind the children that commas can be useful for making the meaning of sentences clearer. Provide children with copies of the Virginia Hall biography extract and ask them, in pairs, to find examples of commas used within sentences. Have them use mini whiteboards to create sentences of a similar structure, using the new content. As individuals read their sentences aloud, have the class make notes of correct punctuation (capital letter(s), comma(s) and a full stop) as they listen.

Shared writing

With the children's input, model writing the next part of the biography. This section could explain an event from early in the inspirational person's life or career. Ask and write answers to questions such as: 'How did they start their journey to become famous?' 'Did they have an ordinary job but write or train in their spare time?' 'Did any family events (such as house moves or bereavements) affect them?' Encourage the children to imagine being the reader of the biography and discuss what information they would want to know. Ask children to consider whether enough detail has been included. Include an example of the VGP focus on using commas to make meaning clearer, especially if you have used any long sentences.

Independent writing

The children can now write their own second section, applying the VGP focus on including commas to help clarify meaning. Some children may benefit from guided group writing or peer-paired writing at this stage.

Plenary

At the end of the lesson, invite children to share their writing with groups or the whole class. Ask the children questions to help them focus on their progress and what they have created during that lesson, for example: 'How have you made your biography engaging as well as informative for the reader?' 'How does the order of events contribute to reader interest?' 'How has your partner used commas in their clause structure?'

Lesson 3

Starter (VGP focus) – Vocabulary: Synonyms

Explain to the children that synonyms are words that have the same meanings as one another. They can be found using a dictionary or thesaurus. Ask children why they might need to find words that are similar (to improve their writing by finding a more appropriate word; to extend their vocabulary knowledge). Ask children, in pairs, to choose three sentences from the Virginia Hall biography text and use synonyms to change the vocabulary in the sentences. Discuss the impact on the sentence and on the reader.

Shared writing

With the children's input, model writing the third part of the biography. This could be the main body of information about how the inspirational person has achieved success or recognition for their hard work or dedication to their cause. Encourage children to reflect upon the qualities required to make a difference, or succeed, such as perseverance, dedication and commitment. Discuss how you can craft the language in the biography to be inspirational to the reader. Ask and write answers to questions such as: 'Were there any barriers to the inspirational person's success?' 'Did it look like they might fail?' Discuss including images: 'How might images enhance the biography?' 'Which images should be included?'

Independent writing

The children can now write their own third section, applying the VGP focus by thinking about the language they are using and whether there might be a better synonym to use. Some children may benefit from guided group writing or peer-paired writing at this stage.

Plenary

At the end of the lesson, invite children to share their writing with groups or the whole class. Ask the children questions to help them focus on their progress and what they have created during that lesson, for example: 'How have you made your writing clear for the reader?' 'How might your synonym choices be improved?' 'How have you made your biography inspirational as well as informative?' 'How does the order of content create interest for readers?'

Year 6, Sequence 15
Non-fiction: Biographies

Lesson 4

Starter (VGP focus) – Grammar: Using the passive voice

Inform children that we often use the passive voice when an action is more important than who or what did it. Write the following example on the board.

'A hunting expedition was attended by Virginia.'

Explain that the hunting expedition is the subject of the sentence. However, it did not perform the action in the sentence, the action happened to it.

Write the following three sentences on the board and ask children to change them into passive voice sentences on their mini whiteboards.

'Virginia slipped on the wet grass.'

'Her companions tore off strips of their clothing.'

'The surgeon amputated Virginia's foot.'

Shared writing

With the children's input, model writing the final part of the biography. This could be about the end of the inspirational person's life or what they are doing now. Sometimes retired sports stars go on to do lots of charity work after the peak of their career. An author might still be writing children's books until they are very elderly. Ask and write answers to questions such as: 'Where do they live now?' 'Who do they live with?' 'Are they happy?' 'Did they receive any awards for their achievements?' You could also include a conclusion giving information about where the reader could learn more information, for example, from the inspirational person's own website. Or you could conclude by relating the text to the readers' own lives by suggesting how they can follow the inspirational person's steps, for example, by joining a local sport's club.

Independent writing

The children can now write their own final section, applying the VGP focus by thinking about whether they are using the active or passive voice and the impact on the reader. Some children may benefit from guided group writing or peer-paired writing at this stage.

Plenary

At the end of the lesson, invite children to share their writing with groups or the whole class. Ask the children questions to help them focus on their progress and what they have created during that lesson, for example: 'How have you used the passive voice to present information?' 'How does the order of content support inspiration and engagement in readers?'

Rehearsing and performing

Once the children have written their biography, encourage them to present it to the class. Discuss how different or similar the biography is to the original biography about Virginia Hall.

Review of the Big Picture

Once you have completed all the lessons for this phase, remind the children of the sequence's Big Picture. Discuss what they have learned during Phase 3.

Year 6, Sequence 15
Non-fiction: Biographies

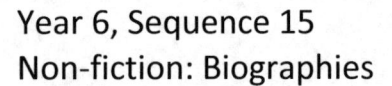

Phase 4: Write independently

This final phase brings all the children's learning and writing skills together so that they can write their own biographical text about an inspirational person of their choice. Through their writing, they will be able to utilise the different VGP focuses that they have been investigating and applying to their shared writing in the previous phases.

> **Programmes of study: Year 6**
> - **Composition:** Select appropriate grammar and vocabulary, understanding how such choices can change and enhance meaning.
> - **Composition:** Use a wide range of devices to build cohesion within and across paragraphs.
> - **Composition:** Use further organisational and presentational devices to structure text and to guide the reader.
> - **Composition:** Assess the effectiveness of their own and others' writing and suggest improvements.
> - **Composition:** Propose changes to grammar and vocabulary to enhance effects and clarify meaning.
> - **Composition:** Proofread for spelling and punctuation errors.
> - **Composition:** Perform their own compositions, using appropriate intonation, volume and movement so that meaning is clear.

Introduction

Introduce this phase by highlighting the overall Big Picture to the children. Recap on learning and progress through Phases 1–3 and explain that in Phase 4 they will be applying their learning to write their own biographical text independently. Discuss and list examples of features that should be included in the biography such as chronological order, use of the third person and past tense, life events, description, and subheadings. Discuss and list potential inspirational people relevant to the children and their current classroom learning.

Writing

Give each child a Non-fiction planner and instruct them to start planning and writing each section of their own biographical text. Display the class planning structure and a copy of the model text, the extract from Virginia Hall's biography, for reference. All the children should be encouraged to try to write independently to the best of their ability. Ask open questions such as: 'How will you relate the information to the readers' own experience?' 'How will you hook the reader to read more?' Avoid telling children what to write. Some children may benefit from guided composition. Focus on perseverance and resilience in their independent application.

Proofreading and redrafting

Have the children proofread their work periodically as they write. Proofreading and improvement without support means that the writing may happen over a few lessons. Offer the children the Editor's checklist or create your own checklist that includes the VGP and spelling focuses covered throughout the sequence. Highlight the importance of redrafting, linking their efforts to the overall Big Picture.

Self- and peer-assessment

Encourage the children to take time to self-assess their own writing as well as assess that of others in their group. Offer them a set of self-assessment questions, such as: 'How does the biography explain the information clearly to the reader?' 'Which features have worked particularly well and why?' 'What could be improved next time?' 'Which parts were challenging and what helped?'

Rehearsing and performing

Once the children have written their biographical text about an inspirational person, encourage them to present it to the class. Discuss how different or similar the biography is to the original model text, Virginia Hall's biography. Encourage the children to feed back on one another's writing and presentations.

Final review of the Big Picture

Individually or with partners, have children reflect on what they have learned from this sequence and what they will apply in their future writing.

Year 6, Sequence template

Use this template to plan your own teaching sequence.

Sequence title

Approximate duration:

Big Picture

Phase 1: Enjoy and immerse

Phase 2: Capture and organise

Phase 3: Collaborate and compose

Phase 4: Write independently

Main source text

Spoken outcome

Extra source texts

Writing outcome

Background knowledge

Prior knowledge

© HarperCollins *Publishers* 2015

Year 6, Sequence template

Diagnostic assessment options

Treasure House links

Cross-curricular links

Resources

Year 6, Sequence template

Phase 1: Enjoy and immerse

Programmes of study: Year 5
- Comprehension:
- Comprehension:
- Comprehension:
- Comprehension:
- Composition:
- Vocabulary, grammar and punctuation:
- Spelling:

Sparking interest

Drama and storytelling

Reading and discussion

Year 6, Sequence template

Incidental writing

Phonics and spelling

Analyse

Review of the Big Picture

Grammar

Year 6, Sequence template

Phase 2: Capture and organise

Programmes of study: Year 5
- Comprehension:
- Comprehension:
- Composition:
- Composition:
- Spelling:

Introduction   **Drama and storytelling**

Discussing ideas

Year 6, Sequence template

Incidental writing

Phonics and spelling

Organising into a structure

Review of the Big Picture

Year 6, Sequence template

Phase 3: Collaborate and compose

Programmes of study: Year 5
- Composition:

- Composition:

- Composition:

- Composition:

- Composition:

Introduction   **Independent writing**

Lesson 1

Starter (VGP focus)

Daily plenary

Shared writing

© HarperCollins *Publishers* 2015

Year 6, Sequence template

Lesson 2
Starter (VGP focus)

Shared writing

Independent writing

Daily plenary

Lesson 3
Starter (VGP focus)

Shared writing

Independent writing

Daily plenary

Year 6, Sequence template

Lesson 4
Starter (VGP focus)

Rehearsing and performing

Shared writing

Review of the Big Picture

Independent writing

Daily plenary

Year 6, Sequence template

Phase 4: Independent writing

Programmes of study: Year 5
- Composition:

- Composition:

- Composition:

- Composition:

- Composition:

Introduction

Self- and peer-assessment

Writing

Rehearsing and performing

Proofreading and redrafting

Final reflection on learning

© HarperCollins *Publishers* 2015

Editor's checklist

I / we have checked that:

Purpose, audience and language choices:

- [ ] sentences make sense and there are no missing words
- [ ] the writing fits the intended purpose and audience throughout
- [ ] dialogue has not been over-used in narrative
- [ ] style is appropriately formal / informal in non-fiction
- [ ] style is appropriately personal / impersonal in non-fiction

Punctuation:

- [ ] capital letters and full stops (question marks and exclamation marks) are used correctly
- [ ] commas are never used to join separate sentences
- [ ] apostrophes have been used correctly

Grammar:

- [ ] appropriate verb tenses have been used throughout
- [ ] the verb in each sentence agrees with the subject

Spelling:

- [ ] correct spelling of familiar words has been used
- [ ] suffixes have been spelt correctly

Handwriting:

- [ ] handwriting is legible and well-presented

Personal targets:

- [ ] _____
- [ ] _____

© HarperCollins *Publishers* 2015

My writing checklist

Name: _____

Title: _____

Writing checklist	✓	✗	Comments
I can identify the audience for and purpose of my piece of writing.			
I have selected the appropriate form and used similar writing as a model for my own.			
I have used appropriate grammar and vocabulary.			
In narratives I have described settings, characters and atmosphere, and integrated dialogue to convey character and advance the action.			
I have used a wide range of devices to build cohesion within and across paragraphs.			
I have used organisational and presentational devices to structure text and guide the reader.			
I have assessed the effectiveness of my own and others' writing.			
I have proposed changes to vocabulary, grammar and punctuation to enhance effects and clarify meaning.			
I have consistently used the correct tense throughout my piece of writing.			
I have used correct subject and verb agreement when using the singular and plural.			
I have distinguished between the language of speech and writing and I have chosen the appropriate register.			
I have proofread my work for spelling and punctuation errors.			

© HarperCollins *Publishers* 2015

Story planner

Use this planning sheet to help you think about the story you will write.

> What is the purpose of the story? How do you want readers to feel?

> Who are the characters? Where is the setting? What tense or narrative style will you use?

> What will happen in the opening section? How will you hook readers so they want to read more?

> What will happen in the main body of the story? What will the dilemma be? How will you keep the story progressing? How will the characters feel?

> How will the story end? Will it be resolved or left open? Will there be a twist? How will the characters feel? How will the reader feel?

© HarperCollins *Publishers* 2015

Non-fiction planner

Use this planning sheet to help you think about the text you will write.

What is the purpose of the text? How do you want readers to respond to the text?

What are the characteristics of this text type that you will need to include? Is it formal or informal? Personal or impersonal?

What will you include in the introduction section? How will the reader be engaged to read more?

What will you include in the main body of the text?

How will the text conclude? Do you need to plan for any specific illustrations or diagrams?

© HarperCollins *Publishers* 2015

Poetry planner

Use this planning sheet to help you think about the poem you will write.

> What is the purpose of the poem?
> How do you want to make readers feel?
> What is it about?

> What will the structure of your poem be like? How many stanzas? Will it have a set rhythm or amount of syllables per line? What will be the theme for each stanza?

> What poetic devices will you include?
> Will you include any similes, metaphors, alliteration or onomatopoeia?
> Note down ideas for vocabulary

© HarperCollins *Publishers* 2015

Year 6: Challenge questions

Comprehension

These Challenge questions can be used in conjunction with the Treasure House Pupil Book units. They provide an additional activity to stretch children and give them the opportunity to apply their learning in a more challenging context.

Unit 1

The extract mentions a conversation between Amy and her mum about what Amy should call Richard. Write the part of the story that features that conversation. Is Richard there too? Think carefully about how you can show the characters' feelings and opinions through the things they say and the way they respond to one another.

Unit 2

Think carefully about the moral of the story. Write your own short story based on this moral or a similar one, but use human characters instead of animal characters. What might your main character learn during your story?

Unit 3

With a partner, improvise a TV advert for Strobers trainers. What information will you include? Will you show a scene featuring people wearing them, or might a presenter be talking straight to the camera? Create a storyboard for your advert, and write it as a playscript.

Unit 4

Do some research using the internet or reference books about climate change. Then read the extract again. Using your new knowledge, write an email to Josh and his grandad about what you think. What could Josh tell Pete? What do you think he should include in his project?

Unit 5

Imagine you have a naughty younger brother or sister. Write a poem similar to the one in the extract, trying to persuade them to go to bed at night. What exaggerated things will you say to try and make them do what you're asking?

Unit 6

Do some research using the internet or reference books about Native American ('American Indian') stories and legends. Choose one legend. Write the legend as a poem in the same style and rhythm as the extract.

Unit 7

Turn your story about what happens when the highwayman returns into a poem, with the same style and structure as the extract.

Unit 8

Imagine that the water shortage has become even worse. Write a news report urging people to take water saving measures, referring to the extract for information and ideas.

Unit 9

Research and write a fact file about cold deserts. Draw and label a world map to show where they are, and add a diagram to help you to explain how they are formed. Use a heading and sub-headings, and add one new section. Perhaps you could research whether any wildlife lives in cold deserts. If so, how does it survive?

Year 6: Challenge questions

Unit 10

Using your mind map and your diary entry for ideas, make notes about positive and negative ways that you could write about summer. Using the poems in the extract as guides, write two poems about summer, one from the perspective of someone who enjoys it and one from the perspective of someone who is unable to enjoy it. Try to use a simile, a metaphor and an example of personification. Try to think about how changing your rhythm might affect one line's meaning.

Unit 11

Talk with a partner about the differences between 'literal' meanings and 'figurative' meanings. Use a dictionary if you need to. Stories like the one in the extract can create interesting effects by using both literal and figurative meanings. Think of a phrase or saying that could have both kinds of meaning. If you like, you can use the saying 'time flies'. Write a silly short story that uses both the literal and the figurative meaning of your phrase or saying.

Unit 12

As a class, discuss all the clues you have gathered that might help you to guess what has happened. Make a class mind map to note down all the facts, deductions and ideas. What do most people think has happened? Does the evidence support this?

Once an agreement has been reached, work alone to add a scene to the story in which Roberta asks Mother some direct questions and Mother answers them in the way the class has decided is most likely.

Unit 13

Rewrite the events from the extract from the perspective of one of the little people. How did you or one of your fellows discover this giant? Why did you tie him down? How did you try to communicate with him?

Unit 14

Write the next scene of this playscript. If you like, you could improvise it in groups first. Think carefully about how the characters would act: can Compere Lapin get out of being burned by the king's guards? Might he and Compere Tig start to work together, or will they keeping tricking one another? Remember to include the features of play scripts, such as stage directions and who says what.

Unit 15

Write a short autobiography of your life so far. Make sure you have everything noted down in the correct order before you begin to write, and try to think about how you could link your earliest memories with who you are and how you live now.

Year 6: Challenge questions

Composition

These Challenge questions appear at the end of 'Now try these' in the Treasure House Pupil Book units. They provide an additional activity to stretch children and give them the opportunity to apply their learning in a more challenging context.

Unit 1

Authors often spend a long time researching the topic they are writing about to help them get the details of the story right and to help them decide exactly what it is they want to say. Spend time researching your topic and find out as much as you can about it. Go back to your story plan and check that all your ideas still work with what you know now. Make any changes you need to and add any ideas you have had as a result of your research. When you are ready, write a scene from your story. It can be the beginning, or any other scene that is particularly clear in your mind.

Unit 2

A blurb is a short description of a book written to help people decide whether or not they want to read the book. Most blurbs summarise key information about the book such as settings, characters, themes and a small part of the plot. But the main aim of a blurb is to persuade people to read the book, so the blurb cannot give away too much information. Choose a book that you have enjoyed reading and write its blurb. Summarise the key information and try to make the book sound really appealing. What information can you summarise about it without giving too much away?

Unit 3

Using your notes and ideas, write the playscript of the beginning of your chosen scene. Remember to follow the rules for correctly for writing and setting out a playscript:

- Write the details of where the scene is set at the beginning.
- Don't use speech marks to show who is speaking.
- Write a name followed by a colon to show who speaks each line.
- Start a new line each time a character starts to speak.
- Write stage directions to tell the performers what to do.

Unit 4

Write a descriptive paragraph, using as many examples of personification as you can, on one of these subjects:

- a moonlit night
- a storm at sea
- a forest fire

Unit 5

Now write your autobiography. Remember to keep chronological order, to write in the first person and the past tense, and to organise your autobiography into paragraphs. Include lots of facts about your life and you can include your thoughts and feelings about your life too.

Unit 6

Write a science report for your experiment. Set it out like Kate's science report: use sub-headings for each section; present the equipment in a bullet-pointed list; write the method as a numbered set of instructions; present the results in a table (if appropriate); write the aim and conclusion in full sentences.

Year 6: Challenge questions

Unit 7

Using the ideas and notes from your planning, write the full newspaper report. Describe the event as it happened and include quotes from the people who were there.

Unit 8

Now write your humorous story. Use the notes you made previously and pay attention to the techniques you use to make it funny. Once you have finished, test your story on a partner. Give it to them to read or read it to them. Do they think it's funny? Were there any bits that didn't work? Make any improvements and then test it again on someone else.

Unit 9

Using your notes, write your poem on the theme of loneliness. When it is written, 'perform' your poem by recording it or reading it to a partner. Take feedback from your partner and do the same for them and their poem. If you have recorded your poem, listen back to it. What have you done well? Could you improve anything?

Unit 10

Plan and write Chapter 4, the final chapter. Plan the ending, deciding what type of narrative ending you want to use. Read it through, checking for effect. Is there anything you would like to improve?

Unit 11

Write your diary entry about the time you made this item of food. Remember that a diary account will:

- describe the event;
- record your thoughts and feelings at the time;
- be written in the past tense;
- contain connecting words and phrases.

Unit 12

Using your plan, write an information text about your chosen hobby or sport. Use the checklist you composed to make sure you are using sections and paragraphs correctly.

Unit 13

Write your own short story. Your paragraphs must structure the story. Use your checklist to help you. Choose one of these titles or use one of your own:

- The lost purse
- The match
- Aliens in the High Street!

Unit 14

Write the leaflet, referring to the notes you made earlier. Remember, you want people to visit Morocco so use persuasive language and tell them enticing things. Use organisational features to format the information you're providing. Think carefully about how you present the different types of information. Try to make your leaflet as reader-friendly and usable as possible.

Year 6: Challenge questions

Unit 15

Think of a story you have read, watched or listened to where you really didn't like the ending. Write a review of the story, explaining exactly why you didn't like the ending. Here are some questions to help you decide why you didn't like it:

- Did the ending make sense?
- Do you think it was planned well enough?
- Did it seem false or not fit with the rest of the story somehow?
- Was it too sudden, abrupt or just not really an ending at all?
- Was it too complicated? Did too much happen at once?
- Was the problem that questions were left unanswered and loose ends not tied up? If so, do you think that was deliberate or a mistake made by the author?
- Is it just a matter of personal taste?

Year 6: Challenge questions

Vocabulary, Grammar and Punctuation

These Challenge questions can be used in conjunction with the Treasure House Pupil Book units. They provide an additional activity to stretch children and give them the opportunity to apply their learning in a more challenging context.

Vocabulary Unit 1

Copy out a passage from a book you are reading. Then, using a thesaurus, go through the passage and change as many words as you can. How have your changes affected the piece of text?

Vocabulary Unit 2

Write a list of ten ordinary words and then swap your list with a partner. Use a thesaurus to find a synonym for each word that is more unusual, interesting or powerful. Then find an antonym for each word. Present your findings in a leaflet, poster or presentation to help others to learn this new vocabulary.

Vocabulary Unit 3

Pretend you have been asked by a sportswear company to try out the latest design of trainers with some friends. Use both formal and informal language to write them a short, positive review that features quotes from children who have tried the trainers.

Grammar Unit 1

Write a formal letter using as many examples of the subjunctive form as you can. Ideas you could include are:

- The situation demands that …
- I request that …
- It is desirable that …
- It is vital that …
- If I …
- Suppose we …

Grammar Unit 2

Rewrite a simple story that you know well, such as a fairy tale, using only passive sentences.

Grammar Unit 3

Write a paragraph describing a club you attend or a sport you play. Use four different relative clauses to give lots of detailed information about your activity. You could write about what it is, where it is, who goes there, when you attend and about any special events.

Grammar Unit 4

Write three short paragraphs on the topic of birthdays. Show the links between your paragraphs by using repetition and connecting adverbials.

Punctuation Unit 1

Think up a sentence that changes its meaning if you change the position of the comma, or remove the comma completely. Can you explain the different meanings?

Year 6: Challenge questions

Punctuation Unit 2

Think up a sentence that changes its meaning if you change the position of the hyphen, or remove the hyphen completely. Can you explain the different meanings?

Punctuation Unit 3

Write a short paragraph that would begin an adventure story of your own, using parenthesis marked in different ways.

Punctuation Unit 4

Write a short story about a group of people making their way through a forest on a mission. Use colons, semi-colons and dashes to join some sentences, instead of separating them with full stops and capital letters.

Punctuation Unit 5

Write a list of your own to tell the reader about a club or hobby you attend, perhaps explaining equipment you need or activities you do. Make sure you use: an introduction with a colon; items that are phrases, containing commas; and semi-colons at the ends of your items.

Punctuation Unit 6

Use bullet-pointed lists to make notes for a book review. Ideas for your lists could include 'Things I liked', 'Things I didn't like', 'Characters', 'Settings', 'Events' and 'Features'.

Year 6: Challenge questions

Spelling

These Challenge questions can be used in conjunction with the Treasure House Pupil Book units. They provide an additional activity to stretch children and give them the opportunity to apply their learning in a more challenging context.

Unit 1

Look up the related noun for each adjective and then write the meaning of each word.

1. tenacious
2. audacious
3. capacious
4. voracious
5. ferocious
6. anxious

Can you find any more nouns and adjectives that follow this pattern?

Unit 2

Change these adjectives to adverbs by adding the suffix **-ly** after **-cial** or **-tial**. Then use them to write sentences.

crucial
partial
official
special
potential
essential
martial
substantial
beneficial
social

Unit 3

There are many words that do not follow the rules for adding the suffixes **-ant**, **-ance / -ancy**, **-ent**, **-ence / -ency**. Think of ways to remember how to spell these words.

grievance, inheritance, audience, sentence, patience, efficiency

Unit 4

Using an etymological dictionary, investigate the origins of the suffixes **-able** and **-ible**.

Unit 5

Investigate the suffixes **-ed**, **-ing**, **-ence**, **-ee** and **-al**. How does each suffix change the meaning of the verb **refer**?

Unit 6

Use a dictionary to find words that have one meaning with a hyphen and another meaning without. Using the words you have found, write pairs of sentences to show their different uses.

Unit 7

ei does not always spell the **ee** sound. Investigate how many different sounds the spelling pattern **ei** makes. Find examples, make a list and then group the words according to the sound **ei** makes.

Year 6: Challenge questions

Unit 8

Devise a rhyming game for younger children to help them learn how to spell words containing the letter-string **ough**.

Unit 9

There are many words containing 'silent' letters. Use a dictionary to make a list of as many as you can. Sort the words you find according which letter is silent. What patterns can you find?

Unit 10

How would you help someone to remember how to spell these words:

desert, dessert, wary, weary, affect, effect, complement, compliment, precede, proceed

Are there any clues in the way the words are pronounced? Read them aloud and work out some helpful suggestions.

Unit 11

Use a dictionary to research homographs. What is a homograph? Which words in this unit are homographs? How many more homographs can you find?

Unit 12

Read aloud the sentences you have written. Are there any pairs of words where the pronunciation is slightly different? How might this help you to remember the spelling? Make up a rule for this.

Unit 13

Some people make up mnemonics (such as songs, rhymes, stories or phrases) to help them remember how to spell words. What mnemonics could you write to help other children remember how to spell the difference between these words?

1. **aisle** and **isle**
2. **principle** and **principal**
3. **draft** and **draught**

Unit 14

Some people make up mnemonics (such as songs, rhymes, stories or phrases) to help them remember how to spell words. What mnemonic could you write to help other children remember how to spell any of these homophone pairs?

whose, who's; ascent, assent; descent, dissent; father, farther; morning, mourning; steal, steel; bridal, bridle; profit, prophet

Year 6: Challenge question answers

Comprehension

Unit 1
Open-ended question: Look for relevance to task, consistency of characters and theme, imagination, presentation and correct spelling, grammar and punctuation.

Unit 2
Open-ended question: Look for a story that appropriately illustrates this or a similar moral. The story should feature humans and a lesson learned.

Unit 3
Open-ended question: Look for relevance to task, development of characters and theme, imagination and presentation. In the storyboards, look for awareness of how scenes may look on TV screens. In the written scripts, look for playscript features such as layout and stage directions.

Unit 4
Open-ended question: Look for relevance to task, consistency of characters and theme, interesting research facts, email style, imagination and presentation.

Unit 5
Open-ended question: Look for relevance to task, consistency of characters and theme, imagination, presentation and similarities with the form of the extract.

Unit 6
Open-ended question: Look for relevance to task, sensitivity to subject matter, consistency of characters and theme, imagination, presentation and poetic form with the same style and rhythm as the extract.

Unit 7
Open-ended question: Look for relevance to task, consistency of characters and theme, imagination, presentation and poetic form with the same style and structure as the extract.

Unit 8
Open-ended question: Look for relevance to task, imagination, presentation and use of newspaper report conventions as demonstrated by the extract.

Unit 9
Open-ended question: Look for relevance to task, consistency of theme, imagination, presentation, interesting and accurate facts about cold deserts, a labelled world map, a diagram explaining formation, a heading, subheadings and one new section. The suggested topic for the new section (wildlife living in cold deserts) may or may not be used.

Unit 10
Open-ended question: Look for relevance to task, development of characters and theme, imagination, presentation, two distinct perspectives, a simile, a metaphor, an example of personification and, possibly, a change in rhythm that affects a line's meaning.

Unit 11
Open-ended question: Look for relevance to task, consistency of theme, imagination, presentation and good understanding of the two different meanings of the phrase or saying chosen (e.g. flying = going quickly / travelling through the air). The saying suggested, 'time flies', may or may not be used.

Unit 12
Open-ended question: Look for good clues spotted and reasonable deductions made (see answer to 'Now Try These' Question 4). In the written scenes, look for relevance to task, consistency of characters and theme, imagination, presentation and use of the class decision.

Unit 13
Open-ended question: Look for relevance to task, consistency of characters and theme, imagination, presentation and attempts to judge the events of the extract from the perspective of the little people.

Unit 14
Open-ended question: Look for relevance to task, consistency of characters and theme, imagination and presentation. In the written scripts, look for playscript features such as layout and stage directions.

Unit 15
Open-ended question: Look for relevance to task, coverage of the basic facts of children's lives, a chronological order, imagination and presentation. Autobiographies could include date and place of birth, family life, childhood and schooling, hobbies, achievements, plans, feelings and any life-changing events. Look specifically for ways children have tried to link their earliest memories with who they are and how they live now.

Composition

Unit 1
Children research the topic they are writing about to check their facts and make improvements. Look for a scene (any scene) from the story planned previously. Look for evident attempts to gain the reader's sympathy, address the chosen topic and / or to inspire the reader to take action. Reward creativity, good writing and language skills.

Year 6: Challenge question answers

Unit 2
The blurb should successfully summarise key information about the book such as settings, characters, themes and a little bit of the plot, but should not give too much away and should aim to persuade the reader to read the book. Reward creativity, good writing and language skills.

Unit 3
Children write a playscript adaption of a scene from a chosen book using the planning from the previous section. The work must correctly follow the conventions of a script. Look for correctly formatted dialogue, actions or feelings successfully converted into stage directions, and an accurate setting description. Reward fidelity to the original extract, attention to detail, creative problem solving and usability of the script for staging a play.

Unit 4
Children should write a descriptive paragraph on the chosen subject which uses personification correctly. Reward particularly effective examples.

Unit 5
Look for a completed autobiography written in the first person and the past tense, in paragraphs, and which describes events in chronological order. Autobiographies can include thoughts, feelings and opinions about facts and events. Reward good writing and language skills.

Unit 6
Look for the same science experiment written as a science report following the format of the example text: using the same subheadings for each section; presenting the equipment in a bullet point list; writing the method as a numbered set of instructions; presenting the results in a table (if appropriate); writing the aim and conclusion in full sentences.

Unit 7
Look for a full newspaper report based on the previous planning. Reports should include details on the questions: What? Where? When? Why? Who? They should also include a headline and an interview with a quote. Reward creativity, good writing and language skills.

Unit 8
Look for a completed humorous story based on previous planning. Reward creativity, promising ideas, good writing and language skills, evident attempts at humour and anything that is genuinely funny. Allow for the fact that humour is very subjective. Children should test their stories on a partner, discuss what worked and make improvements.

Unit 9
Children should write a completed poem on the theme of loneliness using the previous planning. Reward creativity, use of poetic language and devices, good poetic structure, good writing skills and interesting, original and / or sensitive treatment of the subject.

Unit 10
Look for a completed final chapter. Children should decide what type of narrative ending they want to use. Reward creativity, good writing and language skills. Children should read through their first draft, checking for effect and then making improvements.

Unit 11
Children should write a diary entry describing the time they made the item of food they have written instructions for. Diary entries should describe the event; record their thoughts and feelings at the time; be written in the past tense; and contain connecting words and phrases. Reward good description, attention to detail, and good writing and language skills.

Unit 12
Look for an information text on the chosen hobby or sport using the planning from the previous section. Reward good organisation of information, knowledge of the subject, attention to detail, and good writing and language skills.

Unit 13
Look for a narrative where the storyline has been organised into paragraphs. It should be clear as to why there is a change in paragraph. Reward creativity, good structure and good writing and language skills.

Unit 14
Look for a tourist information leaflet using the planning done previously. The leaflet should aim to persuade people to visit Morocco. It should include organisational features and aim to be reader-friendly and usable. Reward good gathering, organising and presenting of information and good writing and language skills.

Unit 15
Children should write a review of a bad story ending of their choice. They should consider various questions to determine exactly why they didn't like the ending and then write about why the ending didn't work for them. Better answers will be more objective in their reasons rather than relying entirely on personal taste. Reward good analytical skills, evident understanding of good story structure, good structure of the review, good writing and language skills.

Year 6: Challenge question answers

Vocabulary, Grammar and Punctuation

Vocabulary Unit 1
Children write a short passage from a book they have read and substitute some of the words with synonyms. Check the sentences have been written with correct punctuation and make sense. The changes may have affected the text in several ways for example, by making it more formal or informal. It may also have made it seem more contemporary or old-fashioned.

Vocabulary Unit 2
Children write down any words that are synonyms or antonyms. Check their posters, leaflets and presentations display their results correctly, for example: justify > excuse memorise> forget.

Vocabulary Unit 3
Children write a short review, which includes formal and informal language with quotes from children about a new range of trainers. The quotes are likely to include informal language such as contractions and slang and other features associated with informal spoken language. The body or the review will be more formal.

Grammar Unit 1
Children write a formal letter using the subjunctive in set phrases. Check they have used the correct subjunctive form and that the letter makes sense and has correct letter format.

Grammar Unit 2
Children write a fairy tale or other simple story with a clear structure. Check that they have only used passive sentences throughout.

Grammar Unit 3
Children write a paragraph describing a club or a sport. Check they have used four different relative clauses correctly to give more detailed information.

Grammar Unit 4
Children write three short paragraphs on the topic of birthdays. Check they have linked the paragraphs by using repetition and connecting adverbials.

Punctuation Unit 1
Children think of a sentence that changes its meaning if the position of the comma is changed, or removed completely. They should be able to explain the difference, e.g. *Martha enjoys cooking plants and her cat.* (Martha actually cooks her family and pet) compared with *Martha enjoys cooking, plants and her cat.* (Martha enjoys these three things)

Punctuation Unit 2
Children think of a sentence that changes its meaning if the position of the hyphen is changed, or removed completely. They should be able to explain the difference, e.g. *There's a man eating chicken in the restaurant.* (A man is eating a chicken in a restaurant) compared *There's a man-eating chicken in the restaurant.* (There's a dangerous chicken, which eats men in the restaurant.)

Punctuation Unit 3
Children write a short paragraph that would begin an adventure story. Check they have used parenthesis in at least three different ways: e.g. brackets, dashes or commas (clauses).

Punctuation Unit 4
Children write a short story. Check the structure and punctuation. In particular, make sure they have used colons, semi-colons and dashes to join some sentences together.

Punctuation Unit 5
Children write a list about a club or hobby. Make sure they have used: an introduction with a colon; items that are phrases, containing commas; and semi-colons at the ends of items.

Punctuation Unit 6
Children use bullet-pointed lists to make notes for a book review. Check they have included correctly formed bullet-pointed lists for: 'Things I liked', 'Things I didn't like', 'Characters', 'Settings', 'Events' and 'Features'.

Year 6: Challenge question answers

Spelling

Unit 1
1. tenacity
2. audacity
3. capacity
4. voracity
5. ferocity
6. anxiety

Children may find more nouns that follow the same pattern. A dictionary would support children in their investigation.

Unit 2
Accept sentences with a correctly spelt adverb that follows the rule -ly after -cial or -tial used in the correct context. A dictionary would support children in their investigation.

Unit 3
Children should invent strategies for remembering how to spell grievance, inheritance, audience, sentence, patience and efficiency correctly.

Unit 4

Challenge answer

The suffix -able comes from French -able or Latin -abilis, while the ending -ible comes from French -ible or Latin -ibilis.

Unit 5
Children should investigate the suffixes -ed, -ing, -ence, -ee and -al and their impact on the verb refer. Children may recognise that -ed changes the verb to past tense, -ing changes the verb to present tense, -ence and -al change the verb to a noun, and -ee denotes the person receiving the action of the verb.

Unit 6
Children should find more words that mean one thing with a hyphen and another thing without. Then they should use them in sentences. Check that spellings and contexts are correct. A dictionary would support children in their investigation.

Unit 7
Children should investigate how many different sounds the spelling pattern **ei** makes. Children may find: beige, eight, neigh, neighbour, rein, veil, vein, weight, height, heist, heir.

Unit 8
Accept any rhyming game which would help children to spell this family of words. Year 6 children could try out their rhyming games on younger children.

Unit 9
There are many words in the English language with 'silent' letters in for children to find.

Unit 10
Accept any relevant strategies for remembering the difference between the homophone pairs.

Unit 11
Homographs are words that are spelt the same but are not pronounced the same or have the same meaning. The homograph in this unit is **lead**, which can mean a type of metal (noun), a leash (noun) or to guide (present tense verb) depending on the pronunciation and context. Children may also note that **guest** and **herd** function as both nouns and verbs and that **past** can function as a preposition. There are many more homographs for children to find.

Unit 12
Check that they children have head the slight difference in pronunciation and understand the terms **noun** and **verb**.

Unit 13
Accept any relevant mnemonics for remembering the differences between the homophone pairs **aisle** and **isle**, **principle** and **principal**, and **draft** and **draught**.

Unit 14
Accept any relevant mnemonics for remembering the differences between any of the homophone pairs.

Year 6: Pupil Book answers

Comprehension

Unit 1

Get started

The children are asked to use quotes where they can.

1. For example, Amy didn't want to call Richard "Step-Daddy" because she thought it "sounded daft". [1 mark]
2. For example, Mum said she ironed the nappies because "it looks... nicer" (and that she "can see them", even if no-one else can). [1 mark]
3. For example, Amy's sister is called Debra. [1 mark]
4. For example, Amy has hurt her knee: there is an "elastic bandage around Amy's knee". [1 mark]
5. For example, The stretchy part of Amy's socks were giving way "because she kept tugging at them during lessons". [1 mark]
6. For example, Debra "turned her ankle on the beam on Wednesday. She came down too heavy". [1 mark]
7. For example, Amy's teacher is called Miss Oxley. [1 mark]
8. For example, Amy's mum suggests she write a note to the teacher to request that Amy be let "off games and that for the start of next week", because she thinks Amy should "be careful" as she wants her knee to be "right for Thursday". [1 mark]

Try these

The children's answers may be subjective but should be in their own words and well justified, using evidence from either the text or the children's own experiences.

1. Answers could detect that Amy's mum saying "You never called your dad Michael, did you?" suggests that Amy's dad and Richard are or should be equals in Amy's eyes. Amy's dad, Michael, has died; this is therefore a particularly sensitive subject for Amy. [2 marks]
2. Answers could suggest that Amy's mum may not have liked Amy calling Richard by his name because it seems too impersonal for someone who is a family member, or too like a friend for someone who has become a parental figure. [2 marks]
3. Answers should infer that Amy's sister is a baby as the extract refers to her mum ironing nappies. [2 marks]
4. Answers could detect Amy's sense of duty, formality and awkward politeness towards Richard; the idea that she may not feel (or want to feel) comfortable enough to be more relaxed around him; and her consciousness that her mum is judging (and may criticise) the way she behaves towards him. [2 marks]
5. Answers should refer to Amy's need to practise something in games and her teacher's assertion that she's "the best chance we've got if Debra isn't better". They should conclude that Amy's leg needs to recover for a sports competition on Thursday, perhaps gymnastics (Debra "turned her ankle on the beam"). [2 marks]
6. Answers should refer to Amy's mum's sharp response to the suggestion Amy's leg hurt ("'What do you mean, not too bad?' Mum said, quickly. 'Has it been hurting?'"), her command that Amy "be careful" and her offer to write Amy an off-games note in the run-up to the event on Thursday. [2 marks]
7. Answers could speculate that Richard seems perplexed about Amy kneeling in assembly, and that this question shows his surprise at the idea she prays at school. They could also suggest that the wording of the question shows that Richard was either too surprised to structure it formally, or that he is joking about the idea of kneeling to pray. [2 marks]
8. Answers could refer to the tension between Amy and Richard; the presence of a baby; Amy's injury and the importance of the event happening on Thursday; and perhaps the continued feelings of loss regarding her first husband. [2 marks]

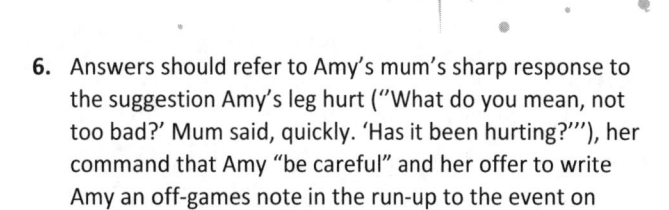

Now try these

The children's answers will be subjective but should be well justified, where appropriate.

1. Answers could refer to Amy's discomfort with Richard, her feelings about her mother's unfairness; her habit of tugging at her socks during class (perhaps revealing a lack of academic interest); her talent at sport and / or her commitment to her team. [3 marks max]
2. Answers could include the image of Amy's mum repeatedly ironing nappies and socks; the memory of her snapping "unreasonably" at Amy about what she calls Richard; the words / phrases: "Mum did not like her calling him Richard", "Mum was folding the napkins into even smaller squares", "Mum would retort", "Mum was looking at her socks but not saying anything", "'What do you mean, not too bad?' Mum said, quickly'", or the sarcasm of "'What did you do in assembly, then?' Mum demanded, unfolding the ironing board. 'Stand on one leg?'". [3 marks max]
3. Answers could refer to Richard teasing Amy's mum about ironing the nappies; his assertion that "Life's too short" to worry about them; his apparent concern for Amy's knee; his surprise at her praying at school; and / or the jokey way he questions her about it. [3 marks max]
4. Answers should acknowledge that the tense of this section is different (it is conditional rather than past): "Richard would ask, sometimes", "Mum would say", "Mum would retort", "Richard would be looking at the laundry basket", "he would say". This contrasts with the next section: "Now he was looking at the elastic bandage around Amy's knee." [3 marks max]
5. Open-ended question: Look for relevance to task, consistency of character and theme, imagination and presentation. [3 marks max]

Year 6: Pupil Book answers

Unit 2

Get started

The children are asked to use quotes where they can.

1. For example, The small pool is described as "a still, muddy pool, stony and weedy, and surrounded by scraggy trees and bushes". [1 mark]
2. For example, The little big fish "kept himself to himself. He was aloof and haughty whenever the others came near him". [1 mark]
3. For example, The older fish "was becoming irritated by the big fish's constant gripes". [1 mark]
4. For example, The little big fish decided he would allow himself "to be swept down into the big river and out of this little pool". [1 mark]
5. For example, The little big fish needed rain and floods for his plan to work. [1 mark]
6. For example, When he reached the river, the little big fish sighed "with anticipation of the good life that lay ahead". [1 mark]
7. For example, The little big fish got away from the black and white fish because he "wedged himself into a crevice in the bank, just out of their reach". [1 mark]
8. For example, The little big fish got back to the small pool "with a leap … into the expanse of flood-water" and then by swimming "against the swirling torrent". [1 mark]

Try these

The children's answers may be subjective but should be in their own words and well justified, using evidence from either the text or the children's own experiences.

1. Answers should explain the description that the little big fish "kept himself to himself. He was aloof and haughty whenever the others came near him". [2 marks]
2. Answers should refer to the little big fish thinking "how much too big and important he was to be living in such a small pool" and the older fish's (sarcastic) suggestion that he go "off to the big river and mix with the other big and important fish". [2 marks]
3. Answers should refer to the fact that the little big fish calls the older fish "my friend". [2 marks]
4. Answers should refer to the fact that the big little fish thinks of the older fish as a friend despite the fact that the older fish is "irritated" by him and speaks to him "sarcastically". [2 marks]
5. Answers should refer to the little big fish's anticipation of a "good life" where he is able to mix with his "equals" and live "among fish of my own size, beauty and intelligence". [2 marks]
6. Answers should refer to the little big fish being told "Out of the way, little fellow! Don't you know this is our hunting ground?" [2 marks]
7. Answers should refer to the river being full of larger fish who are rude to the little big fish or who want to eat him. [2 marks]
8. Answers should refer to the little big fish's decision to return to the safety of the small pool rather than stay in the river (For example, He learnt he would rather be a big fish in a small pond than a small fish in a big river). [2 marks]

Now try these

The children's answers will be subjective but should be well justified, where appropriate.

1. Answers could refer to the little big fish's initial rudeness and elitism; his ambition and hopes about the big river; his joy at arriving there; his confusion and fear at the reality of the river; his decision to return to the pool; his struggle to get there and / or his relief at being back. [3 marks max]
2. Answers could refer to the older fish's irritation, sarcasm, manipulation of the little big fish into leaving and / or solemnness when congratulating the little big fish on 'his' idea. [3 marks max]
3. Answers should grasp that this is the moment the little big fish begins to doubt himself and the wisdom of moving to the river. [3 marks max]
4. The phrase describes the little big fish's return to the pool. Answers could refer to the strength of the description created by the words "struggled", "force" and "swirling torrent" when building up a picture of the homeward journey. They could suggest that the difficulty of this journey proves how desperate the little big fish is to return to the pool. [3 marks max]
5. Open-ended question: Look for relevance to the plot and characters established, and correct punctuation of dialogue. The story's moral could refer to being content with one's circumstances / not being arrogant about one's better qualities / realising there are always people better off, and should acknowledge that the little big fish rejects the challenging world of the river in favour of safety and familiarity. [3 marks max]

Unit 3

Get started

The children are asked to use quotes where they can.

1. For example, Both of these adverts are promoting a new kind of trainers, or "sports shoe". [1 mark]
2. For example, The brand name for the product is "Strobers". [1 mark]
3. For example, You can buy the trainers "in your favourite store" / "from all major department stores and good sports shops". [1 mark]
4. For example, The trainers have "maximum grip all rubber soles", "strong tops and laces" and come in the "latest colour range". [1 mark]
5. For example, James from Express says, "Strobers, they're cool and canny". [1 mark]
6. For example, According to the adverts, "the seriously sporty", and people who "run, jump, kick or just look cool", will want to buy Strobers. [1 mark]
7. For example, The trainers cost from £39.99 to £70 (Advert 1 says "from only £39.99"; Advert 2 says "price £40 – £70 per pair"). [1 mark]

Year 6: Pupil Book answers

8. For example, The colours used on Advert 1 are mostly red, black and white (orange, blue and brown are also used). The colours used on Advert 2 are pale blue and black. [1 mark]

Try these

The children's answers may be subjective but should be in their own words and well justified, using evidence from either the text or the children's own experiences.

1. Answers could suggest that people who like that celebrity will be more likely to like the trainers, and / or that a 'cool' celebrity will make the trainers appear 'cool'. [2 marks]
2. Answers should mention that fans of James may want to copy him / take his advice by buying the trainers, and will also get a free poster of him when they do. [2 marks]
3. Answers should refer to the advert suggesting that the trainers may sell out ("while stocks last") and that the "special introductory price" may expire, and to the advert wanting to create a sense of urgency so people will buy the trainers quickly. [2 marks]
4. Answers should refer to the word "Strobers" being a logo in Advert 1 (it is red, in a different and larger font to the rest of the text and the final letter s has been used to create a line underneath). [2 marks]
5. Answers could refer to the colours breaking up the text to make it clearer and easier to read, making key points such as the price stand out and attracting the viewer's attention. [2 marks]
6. Answers should acknowledge that the "from only £39.99" price shown in Advert 1 is more likely to attract customers because it gives the impression of being cheaper (even though it is only a penny cheaper than the £40 price given on Advert 2). [2 marks]
7. Answers should refer to the advert's efforts to make the trainers appealing to those who do sports as well as those who 'just look cool'. [2 marks]
8. Open-ended question: Look for answers that are well justified and explain the choice made. (Justifications for Advert 2 could include clarity, simplicity and lack of manipulation.) [2 marks]

Now try these

The children's answers will be subjective but should be well justified where appropriate.

1. Answers should grasp that facts are true and certain, whereas opinions are personal beliefs or judgements. [2 marks]
2. Facts could include the trainers' features ("maximum grip all rubber soles", "strong tops and laces", "latest colour range"); where they can be bought ("from all major department stores and good sports shops"); their price (from £39.99); and the fact that buyers "this month" get a "free James poster"). All other features of the advert are opinions. [3 marks max]
3. Open-ended question: Look for explanations of how the language is persuasive and intended to make the trainers appealing to buyers. [3 marks max]

4. Open-ended question: Answers could suggest adding eye-catching images, fonts, colours, features, offers and / or endorsements. [3 marks max]
5. Open-ended question: Look for relevance to task and the character described, details from the adverts, persuasive language, imagination and presentation. [3 marks max]

Unit 4

Get started

The children are asked to use quotes where they can.

1. For example, Josh's school project is "about climate change". [1 mark]
2. For example, "Grandad" is replying to Josh's emails. [1 mark]
3. For example, One of Josh's friends said climate change is made up by journalists. (The children may conclude from later emails that this friend is Pete.) [1 mark]
4. For example, Grandad says that without greenhouses gases "we'd freeze, so we certainly need some". [1 mark]
5. For example, Pete's dad "works for an oil company". [1 mark]
6. For example, Grandad says "the next ice age isn't due here for another 10,000 years". [1 mark]
7. For example, Two emails were sent 'yesterday'. [1 mark]
8. For example, According to these emails, climate change is the Earth "warming up" "more than it should" because "carbon dioxide gas (and some others as well) that is produced when we burn oil and coal" "traps the heat from the sun"; "we must be emitting more greenhouse gases and so climate change must be taking place". (Answers should grasp the point of this, broadly, from the emails.) [1 mark]

Try these

The children's answers may be subjective but should be in their own words and well justified, using evidence from either the text or the children's own experiences.

1. Answers should refer to Josh hearing conflicting information about climate change from different people. [2 marks]
2. Answers may mention that the journalists "like a good story", but should be aware that Pete is repeating information from his father. [2 marks]
3. Answers could refer to any of these assertions by Grandad:
   "we need to look at our planet Earth overall and over several years"
   "with all the gases being pumped out of cars, aircraft, power stations and so on, we must be emitting more greenhouse gases and so climate change must be taking place"
   "At the rate the Earth's climate and oceans are warming, the ice in the Arctic and Antarctic will have melted so much that many low-lying places will have flooded already [i.e. before 10,000 years is over]"

Year 6: Pupil Book answers

"People who study the Earth's climate have found that as it warms up, the weather is going to get more violent and unpredictable. Hurricanes, for example, will become more powerful [...]. Deserts are increasing and places where lots of the Earth's food is grown, like the Great Plains of North America will get drier. Rain will be heavier in other parts of the world so there will be more floods. These things have already started to happen."

He also says that "people who depend on other people using lots of fuel if they are to continue making money [...] don't think there is any climate change. But it doesn't make them right, does it!" [2 marks]

4. Answers could refer to any of these assertions by Josh:
"it's all made up by journalists who like a good story to sell their newspapers"
"it was really cold last winter"
"the temperatures on Earth have always gone up and down." [2 marks]

5. Answers should acknowledge that the specific thing that makes Grandad cross is people with a "vested interest" in fuel businesses thinking (or saying) that climate change isn't happening. [2 marks]

6. Answers should conclude that having a "vested interest" means having a personal interest related to your own well-being / success. [2 marks]

7. Answers could mention that emails are usually shorter and more informal than letters. They do not use features of letter form such as writing the addresses at the top of the page. [2 marks]

8. Answers should suggest that Josh is writing more informally than Grandad is, and could conclude that this is because Grandad is more used to letter form than email. [2 marks]

Now try these

The children's answers will be subjective but should be well justified, where appropriate.

1. Answers could refer to Josh wanting to listen to his friend; seeking further information when confused; his close and trusting relationship with his grandad; and / or his willingness to consider different viewpoints. [3 marks max]

2. Open-ended question: Look for relevance to task, use of the detail in the extract, imagination and presentation. [3 marks max]

3. Open-ended question: Diary entries should be from Pete's point of view, and appreciate that Pete will be at least as confused as Josh: he is being given conflicting information from his father (whom he seems to trust) and at school, during the project. It is likely that Josh (his friend) will also now support the information learned at school. [3 marks max]

4. Answers could note that Grandad uses lots of exclamation marks, starts to answer his own questions and writes more informally than usual (using words and phrases such as "Phooey!" and "You guessed it!"). He also begins to make more personal comments about people with a "vested interest" in denying climate change. [3 marks max]

5. Open-ended question: Look for relevance to task, consistency of characters and theme, imagination, presentation and correct punctuation of dialogue. [3 marks max]

Unit 5

Get started

The children are asked to use quotes where they can.

1. For example, The intended listener in the poem is Darren. [1 mark]
2. For example, Darren's mum is speaking in the poem: she says "This is your mother speaking". [1 mark]
3. For example, The poem takes place in the "early morning". [1 mark]
4. For example, It is windy and rainy outside: Darren's mum says there's "a fresh Force Six blowing and a spot of rain lashing the rooftops". [1 mark]
5. For example, Darren's mum says "Your gerbil has been eaten by the dog". [1 mark]
6. For example, Darren got twenty spellings wrong in total: "eighteen spellings wrong in your Geography homework" and two in the letter he forged from his dad ("you could at least have spelt his Christian name right and the address"). [1 mark]
7. For example, The poem does not say what Darren was doing on Friday afternoon. (It does suggest that he was not really at a dental appointment or at school.) [1 mark]
8. For example, At the end of the poem, Darren's mum has started to pour tea over Darren ("I am about to pour your tea over your head [...] the trickle of water you feel at this moment, is NOT an illusion"). [1 mark]

Try these

The children's answers may be subjective but should be in their own words and well justified, using evidence from either the text or the children's own experiences.

1. Answers should convey that "crack-a-dawn" means 'crack of dawn', which means the very earliest hours of daylight in the morning. [2 marks]
2. Answers should conclude that Darren has been late before, referring to his mum saying "if you want to walk [to school] again" and that he would be making her late for "the third morning running". [2 marks]
3. Answers should recognise that the numbers are a countdown representing the time Darren's mum is giving him to get up. [1 mark]
4. Answers should recognise both that Darren will be late for school and his mum will miss her bus if he does not hurry up. [2 marks]
5. Darren's mum suggests that the letter is from the England football team ("A letter has just arrived, postmarked Wembley, inviting you to play for England next Saturday against Czechoslovakia"). [2 marks]

Year 6: Pupil Book answers

6. Answers should conclude that this means Darren will not be going out as he intends. [1 mark]
7. Answers could suggest that Darren was aware of the poor standard of his homework (i.e. how many spellings he had got wrong). [1 mark]
8. Answers could discuss Darren's mum's cheerful tone at the start of the poem, but also that Darren's lateness will not have come as a surprise. [2 marks]

Now try these

The children's answers will be subjective but should be well justified, where appropriate.

1. Answers should draw their conclusions from what Darren's mum says. They could refer to Darren's habitual laziness; his apparent lack of concern for his mother's job and for his gerbil; his apparent liking for international football; his inability to spell; his lack of concern for handing in homework; his dishonesty (forging the letter) and / or his truancy from school. [3 marks max]
2. True things could include the assertions that Darren's mum has brought him tea and cereal; that it is windy and rainy outside; that the bus is on time; that he got spellings wrong; that he hadn't handed in his Geography homework; that he'd forged and misspelt a letter from his dad and / or that she was pouring tea over him. Untrue things, which begin after Darren's mum counts "FIVE", could include the assertions that the gerbil has been eaten by the dog; that the dog has been eaten by a crocodile; that the crocodile is about to bite Darren's toes and / or that Darren has had a letter from the England football team. [3 marks max]
3. Answers could suggest that the countdown adds to the feel of nagging, the poem's pace and its rhythm, and helps the poem to build towards its climax. [3 marks max]
4. Answers could suggest that the long sentences also add to the feel of nagging and help to express Darren's mum's frustration with Darren. [3 marks max]
5. Open-ended question: Look for relevance to task, consistency of characters and theme, imagination and presentation. [3 marks max]

Unit 6

Get started

The children are asked to use quotes where they can.

1. For example, Nokomis is the "Daughter of the Moon". [1 mark]
2. For example, Hiawatha slept "in his linden cradle, Bedded soft in moss and rushes". [1 mark]
3. For example, He was "Safely bound with reindeer sinews". [1 mark]
4. For example, Nokomis called Hiawatha "My little owlet". [1 mark]
5. For example, Ishkoodah was a comet "with fiery tresses". [1 mark]
6. For example, The pine-trees said "Minne-wawa!". [1 mark]
7. For example, Hiawatha's Chickens were "every bird". [1 mark]
8. For example, Hiawatha learnt "How the beavers built their lodges". [1 mark]

Try these

The children's answers may be subjective but should be in their own words and well justified, using evidence from either the text or the children's own experiences.

1. Answers should grasp that the poem is about the childhood of a young Native American ('American Indian') called Hiawatha. [1 mark]
2. Answers should refer to the setting described in the first verse: the wigwam of Nokomis stands between a dark pine forest and a large body of water. The story is set in America (modern-day USA). [2 marks]
3. Answers should report that "the whispering of the pine-trees" and "the lapping of the water" were the "Sound of music" to Hiawatha. They could suggest that these sounds have lyrics (of a sort) and rhythm in common with music. [2 marks]
4. Answers should give details about the rhythm: there are eight beats (syllables) and four stresses in every line (except "Of all the beasts he learned the language" which has nine beats and four stresses). The stresses fall on beats 1, 3, 5 and 7 (beats 2, 4, 6 and 8 for the exception line). Answers could also discuss the rhythm's effect: the rhythm is regular and helps the poem to flow quickly; it could be thought to sound like drums or mimic the 'music' Hiawatha hears in the "lapping of the water". [2 marks]
5. Answers could suggest that the baby has no-one else to care for him and / or that Nokomis is his grandmother. (Both are true, although this is not revealed in the extract: Hiawatha's mother was Nokomis's daughter, and she has died.) [2 marks]
6. Answers should suggest that Hiawatha calls the animals his brothers because he understands them and is close to them. [1 mark]
7. Answers could suggest that Hiawatha was lonely (he is certainly alone) and / or simply that he is interested in and feels close to nature. [2 marks]
8. Answers should refer to the nature of folk and traditional tales: that they are handed down through generations, that they are used to entertain and educate and / or that they often offer fantastical explanations for things that the culture otherwise did not understand. [2 marks]

Now try these

The children's answers will be subjective but should be well justified, where appropriate.

1. Answers could refer to Nokomis's age; solitary life; love for Hiawatha; knowledge of the natural world; and fondness for folklore and spiritual stories. [3 marks max]
2. Open-ended question: Look for seven lines from Hiawatha's point of view that mimic the style of the poem and detail something Hiawatha has learned in the forest

Year 6: Pupil Book answers

(this could be something mentioned in the extract). [3 marks max]

3. Answers should find good examples and could suggest that the effect of the repetition is to emphasise the meaning of the repeated words, and add to the rhythmic nature of the poem. [3 marks max]

4. Answers could suggest that the word order is chosen to create the rhythm of the poem, that it creates an impression of Native American chants and / or that it enables the poet to start each line with its most important element. [3 marks max]

5. Open-ended question: Look for relevance to task; consistency of characters and theme; imagination; presentation; modern language with natural word order; and no retention of other poetic devices. [3 marks max]

Unit 7

Get started

The children are asked to use quotes where they can.

1. For example, The highwayman approaches the inn at night. This is shown by the description in the first three lines: the wind is "a torrent of darkness", the moon is up ("The moon was a ghostly galleon") and it is the only thing lighting the road ("The road was a ribbon of moonlight"). [1 mark]

2. For example, The highwayman was carrying a "pistol" (a gun) and a "rapier" (a sword). [1 mark]

3. For example, Bess is "the landlord's daughter". She is "black-eyed", "red-lipped", "bonny" (pretty) and has "long black hair". [1 mark]

4. For example, The highwayman "whistled a tune to the window" to signal to Bess that he was there. [1 mark]

5. For example, Bess was "Plaiting a dark red love-knot into her long black hair" at the window. [1 mark]

6. For example, Tim is an "ostler" (a man who looks after horses) who "loved the landlord's daughter". [1 mark]

7. For example, The highwayman couldn't kiss Bess because "He scarce could reach her hand" even when he "rose upright in the stirrups". That is, Bess was in a window too high above him. [1 mark]

8. For example, Instead, Bess "loosened her hair" and let it fall over the highwayman's face and chest; "he kissed its waves". [1 mark]

Try these

The children's answers may be subjective but should be in their own words and well justified, using evidence from either the text or the children's own experiences.

1. Answers should suggest that Bess doesn't want to be seen waiting for the highwayman – they could suggest that she is hiding from her father, Tim or anyone else. [1 mark]

2. Answers should suggest that the highwayman didn't want to be seen either. [1 mark]

3. Answers could repeat the poem's description of the highwayman's clothes, but should conclude that the highwayman dresses carefully and smartly (in "lace", "velvet" and breeches that "fitted with never a wrinkle", and with highly-polished weapons). They could suggest that this demonstrates that the highwayman takes pride in himself – and, perhaps, does not look like a criminal. [2 marks]

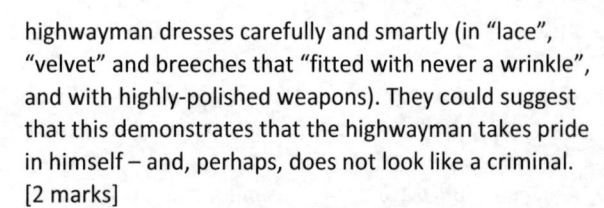

4. Answers should acknowledge that the highwayman is romantically involved with Bess: he calls her his "bonny sweetheart", asks for "one kiss", promises to return to her and, when she lets down her hair to him, "His face burnt like a brand". [2 marks]

5. Open-ended question: Answers are likely to suggest that Bess is not interested in Tim. The reader is told that "he loved the landlord's daughter", but the only other information given about him describes his appearance: in unflattering contrast with the smart highwayman, "His face was white and peaked. His eyes were hollows of madness, his hair like mouldy hay." [2 marks]

6. Answers should show an understanding of a highwayman's activities (robbing coaches on the road) and could refer to the highwayman saying, "I shall be back with the yellow gold before the morning light" and the suggestion that "they" (presumably the law) may "harry" him (not leave him alone). [2 marks]

7. Answers should give details about the poem's structure: there are six verses with six lines each. The number of beats (syllables) per line varies, but lines 1, 2, 3 and 6 of each verse contain six stresses. Lines 4 and 5 contain three stresses each (with the exception of line 5 in the first verse, which contains two stresses). Lines 1 and 2 are a rhyming couplet; line 3 rhymes with line 6; lines 4 and 5 end in the same word (rhyme structure AABCCB). [2 marks]

8. Answers should grasp that the purpose of the poem is to tell the story of the highwayman and his relationship with Bess. They could expand that it intends to create very vivid pictures of the scenes in the story using powerful descriptions and repetitions. [2 marks]

Now try these

The children's answers will be subjective but should be well justified, where appropriate.

1. Answers could refer to Bess's feelings of anticipation while waiting for the highwayman; fear that they may be caught; joy when he arrives; excitement about speaking with him; longing to be able to reach him; happiness when he kisses her hair; sorrow when he leaves; and worry that he will be caught. [3 marks max]

2. Answers could refer to the highwayman's pride in his appearance; dangerous lifestyle; disregard of the law; romantic nature; and / or genuine feelings for Bess. [3 marks max]

3. Answers could suggest that the change of line length helps to break up the verses, and that the repetition draws the reader's attention to a key element in the picture the verse creates. [3 marks max]

Year 6: Pupil Book answers

4. **Metaphors**: "The wind was a torrent of darkness among the gusty trees." / "The moon was a ghostly galleon tossed upon cloudy seas." / "The road was a ribbon of moonlight over the purple moor." Answers should grasp that these help to create a vivid picture of the moonlit scene. They could expand that the images chosen give clues about the rest of the story: "torrent of darkness" suggests rapid and unseen movement; "ghostly galleon tossed upon cloudy seas" suggests a dangerous journey (and death); "ribbon" suggests a woman and recalls Bess's hair. (In the part of the poem not included in the extract, the highwayman's plans to return are reported by Tim, Bess dies trying to warn him and he dies trying to return for her.)

   Similes: "his hair like mouldy hay;" / "Dumb as a dog he listened" / "His face burnt like a brand". Answers should grasp that these help to create vivid descriptions (of touch and smell): "mouldy hay" and "like a dog" give a very unflattering sense of Tim – that he is damp, smelly and animal-like – while "like a brand" exaggerates the heat the highwayman feels (from blushing) when Bess's hair covers him.

   Alliteration: "Over the cobbles he clattered and clashed in the dark inn-yard" / "He whistled a tune to the window, and who should be waiting there". Answers should grasp that these help to create vivid descriptions of sounds: the clattering hooves on cobbles or the soft, airy whistle of the highwayman.
   [3 marks max]

5. Open-ended question: Look for relevance to task; consistency of characters and theme; imagination; and presentation. [3 marks max]

Unit 8

Get started

The children are asked to use quotes where they can.

1. For example, The news report was written by "our Environment Correspondent". [1 mark]
2. For example, The water companies have been given "just three weeks" to write their plans. [1 mark]
3. For example, The plans need to show "how they will respond to the current water shortage and to the long-term need to provide water for homes while, at the same time, protecting our rivers". [1 mark]
4. For example, The report says that "Leakage is the top priority" because "an average of 30% of treated water leaks away before it can be used". [1 mark]
5. For example, The report says that "the government is reserving its position on water meters". [1 mark]
6. For example, The report says that "a third of domestic water goes down the toilet". [1 mark]
7. For example, A leaflet giving tips on how to save water has been produced by the Environment Agency. [1 mark]
8. For example, The report says that "Placing a water-filled bottle in the cistern will help by stopping the cistern from taking in so much water as it refills". [1 mark]

Try these

The children's answers may be subjective but should be in their own words and well justified, using evidence from either the text or the children's own experiences.

1. Answers should grasp that the news report has been produced to inform people about the water shortage and how it has led to water companies being required to produce plans to explain how they will deal with the situation. They may also suggest that the article suggests ways people can help to reduce the water shortage (see below). [2 marks]
2. Answers should grasp that the report will have been intended to inform readers, and to encourage them to save water. Other effects could be that it alarms people who may either be worried about the state of the environment (for example, rivers) or concerned about the possibility they may have to install a water meter. People may also be pleased at the prospect of free leak repairs. [2 marks]
3. Open-ended question: Answers could suggest adding more images, sub-headings, quotes and / or other details, and / or reducing the number of bullet points so the advice is easier to absorb. [2 marks]
4. Open-ended question: Look for suggestions that are relevant to the content and tone of the article (for example, a photograph of a dry, dying garden / a diagram of a water-saving tip in action, such as the bottle in the toilet cistern). [2 marks]
5. Answers should grasp that this suggestion is an opinion rather than a fact: it is in a quote by a "water company spokesman". [2 marks]
6. Answers should recognise that the quote adds an opinion. It also suggests a reason for installing water meters. [2 marks]
7. Answers could refer to people not knowing about leaks or ways to save water; enjoying taking baths rather than showers; needing to run washing machines or dishwashers quickly; wanting to keep their gardens watered and not wanting to use dirty water on them; and / or not caring about the water shortage. [2 marks]
8. Open-ended question: Look for well-reasoned and justified opinions. [2 marks]

Now try these

The children's answers will be subjective but should be well justified, where appropriate.

1. Answers could include the headline and writer; introductory paragraph; the quote from an interview; facts and figures; informative diagram; use of the passive voice; the answers to What? When? Where? Who? How? and Why? questions; and short clear sentences. [3 marks max]
2. 'Do' tips could include: Place a water-filled bottle in the cistern; take showers; snoop for dripping taps and get them fixed; use washing-up water in the garden to water the flowers and vegetables; use a water butt to collect

Year 6: Pupil Book answers

rain water for the garden; turn off the tap while you are brushing your teeth.

'Don't' tips could include: Take baths; use washing machines or dishwashers with half loads; use fresh water in the garden to water the flowers and vegetables; run the tap while you are brushing your teeth; use sprinklers unless essential. [3 marks max]

3. Good points: People would soon be far more conservation minded if they knew they had to pay for every drop of water they use.
Bad points: The extra cost of installing meters; unfairness for people with large families; unfairness for people with medical conditions requiring frequent bathing; unfairness for people whose work makes them dirty. [3 marks max]

4. Open-ended question: Answers should include all of the points included in the chart that answers Question 3. Look in addition for relevance to task; consistency of theme; imagination; and well-structured arguments. [3 marks max]

5. Open-ended question: Look for relevance to task; important information selected from the extract; imagination and presentation. [3 marks max]

Unit 9

Get started

The children are asked to use quotes where they can.

1. For example, The extract says that "Few people in the world live in inhospitable deserts". [1 mark]
2. For example, The extract says that "there are no hot deserts in the far north […] of the Earth". [1 mark]
3. For example, The Equator is "an imaginary line around the centre of the Earth, separating the Northern Hemisphere from the Southern Hemisphere". [1 mark]
4. For example, There are two hemispheres, "the Northern Hemisphere" and "the Southern Hemisphere". [1 mark]
5. For example, The extract says that "Most of the major deserts lie in the two bands north and south of the Equator, along lines of latitude called the Tropic of Cancer and the Tropic of Capricorn". [1 mark]
6. For example, The map shows that the Gobi Desert is in Asia. [1 mark]
7. For example, The map shows that the Kalahari Desert is in Africa. [1 mark]
8. For example, Some winds are very dry because they "have already lost their water vapour because they have dropped it as rain over hills and mountains", because "they are far from an ocean" or "because they are very cold". [1 mark]

Try these

The children's answers may be subjective but should be in their own words and well justified, using evidence from either the text or the children's own experiences.

1. Answers should recognise the two subheadings as "Where are deserts located?" and "How are hot deserts formed?", and suggest a sensible main heading (for example 'All about deserts' or simply 'Deserts'). [2 marks]
2. Answers should recognise that the blue arrows represent wet winds, or "Ocean winds", and that the red arrows represent inland winds, or "Dry winds". [1 mark]
3. Answers should deduce that Death Valley must be in the North American desert. [1 mark]
4. Answers could suggest that the map assists the reader by showing the locations and relative sizes of the world's deserts across the different continents and that it shows their positions relative to the Equator and Tropics of Cancer and Capricorn. [2 marks]
5. Answers should deduce that the air gets water vapour from the ocean: the extract says that "Cold winds blowing across cold ocean currents can't collect much water vapour" and therefore don't cause rain. [2 marks]
6. Answers should deduce from the extract that lines of latitude are 'imaginary' lines around the earth: the extract refers to the Tropics of Cancer and Capricorn as lines of latitude, shows them parallel with (and in the same colour and thickness as) the Equator, and states that the Equator is "an imaginary line around the centre of the Earth". [2 marks]
7. Answers should recognise that Africa spans both Tropics, along which "Most of the major deserts lie". [1 mark]
8. Answers should acknowledge that people need water to survive, and could mention that the extract says deserts are "inhospitable" and that "less harsh" weather is preferable. [1 mark]

Now try these

The children's answers will be subjective but should be well justified, where appropriate.

1. Open-ended question: Look for accurate definitions of the key or more difficult words in the extract (for example, 'continent', 'desert', 'Equator', 'hemisphere', 'inhospitable'). The words should be presented alphabetically. [3 marks max]
2. Open-ended question: Answers should be clear, numbered instructions that contain all relevant details in the extract (i.e. that the wind collects water vapour from a relatively warm ocean and moves it to a cooler place to form clouds; when the water droplets become heavy, they fall as rain). [3 marks max]
3. Answers should appreciate that the diagram illustrates the sentences "sometimes the winds bring very dry air. These winds have already lost their water vapour because they have dropped it as rain over hills and mountains". It adds details about how and where the winds lose their water vapour and how and where "Ocean winds" become "Dry winds"; how landscapes change the higher and further from the ocean they are; and gives a specific example of this happening: from the Pacific Ocean to Death Valley. [3 marks max]
4. Open-ended question: Answers should explain all the detail included in the diagram, including the specifics of the example (i.e. that ocean winds collect water vapour

Year 6: Pupil Book answers

from the Pacific Ocean; become cooler, form clouds and drop rain over the Coast Mountains, San Joaquin Valley and Sierra Nevada Mountains; become dry as they leave the Sierra Nevada Mountains and have no water vapour left to drop over Death Valley). [3 marks max]

5. Open-ended question: Look for relevance to task; consistency of theme; information from the extract; a different structure from that used in the extract; imagination; and presentation. The suggested structure (that the children could start with the wind's journey from an ocean and end with an example of a desert shown on the map) may or may not be used. [3 marks max]

Unit 10

Get started

The children are asked to use quotes where they can.

1. For example, The shared topic of the poems is how people feel about winter. [1 mark]
2. For example, Winter turns "tree stumps into snowmen". [1 mark]
3. For example, Winter turns "houses into birthday cakes". [1 mark]
4. For example, The "young" people catch snowflakes on their tongues. [1 mark]
5. For example, Snow is "slushy when it's going". [1 mark]
6. For example, "Icy tyres" scratch the young girl's hands. [1 mark]
7. For example, Her fingers feel "stiff and numb". [1 mark]
8. For example, The girl is "Alone" while watching the children playing in the snow. [1 mark]

Try these

The children's answers may be subjective but should be in their own words and well justified, using evidence from either the text or the children's own experiences.

1. Answers should recognise that the speaker of Ogden Nash's poem feels positively about winter (For example, that it is exciting / beautiful). [1 mark]
2. Answers should recognise that the speaker of Emma Barnes's poem feels negatively about winter (For example, that it is lonely / destroys her independence). [1 mark]
3. Answers should grasp that the snow prevents the girl from moving herself around freely in her wheelchair. [1 mark]
4. Answers should grasp that independence might be important to someone in a wheelchair as it is harder for them to move without people's help, and could suggest that acting without help is an important part of growing up / being your own person / having freedom / enjoying yourself. [2 marks]
5. Answers should report that, in 'Winter Morning', the rhyme pattern is five rhyming couplets (AABBCCDDEE); in 'Winter in a Wheelchair', lines 2 and 4, and lines 6 and 8 rhyme (ABCBDEFE), although lines 2 and 4 are half-rhymes ("numb" and "sun"). [2 marks]
6. Answers could suggest that the line "Snow is snowy when it's snowing" creates an impression of the continuous, repetitive nature of snowfall, the sounds of walking in snow and / or humour. They should recognise that the effects mentioned are creating by the line's repetition (and, therefore, alliteration). [2 marks]
7. The metaphors are "Winter is the king of showmen, / Turning tree stumps into snowmen / And houses into birthday cakes". Answers could report that, because the metaphors suggest things actually become other things, they emphasise the transforming nature of snow in winter by likening its effects to those of a magician doing tricks. [2 marks]
8. The simile is "My independence melts away, Like a snowman in the sun." Answers could suggest that the simile creates a vivid picture for an abstract concept (the independence vanishing), relates it to the topic of winter, and relates it to the feelings of disappointment other children feel at the *end* of winter, emphasising the speaker's alienation from them. [2 marks]

Now try these

The children's answers will be subjective but should be well justified, where appropriate.

1. Answers should accurately identify personification as the action of attributing human characteristics to non-human subjects. The example they should use from the poem is "Winter is the king of showmen". They could expand by detailing what effect this personification has on the poem: that winter is active, and makes transformations purposefully and magically (the metaphors that follow it emphasise the transforming nature of snow in winter by likening its effects to those of a magician doing tricks). [3 marks max]
2. The different line is "I'm sorry it's slushy when it's going." The change in rhythm is from four stresses per line to three stresses per line. Answers could suggest that this creates the effect of slowing down, interruption or less energy, and relate this to the end of winter and the fun described. [3 marks max]
3. The different pair of lines is "Alone in my chair, / I watch the children play and yell,". The change in rhythm is from pairs of lines with four and then three stresses to a pair of lines with two and then four stresses. Answers could suggest that this emphasises the importance of "Alone in my chair", which: explains the real cause of girl's unhappiness; creates the effect of interruption and / or separateness; or creates a lack of flow. They could relate this to the lack of enjoyment, movement and independence that the girl feels. [3 marks max]
4. Open-ended question: Look for relevance to task, imagination, presentation and appropriate new descriptions. Re-used positive descriptions could include any from 'Winter Morning'; re-used negative descriptions could include any from 'Winter in a Wheelchair'. [3 marks max]
5. Open-ended question: Look for relevance to task; consistency of character and theme; imagination; and presentation. [3 marks max]

Year 6: Pupil Book answers

Unit 11

Get started

The children are asked to use quotes where they can.

1. For example, Milo thinks "almost everything is a waste of time". [1 mark]
2. For example, Milo thinks that "the magical forest of words and numbers" is beautiful. [1 mark]
3. For example, The first thing Milo sees when he looks for who had spoken is "two very neatly polished brown shoes". [1 mark]
4. For example, The boy's feet were "easily three feet off the ground". [1 mark]
5. For example, The writer suggests that "standing" is not the most appropriate word to describe the boy's position because he is "suspended in mid-air". [1 mark]
6. For example, According to the boy Milo meets, you might not think the forest was beautiful "if you happened to like deserts". [1 mark]
7. For example, Even when they are born, everyone in the boy's family is born "with his head at exactly the height it's going to be when he's an adult". [1 mark]
8. For example, The boy says that the idea someone might "start on the ground and grow up" is a "silly system" because "your head keeps changing its height and you always see things in a different way". [1 mark]

Try these

The children's answers may be subjective but should be in their own words and well justified, using evidence from either the text or the children's own experiences.

1. Answers should detect that the extract contrasts Milo's feeling that things are "a waste of time" with his positive feelings about the forest: he feels that way "until he mysteriously finds his way into the magical forest". [2 marks]
2. Answers should detect that, when Milo asked, "'Isn't it beautiful?'", he didn't expect anyone to answer. He was surprised to receive an answer, as he "didn't see who had spoken". [2 marks]
3. Answers should refer to the boy saying, "When we're fully grown up, or as you can see, grown down, our feet finally touch. Of course, there are a few of us whose feet never reach the ground, no matter how old we get". [2 marks]
4. Answers could include: "We always see things from the same angle […]. It's much less trouble that way"; "When you're very young, you can never hurt yourself falling down if you're in mid-air"; and "you certainly can't get into trouble for scuffing up your shoes or marking the floor if there's nothing to scuff them on and the floor is three feet away". [2 marks]
5. Answers should conclude that Milo had "never really thought about" the fact that his head would keep "changing its height" as he got older because that is what is normal for him, and that he hadn't considered that there might be an alternative. [2 marks]
6. Answers should detect the figurative meaning of the sentence: that some people may not think the forest is beautiful, and that the boy thinks Milo should consider different opinions. [2 marks]
7. Answers should detect the literal meaning of the sentence: that growing upwards meaning that your head changes height and that the angle you look at your surroundings will therefore change. [2 marks]

Now try these

The children's answers will be subjective but should be well justified, where appropriate.

1. Answers could refer to the boy's neat and polished shoes; his apparent open-mindedness about others' opinions; his odd changes of subject; his playful nature ("He hopped a few steps in the air, skipped back to where he started, and then began again"); his ridicule of Milo growing upwards; his assertive arguments; and / or his conviction that he is right. [3 marks max]
2. Answers could refer to Milo initially thinking "dejectedly"; his awe and appreciation of the forest; his surprise at meeting the boy; his confusion at the boy's words and ability to float; the fact that he responds to the boy's misunderstanding of his age "seriously"; the fact he is asked to consider his growth system for the first time; and his passive agreement with the boy. [3 marks max]
3. Open-ended question: Look for relevance to task; consistency of characters and theme; imagination; and presentation. [3 marks max]
4. Open-ended question: All the boy's arguments except, perhaps, one ("if Christmas trees were people and people were Christmas trees, we'd all be chopped down, put up in the living room, and covered with tinsel, while the trees opened our presents") could be counted as making sense (they aren't illogical), so answers will be subjective. [3 marks max]
5. Open-ended question: Answers could contend that the boy does not contradict himself if his second assertion is taken literally, i.e. that he feels that you should consider other people's opinions but that seeing your surroundings from a consistent height is more productive. Alternatively, they could contend that the boy suggests, at first, that it is better to see things differently (figuratively and / or literally) and then that it is better to see things in the same way (again, figuratively and / or literally). [3 marks max]

Unit 12

Get started

The children are asked to use quotes where they can.

1. For example, The characters in the extract are Mother, Ruth, Roberta, Phyllis and Peter. Children may also mention Father, who is discussed but does not appear in the extract. [1 mark]
2. For example, Ruth suggests that the bad news could be "a death in the family or a bank busted". [1 mark]

Year 6: Pupil Book answers

3. For example, When Mother returns from the library, "Her dear face was as white as her lace collar, and her eyes looked very big and shining. Her mouth looked just like a line of pale red – her lips were thin and not their proper shape at all." [1 mark]
4. For example, Phyllis protests about bedtime because, she says, Mother "promised we should sit up late tonight because Father's come home". [1 mark]
5. For example, Mother "almost always" brushes the girls' hair. [1 mark]
6. For example, In response to Peter's question, Ruth says "Don't ask me no questions and I won't tell you no lies". [1 mark]
7. For example, Mother went "To London" in the morning. [1 mark]
8. For example, When Mother sat down, Peter "fetched her soft velvety slippers for her". [1 mark]

Try these

The children's answers may be subjective but should be in their own words and well justified, using evidence from either the text or the children's own experiences.

1. Answers could detect that Mother does not want Ruth to frighten the children with her guesses. They could also suggest that Mother does not approve of Ruth talking openly about what is happening. [2 marks]
2. Answers should conclude correctly that Ruth is a servant in the family's household. They could refer to Ruth addressing Mother with the words "Please 'm," or (potentially confusingly) "Mum"; that Mother tells Ruth, "That'll do" and "you can go"; and / or that she seems to have responsibility for tasks such as putting the children to bed or serving their breakfast when Mother isn't there. [2 marks]
3. Answers could suggest that Mother is upset and doesn't want a hug or, more sensitively, that she is trying to prevent Roberta from seeing her crying. They could refer to Mother's eyes being "very big and shining" and to Roberta's realisation later that "Mother doesn't want us to know she's been crying". [2 marks]
4. Answers should refer to the fact that, on that night, "Ruth brushed the girls' hair and helped them to undress" when "Mother almost always did this herself". They could also mention that Mother slips into the children's rooms "Late that night" to kiss them. They could conclude that Mother wanted time on her own, without the children, and that this may be because she was upset (see also previous answer). [2 marks]
5. Answers should acknowledge that Roberta is being sensitive to her mother's wish to keep her grief private, and not talk about what has happened. They could refer to Roberta thinking, "If Mother doesn't want us to know she's been crying, [...] we won't know it. That's all." [2 marks]
6. Answers should acknowledge that the reason Mother gives for the children not to ask her questions is, "I am very worried about it, and I want you all to help me, and not to make things harder for me." They could also conclude that she is trying to protect them from bad news. [2 marks]
7. Answers should refer to Mother saying "And don't you worry. It'll all come right in the end". They could suggest that this may reassure the children as they seem to trust and obey her, or that it will not as it hasn't answered any of the questions they may have about what happened, or told them when Father will return. [2 marks]
8. Open-ended question: Answers should refer to the mysterious upheaval in the children's lives, Mother's silence on the subject and their instructions to be good and not ask questions. They may suggest that Roberta and Peter seem more worried than Phyllis does, as her protestation about staying up late suggests that she hasn't picked up on the seriousness of the situation. [2 marks]

Now try these

The children's answers will be subjective but should be well justified, where appropriate.

1. Answers could refer to Mother's calmness and quietness despite her obviously being upset; her determined action (i.e. going to London alone); her firmness with Ruth and about the children not asking questions; her protection of the children from the news; and / or her kindness to the children: she allows them to "sit up late", "almost always" brushes the girls' hair herself and comes to kiss them goodnight. [3 marks max]
2. Answers could refer to Roberta's worry and mystification about what has happened to Father; her worry for Mother; her quickness in picking up ideas (asking, after Ruth's suggestion, if anyone was dead; noticing that her Mother didn't want to talk; correctly guessing the trouble was "something to do with Government"); and her sensitivity to Mother's feelings. They could also mention her surprise that Mother thought they might "make things harder" for her ("'As if we would!' said Roberta") and her "guilty glances" with Peter when Mother mentions quarrelling. [3 marks max]
3. Answers should recognise that the dash indicates a pause. They could suggest that Mother was ready to say the first part of her sentence ("Father's been called away"), but that she had to think before adding "on business". They could then, correctly, expand that the second part of the sentence is likely not to be true. [3 marks max]
4. Clues could include the bad news and Ruth's suggestions that it meant a death or a "bank busted"; men in boots apparently leaving the house with Father in a cab; Mother saying "Father's been called away – on business" (see answer above); Mother denying that anyone is dead; her grief; her trip to London; her news that "Father will be away for some time" and that she is "very worried about it"; her saying the trouble is "about business" and "something to do with the Government"; and her promise that "It'll all come right in the end." Answers could suggest anything based soundly on the selected evidence, although some ideas (such as Father's death) are

Year 6: Pupil Book answers

contradicted by it (even if Mother weren't telling the truth, it would be unlikely that things would "come right in the end"). (The answer, should you wish to reveal it, is that Father has been arrested for selling Government secrets – a crime of which he is eventually proved innocent.) [3 marks max]

5. Open-ended question: Look for relevance to task; consistency of characters and theme; imagination; and presentation. [3 marks max]

Unit 13

Get started

The children are asked to use quotes where they can.

1. For example, When Gulliver woke up, he realised that he "could not move" (and that "the sun had just begun to rise above the horizon"). [1 mark]
2. For example, Gulliver says that the little people were "not much bigger than my middle finger". [1 mark]
3. For example, Gulliver reports that he was "so astonished" when he first saw the little people that he "roared aloud". [1 mark]
4. For example, After the little people returned, Gulliver reports, "one climbed up to where he could get a full sight of my face" and called out '*Hekinah Degul*!' [1 mark]
5. For example, Gulliver broke the strings that bound his left hand "With a violent pull". [1 mark]
6. For example, After the little people had fired arrows at him, Gulliver decided "not to anger my tiny captors further" and "to think about how to get free later, when they had all gone away and left me alone." [1 mark]
7. For example, When Gulliver was hungry, he says, "I put my finger to my mouth to indicate this". [1 mark]
8. For example, Gulliver thinks he might be in a place called "Lilliput" because "one little man, who seemed to be important" said it "several times" in his "long speech". [1 mark]

Try these

The children's answers may be subjective but should be in their own words and well justified, using evidence from either the text or the children's own experiences.

1. Answers should refer to what Gulliver calls "a great crowd". [1 mark]
2. Answers could suggest that the little people were afraid of Gulliver and / or the damage he could do. They could also, possibly with less justification, suggest that the little people intended to attack Gulliver. [2 marks]
3. As above, answers should refer to the little people's desire to protect themselves. They could also speculate that the people wanted to move / manipulate Gulliver and needed him to stay asleep. [2 marks]
4. Answers could refer to Gulliver's attempt "to catch some of the annoying little creatures", but there is otherwise no evidence that he means to hurt them: he plans to attempt to escape only when "they had all gone away and left me alone". (He does seem to be able to free himself with effort, so seems not to want to alarm them.) [2 marks]
5. Answers could refer to the little people building a tower; the "important" little man giving a speech (presumably about Gulliver); the inhabitants feeding him a lot of "deliciously cooked" food; and / or to their doctors giving him a sleeping potion. They could suggest that this treatment is relatively friendly and that the little people did not really want to hurt Gulliver; they could alternatively suggest that the speech and sleeping potion suggest the little people have unknown and suspicious plans for him. [2 marks]
6. Answers should grasp that Gulliver is unable to see and is therefore unable to describe much of the setting, as his head is pinned to the ground. They could also suggest that the author wants the reader to concentrate on characters and actions instead. [2 marks]
7. Gulliver refers to the little people as "small creatures"; "a tiny human creature not much bigger than my middle finger"; "annoying little creatures"; "tiny captors"; "tiny people"; "one little man"; "quite friendly"; and "inhabitants". Answers could suggest that Gulliver stresses the size of the little people with almost every reference, but also that he changes from calling them "creatures" to "people" and "inhabitants" and that this may suggest he has begun to see them as people and individuals rather than "creatures". [2 marks]
8. Answers could suggest that the phrase reveals that, later, Gulliver must learn to communicate with and learn things from the little people. [2 marks]

Now try these

The children's answers will be subjective but should be well justified, where appropriate.

1. Answers could refer to Gulliver's initial astonishment; knowledge of several languages; understandable irritability; acceptance of his situation and reluctance to fight the little people or make them angry; appreciation of the tiny food; and / or seeming interest in his bizarre surroundings. [3 marks max]
2. Phrases could include any of the following details: "I tried to stand up but found to my astonishment that I could not move. My hands and feet and even my hair seemed to be fastened to the ground. The sun was getting hotter. Then I was horrified to feel some small creatures moving along my left leg and up to my chest"; "I felt my left hand and my face pierced with hundreds of tiny arrows"; "I heard some knocking near my right ear and the sound of a great crowd"; "one little man [...] made a long speech, not a word of which I could understand. He said the word '*Lilliput*' several times"; "They were deliciously cooked"; "someone called out, '*Peplum selam*'"; and / or "At this, they loosened the cords that bound me a little". Answers should recognise the senses described (touch, sound and taste). [3 marks max]
3. Open-ended question: The little people say: '*Hekinah Degul!*' when they first meet Gulliver (answers could

Year 6: Pupil Book answers

suggest 'Greetings Giant!' / 'The giant's awake!' or similar); *Tolgo Phonac*!' just before the tiny archers fire arrows at Gulliver (answers could suggest 'Fire Away!' or similar); and *'Peplum selam'* just before the little people loosen Gulliver's cords (answers could suggest 'Loosen the cords' or similar). [3 marks max]

4. Open-ended question: Answers should grasp that the opening paragraph describes Gulliver's experience as he understands it, adding a small amount of information at a time and detailing the feelings he has before he can see their explanations. [3 marks max]

5. Open-ended question: Look for relevance to the topic; characters and situation; and the important little man's possible plans for Gulliver. The speech should use appropriately formal language. [3 marks max]

Unit 14

Get started

The children are asked to use quotes where they can.

1. For example, The setting for the scene is "A lush green landscape with trees and a clear pool of water on a warm day". [1 mark]
2. For example, The characters in the scene are "A King", "Compere Lapin", "Compere Tig", "The King's guards" and "A wise man". [1 mark]
3. For example, The King knows someone has been in his pool because "The water is murky and dirty". [1 mark]
4. For example, The actor playing the King should be "Thundering" when he says "He must die!" [1 mark]
5. For example, The wise man tells the King, "Compere Lapin is to blame". [1 mark]
6. For example, Compere Tig feels proud when he thinks he is allowed to bathe in the pool (he acts "with pride" and says "What an honour"). [1 mark]
7. For example, When they capture Compere Tig, the guards "wrap him in a bundle and tie him to a tree". [1 mark]
8. For example, Compere Tig lies to Compere Lapin when he tells him, "the King is going to kill me because I refused to marry his daughter. It has nothing to do with the pool of clear water". [1 mark]

Try these

The children's answers may be subjective but should be in their own words and well justified, using evidence from either the text or the children's own experiences.

1. Answers should recognise that Lapin knows he "dirtied the waters" of the King's pool and must have heard the King say, "No-one visits my pool and lives". [1 mark]
2. Answers should recognise that Lapin tells Tig the King has given him permission to use the pool so Tig will be caught and punished for dirtying the pool in his place. [1 mark]
3. Answers should recognise that Tig has successfully tricked Lapin into believing that whoever is in the trap will be able to marry the King's daughter. [1 mark]
4. Answers should recognise that Tig and Lapin are fond of tricking one another, and could expand that the consequences of their tricks could result in death or serious injury; it is therefore likely that they feel strongly against one another. They could further suggest that Lapin appears to have started this antagonism by blaming Tig for dirtying the King's pool. [2 marks]

5. Open-ended question: Answers could suggest that Tig was justified as Lapin had tricked him first, or that tricking Lapin made Tig just as bad. [2 marks]
6. Answers could refer to the stage directions "Compere Tig walks proudly to the pool and dips his paws in" and "Compere Lapin sits washing his ears". [2 marks]
7. Open-ended question: Answers should approximate Tig gloating, jeering or laughing cruelly in Lapin's direction. [2 marks]
8. Answers could suggest that the guards remaining onstage with the glowing iron bar acts as a reminder of the fate awaiting whichever Compere ends up in the bundle. [2 marks]

Now try these

The children's answers will be subjective but should be well justified, where appropriate.

1. Answers could refer to Lapin's sneaky use of the King's pool; panic at the prospect of being caught; deceptive nature; eagerness to marry the King's daughter; and / or foolishness at being tricked by Tig. [3 marks max]
2. Answers could refer to the extract's inclusion of the setting; character list; scene heading; stage directions; character line prompts; and / or direct speech written without speech marks. [3 marks max]
3. Open-ended question: Look for accurate definitions of the technical or more difficult terms in the playscript, including 'upstage', 'downstage', 'stage right' and 'stage left'. The words should be presented alphabetically. [3 marks max]
4. Open-ended question: Look for relevance to task; imagination; presentation and appropriacy of content to the setting; characters; and the reality of a stage. Answers should acknowledge it would not be possible to have a pool or red hot iron on stage, for example, or to string someone up from a 'tree'. [3 marks max]
5. Open-ended question: Look for passages that contain all of the information from the extract as a narrative that doesn't retain any features of a script. [3 marks max]

Unit 15

Get started

The children are asked to use quotes where they can.

1. For example, The extract says that "Jung Chang was born in Yibin, Sichuan Province in China". [1 mark]
2. For example, The extract says that she wrote 'Wild Swans' "partly as her autobiography and partly as a biography describing the lives of her mother and grandmother". [1 mark]
3. For example, Chang was six when she started primary school. [1 mark]

Year 6: Pupil Book answers

4. For example, On her journeys to and from school, Chang searched "for broken nails, rusty cogs, and any other metal objects that had been trodden into the mud between the cobbles". [1 mark]
5. For example, She needed them "for feeding into furnaces to produce steel". [1 mark]
6. For example, The slogans on the walls said "Long Live the Great Leap Forward!" and "Everybody, Make Steel!" [1 mark]
7. For example, Chairman Mao was the leader of China. [1 mark]
8. For example, The cooking woks were replaced by "crucible-like vats". [1 mark]

Try these

The children's answers may be subjective but should be in their own words and well justified, using evidence from either the text or the children's own experiences.

1. Answers should appreciate that an autobiography is an account of the author's own life. [1 mark]
2. Answers could refer to features such as factual information presented in a chronological order and in the first person. The information covers Chang's childhood, its circumstances and their impact. [2 marks]
3. Answers should recognise this sentence assumes that the reader is surprised by the previous piece of information (that the metal objects she collected "were for feeding into furnaces to produce steel, which was my major occupation"). They could add that it answers an assumed question such as 'Did you really have a major occupation at the age of six?' and creates the impression that the author is speaking with the reader rather than just informing them. [2 marks]
4. Answers should grasp that Mao's main aim for China was that it should produce huge amounts of steel. [1 mark]
5. Answers could refer to education, health, healthcare, home life, nutrition and / or agriculture. [2 marks]
6. Answers should grasp that Chang did not agree with Mao's plan, and could refer to her calling it a "half-baked dream". [2 marks]
7. Answers should recognise that Chang mentions an alternative when she says, "But instead of trying to expand the proper steel industry with skilled workers, he decided to get the whole population to take part." [1 mark]
8. Open-ended question: Look for well-reasoned opinions (although it is less likely that children will be able to justify an affirmative answer). [2 marks]

Now try these

The children's answers will be subjective but should be well justified, where appropriate.

1. In addition to worrying about her daughter, answers could refer to Chang's mother having to move out of her home ("the old vicarage") and into a compound; having to stop cooking for her family; having to give up her woks and soft, comfortable bed; and / or her and her husband having to stay in their offices, away from each other and their daughter, "to make sure the temperature in their office furnaces never dropped". [3 marks max]
2. Open-ended question: Look for relevant questions directed at Chang that are not answered by the extract (For example, 'How did you feel about leaving your home and not seeing your parents often?' 'How did you learn to read and write well, without any lessons at school?' 'Did you have any time to make friends?') [3 marks max]
3. Open-ended question: Look for relevance to task; consistency of theme and character; imagination; presentation; and consideration of things that Chang might like or not mind as well as things that make her unhappy. [3 marks max]
4. Open-ended question: Look for relevance to task; imagination; presentation; and inclusion of details about Chang's childhood from the text (For example, her "main occupation", her poor schooling, her life in the compound and her lack of contact with her parents). [3 marks max]
5. Answers should consider the main facts required to write an autobiography: date and place of birth, family life, childhood and schooling, hobbies, achievements, plans, feelings and any life-changing events. [3 marks max]

Composition

Unit 1

Get started

As this is a discussion exercise there are no formal marks for this section. Children think of any books they have read or television programmes with cliff hangers. They discuss what was happening, why it was so exciting, the effect of the reader or view, and what this type of ending is called.

Try these

1. Mr Brownlow and Mrs Mayle [2 marks]
2. Mr Bumble, Mr Sowerberry, Fagin and Bill Sikes [4 marks]
3. Settings: workhouse; an orphanage; an undertaker's shop; London – Fagin's house; London – Mr Brownlow's house [5 marks]
4. When writing a story, you should decide settings, characters and plot. You should also try to have a clear idea of why you are writing. [2 marks]
5. The intended readers were readers of *Bentley's Miscellany*, middle class, British Victorians. [1 mark]
6. This story plan has been organised using subheading and bullet pointed lists. [2 marks]
7. Dickens wrote 'Oliver Twist' to entertain readers (and so make a living); to show readers the terrible state of the poor; and to inspire readers to help the poor. [3 marks]
8. Dickens ends chapters on cliff hangers so that the reader will want to know more and buy the next copy. [1 mark]
9. After meeting the Artful Dodger, Oliver is introduced to Fagin who sends him out to steal for him. This results in Oliver being framed for a theft. After being saved from the

Year 6: Pupil Book answers

police by Mr Brownlow, Oliver is abducted by Bill Sikes, forced to burgle the house and is shot. [2 marks]

Now try these

1. Give 1–10 marks for a completed planning table. Give 1 mark for a suitable choice of topic. Give 1–3 marks for appropriate strategies for creating sympathy and inspiring action. Give 1–2 marks each for details of settings, characters and a plot.
2. Children research the topic they are writing about to check their facts and make improvements. Give 1–10 marks for a scene (any scene) from the story planned previously. Award marks for evident attempts to gain the reader's sympathy, address the chosen topic and / or to inspire the reader to take action. Reward creativity, good writing and language skills. [10 marks]

Unit 2

Get started

1. As this is a discussion exercise, there are no formal marks for this section. Children describe a film they have seen to each other. They consider what details their partner included; what details were left out; what details were included that could have been left out; and what the most important details were.
2. A summary is a shortened version of a piece of writing, which includes the most important details. A summary should be as short as possible, including all and only the important details.
3. Children write a summary of the film they described earlier with close attention to what is and is not included.

Try these

1. Don't include unnecessary details; if you use exact text from the story, put it in quotation marks; the present tense is simplest and most efficient; never copy out whole sentences; paraphrase for the most efficient language. [5 marks]
2. Children rewrite sentences in as few words as possible. Answers may be similar to the following. Give 1 mark per condensed sentence.
   a) Mrs Darling sat by the fire to sew.
   b) Mrs Darling screamed; Nana entered.
   c) Nana closed the window. Peter escaped. His shadow was trapped.
3. Direct speech is when the actual words of the speaker are written enclosed by speech marks. Reported speech is when a speaker's words are reported rather than quoted directly. Reported speech is generally more useful because it can be paraphrased and condensed, so only the meaning need be reported. [3 marks]
4. Paragraph 1: Having given Nana the night off, Mrs Darling has seen her children to bed and to sleep.
   Paragraph 2: Mrs Darling falls asleep by the fire.
   Paragraph 3: Mrs Darling dreams of Neverland and a "strange boy".
   Paragraph 4: A boy and a strange light enter through the window and Mrs Darling wakes up.
   Paragraph 5: Mrs Darling recognises the boy as Peter Pan.
   Paragraph 6: Mrs Darling screams, Nana enters and Peter flees through the window.
   Paragraph 7: Nana has trapped Peter's shadow, which Mrs Darling stores in a drawer.
5. Children's answers may be similar to the following. Give 1–5 marks for brevity, efficient use of language and good choices on what information to keep. Make sure summaries make sense.
   The children and Mrs D. are asleep. Nana is out. Mrs D. dreams of Peter Pan, who appears through the window. Mrs. D screams. Nana returns and traps Peter's shadow in the window as he flees. Mrs D. puts the shadow in a drawer.

Now try these

1. Give 1–10 marks for a summary of a second extract from Peter Pan in less than 50 words. Reward brevity, efficient use of language and good choices on what information to keep. Make sure summaries make sense. [10 marks]
2. Give 1–10 marks for a blurb for a chosen book. The blurb should successfully summarise key information about the book such as settings, characters, themes and a little bit of the plot, but should not give too much away and should aim to persuade the reader to read the book. Reward creativity and good writing and language skills. [10 marks]

Unit 3

Get started

As this is a discussion exercise there are no formal marks for this section.

1. What someone says
   What someone does
   What someone thinks
2. *(sounding doubtful)*
   (confidently)
3. "usual seat" and "What a face he had, now that it was almost level with mine!"
4. Children consider reasons that elements of a story may have to be left out of an adaptation such as lack of space or interest.

Try these

1. Fiona: *(Staring at him)* Did you eat the biscuits? [2 marks]
   Grandpa: *(Scratching his chin)* That is a problem. A dreadful problem. [2 marks]
   Penny: *(Screaming and kicking the fence)* I won't say sorry, I won't! [2 marks]
2. She thought her heart would break: *(Sobbing)* [1 mark]
   I couldn't let him know that I thought it was funny: *(Trying not to laugh.)* [1 mark]
   John had never been so scared in his life: *(Shaking)* [1 mark]
   Maria knew she had to get it right – it was so important: *(Concentrating)* [1 mark]

Year 6: Pupil Book answers

3. Answers may be similar to the following.
   Simret reads the note and laughs. She throws the note in the bin, picks up her school bag and leaves the room. [1 mark]
   Jake sits on the sofa. He changes the channel on the television a few times then plays on his phone for a while. He sighs and puts down the phone. [1 mark]

Now try these

1. Give 1–10 marks for planning an adaptation of a scene from a chosen book. Give 1–2 marks for notes on characters. Give 1–3 marks each for notes on the setting and stage directions. Reward evident understanding and demonstration of the shift in focus that is needed for adaptation. [8 marks]
2. Give 1–10 marks for a playscript adaption of a scene from a chosen book using the planning from the previous section. The work must correctly follow the conventions of a script. Award marks for correctly formatted dialogue, actions or feelings successfully converted into stage directions, and an accurate setting description. Reward fidelity to the original extract, attention to detail, creative problem solving and usability of the script for staging a play. [12 marks]

Unit 4

Get started

As this is a discussion exercise there are no formal marks for this section.

1. Personification is a type of metaphor where non-human things are given human characteristics. Children should use a dictionary to check their definitions.
2. A clock
3. Children take it in turns to solve each other's riddles.

Try these

1. The sun and the wind are personified in the poem. [2 marks]
2. Human qualities you can use include emotions, intentions and speech. [3 marks]
3. Human characteristics used are: self awareness; the need for rest; facial expressions; intention; the ability to make art; antagonism; and conversation. Children may find any or all of these. Give 1 mark per characteristic.
4. It is not possible to use personification on human characters because they are already human. [1 mark]
5. It shows self awareness which is a quality inanimate objects cannot have. [1 mark]
6. **The idea being personified:** Time [1 mark]; Nature [1 mark]; Death [1 mark]; Justice [1 mark]; The government of the United States of America (or, more generally, the country itself) [1 mark]
   Description of the character: Time: An old man with a beard who carries an hour glass and a scythe [1 mark]; Nature: A woman with motherly qualities [1 mark]; Death: A skeleton in a long, black, hooded robe, carrying a scythe. [1 mark]; Justice: A woman wearing a blindfold, holding a sword in one hand and a pair of weighing scales in the other. [1 mark]; The USA: A man with white hair and beard, a white top hat with a blue starry band, a blue coat, white shirt and a red bow tie. [1 mark]

Now try these

1. Stars can't dance: to dance is human. [1 mark]
   Words can't leap: to leap seems human. [1 mark]
   Having no eyes, lights can't wink. Winking seems very human. [1 mark]
2. Danced, leapt, winked [3 marks]
3. Children think of a verb for each inanimate object to give them a human quality. Accept any choice of verb that gives a human quality. Allow for unusual and creative choices. [3 marks]
4. Give 1 mark per sentence showing correct use of personification. [3 marks]
5. Give 1–10 marks for a descriptive paragraph on the chosen subject which uses personification correctly. Award more marks the more correct examples of personification they can give. Reward examples which are particularly effective. [10 marks]

Unit 5

Get started

As this is a discussion exercise, there are no formal marks for this section.

1. A biography is an account of someone's life.
2. Examples of types of biography may include autobiographies, diaries, memoirs, curriculum vitae and timelines.
3. Children discuss biographies they have read or heard of.
4. An autobiography is a biography written by the person it's about.
5. Children discuss autobiographies they have read or heard of.

Try these

1. Charles John Huffam Dickens was born on 7 February, 1812 in Portsmouth. [2 marks]
2. His father was John Dickens, a clerk in the Navy Office. [2 marks]
3. His father was imprisoned for debt so Dickens became the main earner. [2 marks]
4. In 1836 he married Catherine Hogarth. [2 marks]
5. America, Canada, Switzerland, Italy and France [5 marks]
6. 1812: Born
   1821: His father was imprisoned for debt and his education halted. At 12 years old, he worked at Warren's blacking factory.
   1827–1832: He finished his education at Wellington House Academy. He became a clerk, and was then promoted to court reporter.
   1833: He became a journalist for the 'Morning Chronicle.'
   1836: He wrote 'The Pickwick Papers' and became famous.
   1837–1841: He wrote four very successful novels.

Year 6: Pupil Book answers

1842: He toured America.
1857: He toured Europe.
1860–1870: He wrote some of his greatest works.
1870: Died [10 marks]

7. Features may include: date and place of birth; parentage; places of habitation; details of education; hobbies and interests; major achievements; professional details; spouse's and children's names and marriage date; a date and place of death. [Give 1 mark per feature.]
8. A curriculum vitae (CV) is a form of biographical writing that gives a brief account of a person's life, concentrating on education, qualifications and occupations. A CV is usually prepared for job applications. [2 marks]
9. A CV is used for job applications so it would not be needed after a person's death.

Now try these

1. Give 1–12 marks for an autobiography plan. Give 1–2 marks each for date and place of birth; place or places of education; places of habitation; achievements; major events; and any other important information. [12 marks]
2. Give 1–10 marks for a completed autobiography written in the first person and the past tense, in paragraphs, and which describes events in chronological order. Autobiographies can include thoughts, feelings and opinions about facts and events. Reward good writing and language skills. [10 marks]

Unit 6
Get started

As this is a discussion exercise, there are no formal marks for this section.

1. A fact is something that is irrefutably true; an opinion is a view about something.
2. Children give examples of facts and opinions.
3. Almost any type of text can be used to report facts (most of which are also used to report opinions and interpretations of the facts). Examples may include: newspaper reports, non-fiction books, police reports, reference books, encyclopaedias, essays.
4. Some text types are more fact-focused than others. For example, an encyclopaedia should include nothing but facts where as an essay aims to give an interpretation of the facts, and editorial articles focus on the writers' opinions about the facts.
5. Diaries are not really suitable for recording facts because diary entries focus on subjective experiences and are written for the writer, so any other reader may have to read carefully to separate fact from opinion.

Try these

1. Lists of features may include: a narrative of events; reported speech; full sentences and paragraphs; first person; past tense; reported opinions; unreliable reporting. Give 1 mark per feature identified.
2. Lynn has used paragraphs to organise her writing. [1 mark]
3. Lynn has written in the first person, past tense. [1 mark]
4. Lists of features may include: sub-headings; short sentences; a bullet-point list; a statement of the aim; a list of equipment; a set of instructions; a table of results; a conclusion. Give 1 mark per feature identified.
5. Kate has used a numbered list to emphasise the order of events. [1 mark]
6. Kate has used imperative verbs in the Method section because it is a set of instructions for carrying out the experiment. [1 mark]
7. fill, add, put, shake, leave, record, repeat [1 mark]
8. Kate has presented the results in a table. [1 mark]
9. Kate's text is the most appropriate way to present scientific research.
10. Lynn's text is most appropriate for a diary entry.

Now try these

1. Give 1–10 marks for an account of a science experiment using the first person and the past tense, and describing events in chronological order. Accounts should address these questions: What was the aim of the experiment? What equipment or resources were used? What happened? What were the results? Was anything proved or disproved? Reward attention to detail. [10 marks]
2. Give 1–10 marks for the same science experiment written as a science report following the format of the example text: using the same sub-headings for each section; presenting the equipment in a bullet-point list; writing the method as a numbered set of instructions; presenting the results in a table (if appropriate); writing the aim and conclusion in full sentences. [10 marks]

Unit 7
Get started

As this is a discussion exercise, there are no formal marks for this section.

1. Children explain what is meant by 'journalism' (the writing and production of newspapers and magazines). They give examples to support their answer.
2. Children discuss what they think the job of a journalist involves and whether it is a job they think they would enjoy.
3. Children discuss how important they think journalism is.
4. Children discuss how important they think it is for journalists to be truthful and whether they should always present a balanced opinion.
5. Children discuss freedom of the press.

Try these

1. **What**: Two Americans landing and walking on the moon. [1 mark]
2. **Where:** They blasted off from Houston and travelled to the moon. [1 mark]
3. **When:** 21st July, 1969. Landed at 3.18 p.m. Earth time. [1 mark]
4. **Why:** Space exploration, to be the first to land on the moon. [1 mark]

Year 6: Pupil Book answers

5. **Who:** Neil Armstrong, Edwin Aldrin and, in the orbiting spacecraft, Michael Collins [1 mark]
6. Direct speech:
   "That's one small step for a man, a giant leap for mankind"
   "Beautiful, beautiful. A magnificent desolation."
   "The surface is fine and powdered, like powdered charcoal to the soles of the foot,"
   "I can see the footprints of my boots in the fine sandy particles."
   "Here man first set foot on the moon, July 1969. We came in peace for all mankind."

Now try these

1. Give 1–10 marks for a plan of a newspaper article on a fictional local event. Plans should address the questions: What? Where? When? Why? Who? They should also include details of a headline and a person to be interviewed. Reward creativity and promising ideas. [10 marks]
2. Give 1–10 marks for a full newspaper report based on the previous planning. Reports should include details on the questions: What? Where? When? Why? Who? They should also include a headline and an interview with one or two quote. Reward creativity, good writing and language skills.

Unit 8

Get started

As this is a discussion exercise, there are no formal marks for this section.

1. Children discuss what they think makes a humorous or funny story.
2. Children talk about humorous stories they have read. Then they provide anecdotes of the funniest thing they have ever seen, heard or read.
3. Children discuss stories, cartoons, films and television programmes that they find funny.
4. Children tell each other jokes and discuss whether they found them funny or not.

Try these

1. A humorous story is a story that people find funny.
2. Reactions to Stanley's accident are all strangely calm. Accept any examples of calm or blasé reactions to Stanley's accident and / or flattened state.
3. The story contrasts the bizarre with the mundane. Accept any examples of this contrast.
4. If a boy were crushed in real life people would be shocked, panicked and upset.
5. The Lambchops are a bit surprised and puzzled by Stanley's accident but not overly concerned and do not panic.
6. Lambchops have associations of hearty dinners and very British homeliness and normality.
7. The language the Lambchops use is overly formal and polite.

8. Children may make some or all of the following observations and may make others also. Give 1 mark per valid observation.
   Realistic everyday things: Bulletin boards to pin pictures on [1 mark]; Breakfast [1 mark]; A normal family in a normal house [1 mark]; A visit to the doctor [1 mark]; Children needing new clothes / having clothes altered [1 mark]; A ring falling down a drain [1 mark]
   Things that could never happen: A boy surviving being flattened and continuing to live in that state [1 mark]; A boy being able to slide under doors [1 mark]

Now try these

1. Give 1–10 marks for a plan for a humorous story based on a previous event. Plans should include ideas for some or all of these: silly names or surnames; understatement; a contrast between the ordinary and the bizarre; impossible events; unusual behaviour; any other ideas they may have. Reward creativity and promising ideas. Allow for the fact that humour is very subjective. [10 marks]
2. Give 1–10 marks for a completed humorous story based on previous planning. Reward creativity; promising ideas; good writing and language skills; evident attempts at humour; and anything that is genuinely funny. Allow for the fact that humour is very subjective. Children should test their stories on a partner, discuss what worked and make improvements. [10 marks]

Unit 9

Get started

As this is a discussion exercise, there are no formal marks for this section.

1. The main theme of both these poems is loneliness at school.
2. Children discuss the topics of other poems they know of, including their favourite poem if they have one.
3. Children make a list of all the poems they can think of and what each poem is about.
4. Children compare and contrast any poems that deal with the same topics, themes or issues.

Try these

1. **The Loner:** Number of verses: 4; Number of lines per verse: two verses of 7 lines, two verses of 6 lines; Rhyme scheme: variable [3 marks]
   The New Boy: Number of verses: 7; Number of lines per verse: 4; Rhyme scheme: ABCB [3 marks]
2. The boy is afraid of the other children. He stays by himself to protect himself but he is also trapped by his loneliness. [1 mark]
3. followed, rang, shattering, barged, banged, flew, pursued, snapped, clanged, hung, pushing, shoving, pinned [13 marks]
4. They are mostly verbs about action and there are a lot of them. They make the scene seem very lively, active, and noisy. [1 mark]

Year 6: Pupil Book answers

5. Both poems portray school as a rough and pitiless place but also a place that's fun so long as you have friends (and a terrible, scary place if you don't have friends). [1 mark]
6. 'The New Boy' has a happy ending. 'The Loner' has a thoughtful, wistful ending (though the whole poem is quite sad). [1 mark]
7. You don't get to know the lonely boy at all. The poem is from the perspective of another child who observes him. He remains an enigma. [1 mark]
8. Children write which poem they like best and why.

Now try these
1. Give 1–10 marks for a plan of a poem on the theme of loneliness. Plans should include notes on setting, character(s), verses, rhyme scheme, powerful vocabulary, figurative language, and perspective. Reward creativity and promising ideas. [10 marks]
2. Give 1–10 marks for a completed poem on the theme of loneliness using the previous planning. Reward creativity, use of poetic language and devices, good poetic structure, good writing skills and interesting, original and / or sensitive treatment of the subject. [10 marks]

Unit 10
Get started
As this is a discussion exercise, there are no formal marks for this section.
1. Children think of examples of chapter books they have read.
2. Children discuss why they think longer stories are divided into chapters.
3. Children describe the first two chapters of a book they have read, then listen to their partner do the same.
4. Children discuss the chapters they described, looking at what they have in common and what characters and plot elements are introduced.

Try these
1. Characters' personalities; descriptions of settings; character descriptions; details of the plot up to the end of the second chapter. [4 marks]
2. Characters, setting and plot [1 mark]
3. Other elements listed may include: intended readers, themes, aims of the story, and strategies for achieving aims. Give 1 mark per relevant addition to a story plan.
4. Chapter 1 is set in a kitchen on a farm. Chapter 2 begins in the kitchen, moves outside to the farmyard, then to a barn. [3 marks]
5. How many characters; ages; physical descriptions; what they're wearing; personalities; motivations [5 marks]
6. In Chapter 1 "Reader must learn that they are on holiday at auntie's house." [1 mark]
7. Auntie Betty is the new character introduced in Chapter 2. [1 mark]
8. The children find a cupboard in the barn with strange lights and sounds coming from it. [1 mark]

Now try these
1. Give 1–5 marks for completed planning with notes on: what is in the cupboard; where the children go and what they do next; the introduction of a new character (the villain); and a cliff-hanging chapter ending. Give 1–10 marks for completed writing of this chapter. Reward creativity, good writing and language skills. [15 marks]
2. Give 1–10 marks for a completed final chapter. Children should decide what type of narrative ending they want to use. Reward creativity, good writing and language skills. Children should read through their first draft, checking for effect and then making improvements. [10 marks]

Unit 11
Get started
As this is a discussion exercise, there are no formal marks for this section.
1. To explain something is to make something clear by providing the relevant facts.
2. Explanation texts can be formatted in many ways. Text types include: lists (numbered and bulleted), non-fiction books, essays, reports, instructions, and diagrams.
3. Children discuss the advantages and disadvantages of each format.
4. A set of instructions is the best format for explaining how to do something.
5. A diary entry is the most obvious format in which to explain personal motivations. Other appropriate text types may include biographies, memoirs, letters and confessions.

Try these
1. The intended reader of Tom's diary entry is the writer, Tom.
2. The intended reader of the instructions is whoever wants to put the tent up (most likely the owner of the tent).
3. Tom's diary entry records memories, thoughts and feelings.
4. The aim of an instruction text is to explain to the reader how to do something.
5. Tom's diary entry is written in full sentences and paragraphs. Events are told chronologically.
6. The instruction text needs a diagram to show where to fix the guy ropes.
7. The order of things is important because they tell you what to do, step-by-step.
8. The instructions text uses "should" a lot because it is telling the reader what they should do and how things should be.
9. Features listed may include: narrative and anecdote, reported conversations, informal figures of speech, opinions and observations, use of personal pronouns. Give 1 mark per feature listed.
10. Features listed may include: full sentences and paragraphs; efficient language; chronological order;

Year 6: Pupil Book answers

imperative verbs; use of the word should. Children may make other observations. Give 1 mark per feature listed.

Now try these
1. Give 1–10 marks for a set of instructions (a recipe for food which they have prepared in the past) which follow the correct structure and language features for an instructional text. Award marks for good structure and organisation of information, and any use organisational devices. Reward attention to detail and efficient language. [10 marks]
2. Give 1–10 marks for a diary entry describing the time they made the item of food they have written instructions for. Diary entries should describe the event; record their thoughts and feelings at the time; be written in the past tense; and contain connecting words and phrases. Reward good description, attention to detail, and good writing and language skills. [10 marks]

Unit 12
Get started
As this is a discussion exercise, there are no formal marks for this section.
1. A paragraph is a group of sentences that deal with a single topic, theme or idea.
2. It is important to use paragraphs in non-fiction writing because they organise information and break up the text into readable chunks.
3. Children find examples of when they have used paragraphs previously and explain why they used them.
4. Children discuss whether their reasons for using paragraphs are the same for fiction and non-fiction.
5. Checklist for the use of paragraphs in non-fiction:
   - Longer pieces of text should be divided into paragraphs or sections.
   - A section of text should be indicated by a new line.
   - The section or paragraph will usually comprise of more than one sentence, dealing with a single theme, topic or idea.
   - Paragraphs within each section begin on a new line.
   - The first lines of paragraphs within each section are indented.
   - Subheadings indicate new sections of text.
   - Sections or paragraphs in information texts do not have to be ordered chronologically (in time order).

Try these
1. There are four headings in the text about Usain Bolt. [1 mark]
2. There are 10 paragraphs in the text about Usain Bolt. [1 mark]
3. **Section 1:** Introduction with information on why Bolt is famous. [1 mark]
   Section 2: Information on Bolt's early life including where he was born, early interests and achievements and his nickname. [1 mark]
   Section 3: Information on Bolt's career 2004–2007, including some achievements and some difficulties. [1 mark]
   Section 4: Information on the height of Bolt's career, listing his record breaking achievements in 2008–2012 and concluding with his statement that he has nothing more to prove. [1 mark]
4. The text on Mo Farah has no paragraph breaks. [1 mark]
5. Allow for differences of opinion. Accept all reasonable choices. Suggested answers:
   Heading 1: Mo's early life; Information: Up to "... English school titles" [example];
   Heading 2: His ambition grows [1 mark]; Information: From "In 2005 ..." to "he said." [1 mark];
   Heading 3: British records and European champion [1 mark]; Information: From "Soon after ..." to "... chemicals in his blood." [1 mark];
   Heading 4: Britain's greatest male distance runner [1 mark]; Information: From "Once this was sorted out" to "... Britain has ever seen." [1 mark];
   Heading 5: 2012: Double Olympic champion [1 mark]; Information: From "On 4 August 2012 ..." to the end. [1 mark]

Now try these
1. Give 1–10 marks for a completed planning diagram with information on children's favourite hobby or sport. Notes should be organised into sections relevant to the topic as suggested by the layout of the diagram. Children can fill in any or all of the sections suggested and may wish to add some of their own. Reward knowledge of the subject, attention to detail, promising ideas and properly organised material. [10 marks]
2. Give 1–10 marks for an information text on the chosen hobby or sport using the planning from the previous section. Reward good organisation of information, knowledge of the subject, attention to detail, and good writing and language skills. [10 marks]

Unit 13
Get started
As this is a discussion exercise, there are no formal marks for this section.
1. Children find examples of when they have used paragraphs in fiction writing and explain why they used them.
2. Use a new paragraph: whenever the narrative changes time; whenever the narrative changes place; whenever the narrative changes topic; whenever the narrative changes speaker; when a new character is introduced; when the writer wants to control the pace of the narrative and create dramatic effects, for example, a very short paragraph for dramatic effect.
3. Children look at examples of fiction texts. They find the shortest paragraph, the longest paragraph, discuss the effects of different lengths of paragraph, identify reasons

Year 6: Pupil Book answers

for paragraph breaks, clarify any they don't understand and identify any they disagree with.

Try these

1. **Paragraph 2**: First sentence: When dad disappeared, mum said we couldn't afford to live there anymore. [1 mark] Reason: Changes topic and moves back in time to when dad disappeared [2 marks];
   Paragraph 3: First sentence: I watched as the house seemed to disappear behind a mist of fog. [1 mark] Reason: Time moves back to the story present [1 mark];
   Paragraph 4: First sentence: The day seemed to roll by as we travelled along the motorway. [1 mark] Reason: Location changes from house to motorway and time also changes to later in the day [2 marks];
   Paragraph 5: First sentence: She hadn't spoken much at all these last few months. [1 mark] Reason: Time changes to look back at the last few months [1 mark];
   Paragraph 6: First sentence: "Mum ..." I began. [1 mark] Reason: A character begins to speak [1 mark];
   Paragraph 7: First sentence: It was getting dark. [1 mark] Reason: Change in time from daytime to evening [1 mark];
   Paragraph 8: First sentence: We pulled into the drive. [1 mark] Reason: Change of location: arriving at the new house [1 mark]
2. Give 1–6 marks for three paragraphs describing what happens next in the story. 1 mark per paragraph, and 1 mark for each reason for a paragraph break. [6 marks]

Now try these

1. Award marks for correct paragraph breaks and explanations. [10 marks] Suggested answers:
   Paragraph 1
   It was a cold, damp day. The rain had been falling all morning and there had been no chance of going out at all. Kamal really wanted to meet his friends and play football. But here he was, stuck inside with no sign of brighter weather. He would have to stay indoors and watch the television.
   Paragraph 2 (Change of place)
   All of a sudden the phone rang in the other room and he ran to answer it. It was his cousin, Hamid, asking him to come over to play on his new computer game. It had been a present for his birthday and he was longing for someone to play it with him. The offer was irresistible! Kamal agreed, promising to be there in half an hour.
   Paragraph 3 (Change of place)
   He rushed to the hall to get his coat and search for his trainers. It was then he remembered the hole! The last time he wore his trainers playing football he had noticed large holes in the soles of both trainers, made worse by continually playing football! His feet would get soaked but that new game was something special and he couldn't resist the invitation. He put them on, opened the door and rushed outside.
   Paragraph 4 (Change of place)
   Rain fell in sheets, and a cold wind blew, but still Kamal ran on to his cousin's house. By the time he reached the end of his road, his feet were soaked through. His socks were wet, his toes were freezing cold and he felt sure there was a blister on his left heel. He saw his cousin's house in the distance and leaping over puddles like small lakes he finally rang the door bell.
   Paragraph 5 (Introduce new character)
   "Hello Kamal," said his cousin. "You'd better come in and get dry. I don't know what we can do though; there's been a power cut due to the storm and the computer isn't working."
   Paragraph 6 (short paragraph for effect)
   The look on Kamal's face said it all. Cold, wet and no computer game. What a day!
2. Give 1–10 marks for a narrative where the storyline has been organised into paragraphs. It should be clear as to why there is a change in paragraph. Reward creativity, good structure and good writing and language skills. [10 marks]

Unit 14

Get started

As this is a discussion exercise, there are no formal marks for this section.

1. There are different ways to convey factual information. These include: diaries, letters, reports, newspaper articles, maps, lists and diagrams.
2. The method chosen depends on who will be reading it and what they need to know. Children consider the advantages and disadvantages of the different ways they have thought of.
3. We can use a colon instead of a full stop after a clause when the next clause explains the first. The clause after the colon gives more information about the clause before the colon.
4. We can use a semicolon to join two main clauses without using a conjunction. A semicolon is a stronger break than a comma, but not as strong as a full stop. It can be used instead of the words 'and', 'but' or 'so'.

Try these

1. A map can show things (such as the shapes of countries) that are impossible to put into words. [1 mark]
2. There is a lot of information (such as historical or cultural information) that cannot be presented visually. [1 mark]
3. The pictures in the information book show the reader what Morocco looks like. [1 mark]
4. The information book extract mentions: the history of the name of the country; the facts that some parts of the country are mountainous and other parts are barren; that Morocco is the nearest North African country to Europe. [1 mark]
5. The shape of the country; the location of the capital city, Rabat; that Morocco has Mediterranean coastline. [1 mark]

Year 6: Pupil Book answers

6. The size of Morocco is listed in both the reference and the information book.
7. A scale could be added to the map to give the reader an idea of the size of Morocco.
8. The reference book uses colons to organise information.
9. The subheadings are for organising the information and to enable the reader to find information within the text more quickly.

Now try these

1. Give 1–10 marks for planning of a promotional leaflet for the Moroccan tourist board. Planning should include notes about places to visit and things to do while in Morocco. It should also include details on what the sub sections will be and how information will be presented, considering layout, maps, illustrations, bullet-point lists and anything else they can think of. The leaflet should aim to encourage tourism. [10 marks]
2. Give 1–10 marks for a tourist information leaflet using the planning done previously. The leaflet should aim to persuade people to visit Morocco. It should include organisational features and aim to be reader-friendly and usable. Reward good gathering, organising and presenting of information, good writing and language skills. [10 marks]

Unit 15

Get started

As this is a discussion exercise, there are no formal marks for this section.

1. Children describe endings of stories they have read, watched or listened to.
2. Children discuss what types of endings they prefer.
3. Children describe, in written form, how they like stories to end.

Try these

1. The term 'cliff hanger' refers to an ending that leaves the audience in suspense.
2. A 'prequel' is a story written after an original story, but set before the time frame of the original work. A 'sequel' is a story written after an original story that follows on from events in the original.
3. A 'cyclical' story has a plot that ends at the beginning.
4. An 'ambiguous' ending leaves questions unanswered.
5. Happy endings and endings where everyone learns something are most suitable for young children.
6. Accept any suitable ending for each genre. See suggestions below. Give 1 mark per appropriate ending.
   How the story might end: A fairytale / Happily ever after; A murder mystery / The murderer is discovered, the mystery solved; A romance / The lovers admit their love for each other; A moral story / Everyone learns a valuable lesson; A tragedy / All the good characters die; A comedy / A funny twist at the end; A survival story / The characters make it home alive

Now try these

1. Give 1–10 marks for a story ending to the 'The Mountain Climbers.' Children can choose the type of ending and should try to achieve the chosen effect. Reward creativity, good writing and language skills. Children should share the ending with a partner, take their feedback, and then do the same for their partner and their story ending.
2. Give 1–10 marks for a review of a bad story ending of their choice. They should consider various questions to determine exactly why they didn't like the ending and then write about why the ending didn't work for them. Better answers will be more objective in their reasons rather than relying entirely on personal taste. Reward good analytical skills, evident understanding of good story structure, good structure of the review, good writing and language skills. [10 marks]

Vocabulary, Grammar and Punctuation

Vocabulary Unit 1

Get started

All answers will depend on the thesauruses available.

1. sour, old, decayed, musty, fusty [example]
2. For example, cloudy, overcast, grey, gloomy, leaden [1 mark]
3. For example, spotless, unsoiled, fresh, sparkling, hygienic [1 mark]
4. For example, protect, but, except, bar, excluding [1 mark]
5. For example, appearance, expression, air, aspect, guise [1 mark]
6. For example, cheerful, contented, delighted, ecstatic, elated [1 mark]
7. For example, bound, dance, fly, hop, scamper [1 mark]
8. For example, alarming, chilling, creepy, eerie, horrifying [1 mark]

Try these

1. The pop star was <u>swamped</u> with fan mail when she finally returned home from touring. [example]
2. For example, The curious explorer, waiting patiently, wondered with anxiety what would <u>come out</u> from the cave in front of her. [1 mark]
3. For example, The old man realised his mistake and <u>took back</u> his statement in court. [1 mark]
4. For example, Old Major Faversham, who's a friend of my Gran, <u>asked</u> what my name was. [1 mark]
5. For example, The full moon was <u>shining</u> in the black, starry sky. [1 mark]
6. For example, The pantomime we saw in London last Christmas was very <u>entertaining</u>. [1 mark]

Year 6: Pupil Book answers

Now try these

1. Open-ended task: accept any well-explained substitutions. (For example, 'elderly' and 'saturated' exaggerate the man's weakness and wetness.) [2 marks]
2.–5. Open-ended tasks: accept any well-explained substitutions. [2 marks per question]
6. Open-ended task: accept any well-explained substitutions. [3 marks]

Vocabulary Unit 2

Get started

All answers will depend on the thesauruses and dictionaries available.

1. The king had returned from a long journey and <u>consumed</u> his welcome-home feast quickly. [example]
2. For example, The beautiful, wild hawk <u>balanced</u> high in the branches of an old oak tree. [1 mark]
3. For example, The <u>delicate</u> ballerina danced beautifully across the stage in her bright pink costume. [1 mark]
4. For example, It was only by the smallest chance that the <u>fortunate</u> rabbit got away from the fox. [1 mark]
5. For example, I wanted some of the mushroom pizza, but there was only a <u>miniscule</u> bit left! [1 mark]
6. For example, Three large, gentle cows with black spots stood <u>munching</u> grass in the field. [1 mark]
7. For example, Caroline held onto her new puppy's lead <u>firmly</u>, so he couldn't run off. [1 mark]

Try these

1. Dan was <u>active</u> in his hunt for the missing money. [example]
2. For example, The test was tough, and Lola felt <u>defeated</u>. [1 mark]
3. For example, Xander felt <u>confident</u> about the school play. [1 mark]
4. For example, The new teacher was making everyone very <u>tense</u>. [1 mark]
5. For example, Mum seemed very <u>calm</u> when we got home from school. [1 mark]
6. For example, There's a huge dog living next door, and it seems very <u>hostile</u>. [1 mark]
7. For example, Chloe's younger sister looks so <u>diminutive</u> next to her! [1 mark]
8. For example, Giles had always wanted to be <u>famous</u>, so he trained to become an actor. [1 mark]

Now try these

1. For example, favourable / promising; ominous / unlucky. The weather forecast seemed favourable. The dark clouds looked ominous. [3 marks]
2. For example, old-fashioned / obsolete; modern / new-fangled
   Open-ended question: accept any appropriate sentences that include a chosen synonym and a chosen antonym. [3 marks]
3. For example, hot / scorching; chilly / frozen
   Open-ended question: accept any appropriate sentences that include a chosen synonym and a chosen antonym. [3 marks]
4. For example, abandon / reject; keep / cherish
   Open-ended question: accept any appropriate sentences that include a chosen synonym and a chosen antonym. [3 marks]
5. For example, ugly / grotesque; beautiful / stunning
   Open-ended question: accept any appropriate sentences that include a chosen synonym and a chosen antonym. [3 marks]
6. For example, clamorous / deafening; quiet / muted
   Open-ended question: accept any appropriate sentences that include a chosen synonym and a chosen antonym. [3 marks]

Vocabulary Unit 3

Get started

Precise wording will vary.

1. I <u>don't</u> <u>like</u> this flavour. [example]
2. For example, In the film <u>we're</u> watching, the aliens are angry. [2 marks]
3. For example, They <u>don't</u> know how to <u>talk</u> <u>to</u> humans well. [2 marks]
4. For example, <u>Because</u> <u>of</u> <u>this</u>, the misunderstanding meant <u>there'd</u> be a large battle. [2 marks]
5. For example, Fortunately, the aliens <u>couldn't</u> <u>beat</u> the humans. [2 marks]
6. For example, Now <u>they've</u> found someone who is <u>good</u> at speaking both languages. [2 marks]
7. For example, <u>I'm</u> <u>sure</u> that things will improve now <u>they're</u> understanding each other. [3 marks]
8. For example, All in all, <u>I've</u> only found the film <u>OK</u>: I <u>don't</u> really <u>like</u> war scenes. [4 marks]

Try these

Precise wording will vary, but no contractions should remain.

1. We watched an excellent film recently. [example]
2. For example, We did not get bored because it was extemely exciting. [1 mark]
3. For example, It was about a family visiting from the United States of America. [1 mark]
4. For example, They had been escaping from their own country. [1 mark]
5. For example, They had been caught stealing things from large banks. [1 mark]
6. For example, They had decided to come to this country. [1 mark]
7. For example, In the end, they were deported from the new country and handed over to the police! [1 mark]
8. For example, I could not stop thinking about it afterwards. [1 mark]

Now try these

1. Open-ended question: accept any informal text message to a friend about meeting up. [1 mark]

Year 6: Pupil Book answers

2. Open-ended question: accept any formal letter complaining to a restaurant. [1 mark]
3. Open-ended question: accept any informal email to a family member about some plans. [1 mark]
4. Open-ended question: accept any short, formal report on a recently read book. [1 mark]
5. Open-ended question: accept any short scene between two children talking informally in the playground. [1 mark]
6. Open-ended question: accept any short, formal speech suitable for a school prize day or parents' evening. [1 mark]

Grammar Unit 1
Get started

1. Mum wishes that my brother <u>keep</u> his room tidy, but of course he disagrees. [example]
2. It is important that Ruchi <u>practise</u> netball if she wants to become good enough for the county team. [1 mark]
3. I suggested that Pippa <u>come</u> to the cinema, as I haven't seen her for months. [1 mark]
4. On the day of the school play, Ms Cox insisted we <u>be</u> at school early. [1 mark]
5. The teacher recommends that we <u>write</u> carefully during our exam, so the marker can read it. [1 mark]
6. We've packed a huge picnic – the day would be ruined if it <u>were</u> raining! [1 mark]
7. Liam demanded that our project <u>include</u> his name on the title page. [1 mark]

Try these

1. were [example]
2. For example, play [1 mark]
3. For example, brush [1 mark]
4. For example, were [1 mark]
5. For example, attend [1 mark]
6. For example, try [1 mark]
7. For example, be [1 mark]
8. For example, join [1 mark]

Now try these

1.–6. Open-ended questions: accept any appropriate answers including a subjunctive verb. [1 mark each]

Grammar Unit 2
Get started

1. <u>The heavy black curtains</u> were drawn quickly by Sadia. [example]
2. During the afternoon, <u>the tea</u> (with sandwiches, scones, clotted cream and jam) was made by Tyler. [1 mark]
3. With an enormous clatter, <u>the study window</u> had been broken to bits by a branch swinging around in the storm. [1 mark]
4. Mysteriously, <u>the long line of footsteps</u> had been left by someone with larger feet than any of us. [1 mark]
5. <u>My hot bath</u> is, very nicely, always run for me on Sunday afternoons. [1 mark]
6. That evening, <u>my grandfather's favourite spy film</u> was watched by all the children in our family. [1 mark]
7. <u>The film</u>, much to my grandfather's surprise, was enjoyed by us all. [1 mark]

Try these

1. by the builders. [example]
2.–8. Open-ended questions: accept any appropriate answers that add an agent (For example, by Sophie.) [1 mark per question]

Now try these

1. Harry was seen by the kind doctor. [1 mark]
2. The heavy book was grabbed by Helena. [1 mark]
3. The homework was finished by Samir. [1 mark]
4. The large, pear-shaped balloon was popped by AJ. [1 mark]
5. The potted cactus was knocked over by the frightened tabby cat. [1 mark]
6. My favourite green hat was lost by my irritating little sister. [1 mark]

Grammar Unit 3
Get started

1. We visited the town <u>where</u> my friend Jayati lives. [example]
2. There is the teacher <u>who</u> teaches me Science at school – she's always very kind. [1 mark]
3. They found the buried treasure <u>that</u> the pirates stole from the old castle. [1 mark]
4. Diana is the lady <u>whose</u> car mum borrowed because ours broke down. [1 mark]
5. I loved the time <u>when</u> we stayed up really late and watched old movies. [1 mark]
6. That's the lady <u>whose</u> dog keeps barking at me when I go to the post office. [1 mark]
7. Next we have art, <u>which</u> is Callum's favourite subject of all. [1 mark]
8. Can you see the dark mark <u>where</u> we spilled black paint on the new rug? [1 mark]

Try these

1. We went shopping on the street where my mum's favourite café is. [example]
2.–8. Open-ended questions: accept any appropriate sentence beginnings. [1 mark per question]

Now try these

1.–6. Open-ended questions: accept any appropriate relative clauses. [1 mark per question]

Grammar Unit 4
Get started

The features identified may vary slightly.

1. <u>The first thing</u> we must recognise is that eating healthily is important. [example]

Year 6: Pupil Book answers

2. The <u>importance</u> of this is, <u>secondly</u>, something on which many people agree. [2 marks]
3. <u>However</u>, such <u>agreement</u> is not enough to make sure everyone is <u>eating healthy</u> food. [3 marks]
4. <u>Instead</u>, fast <u>food</u> is popular because it is easy and cheap. [2 marks]
5. <u>Nevertheless</u>, there are many issues that arise from eating too much <u>fast food</u>. [2 marks]
6. Some of these <u>issues</u> can be helped by exercise. [1 mark]
7. In conclusion, we should <u>eat healthily</u> most of the time, and balance <u>exercising</u> with treats such as <u>fast food</u>. [3 marks]

Try these

The connectives chosen will vary.

1. <u>Some people say that</u> mobile phones are not suitable for children. [example]
2. For example, <u>Another argument is that</u> some children use them too much of the time. [1 mark]
3. For example, <u>In addition</u>, they are expensive. [1 mark]
4. For example, <u>However</u>, some people argue that mobiles are useful. [1 mark]
5. For example, <u>Furthermore</u>, these phones can help children to stay safe. [1 mark]
6. For example, <u>In contrast</u>, many parents worried about their children before mobile phones were available. [1 mark]
7. For example, <u>In conclusion</u>, there are arguments on both sides of the issue. [1 mark]
8. For example, <u>As a compromise</u>, perhaps an age limit could be agreed. [1 mark]

Now try these

1.–6. Open-ended questions: accept any appropriate paragraphs that are linked together using repetition and connecting adverbials. [5 marks max per question]

Punctuation Unit 1

Get started

1. eggs, bread, fruit and vegetables. [example]
2.–8. Open-ended question: accept any appropriate lists that are correctly punctuated with commas. [1 mark per question]

Try these

1. Last month**,** after Tilly's birthday**,** we went on a family holiday to France. [example]
2. We travelled comfortably, gradually getting more and more excited. [1 mark]
3. I took my waterproof coat with me, thinking it might rain. [1 mark]
4. My sister Maheswari, who is only four, forgot her favourite teddy bear. [1 mark]
5. She cried all day, even when Mum gave her a one of the sweets she likes most. [1 mark]
6. We got changed into clean clothes at the hotel, hurrying to go for lunch. [1 mark]

7. We found a café and the food, which was delicious, was brought quickly. [1 mark]
8. If it were up to me, we would go back to the same place every year. [1 mark]

Now try these

1. "Let's eat, Mum," said Florence, thinking about sandwiches.
   For example, The comma makes it clear that Florence does not want to eat her mum. [2 marks]
2. The garden was full of buzzing bees, and flowers.
   For example, The comma makes it clear that the flowers are not buzzing. [2 marks]
3. "I can't believe it's so late," said Leon, suddenly noticing the clock.
   For example, The comma makes it clear that Frank doesn't speak suddenly. [2 marks]
4. Courtney called her cat, and she came running.
   For example, The comma makes it clear that the cat, not Courtney, came running. [2 marks]
5. Let's see, Carrie thought in confusion.
   For example, The comma makes it clear where Carrie's thought ends. [2 marks]
6. In the street there were lots of crying babies, and mothers.
   For example, The comma makes it clear that the mothers are not crying. [2 marks]

Punctuation Unit 2

Get started

Precise wording will vary.

1. An old lady who has poor sight [example]
2. For example, A warning that sounds at high tide [1 mark]
3. For example, My sandwich that is half eaten [1 mark]
4. For example, That baby who has curly hair [1 mark]
5. For example, A laugh that indicates a light heart [1 mark]
6. For example, That noise that sounds horrid [1 mark]
7. For example, A scream that makes the spine tingle [1 mark]
8. For example, The liquid for cleaning the floor [1 mark]

Try these

1. <u>The fast-moving car</u> zipped past us, its horn blaring. [example]
2. <u>A fifty-year-old house</u> stood on the corner of our street. [1 mark]
3. <u>Her old-fashioned blue coat</u> was her favourite. [1 mark]
4. <u>My long-lost aunt Robyn</u> was coming to stay with us over the holidays. [1 mark]
5. <u>The large flat-bottomed</u> cup could hold such a lot of tea! [1 mark]
6. <u>A long-haired ginger cat</u> followed my brother all the way home. [1 mark]

Year 6: Pupil Book answers

Now try these

Precise wording will vary.

1. a) For example, Five children who are one year old [1 mark]
   b) For example, Children who are five years old [1 mark]
2. a) For example, Grass that is chewing sheep [1 mark]
   b) For example, Sheep that is chewing grass [1 mark]
3. a) For example, If plural ('cubes'), this would mean: Sam's blocks, which are both many and coloured [1 mark]
   b) For example, Sam's block, which has many different colours [1 mark]
4. a) For example, The train that is both slow and travelling [1 mark]
   b) For example, The train that is travelling slowly [1 mark]
5. a) For example, Her hat that is both green and feathered [1 mark]
   b) For example, Her hat that features green feathers [1 mark]

Punctuation Unit 3

Get started

Accept brackets, dashes or commas to mark each parenthesis.

1. Mythical creatures may have existed (or so they say). [example]
2. Once such creature – from ancient Greek myths – was called Nessus. [1 mark]
3. Nessus, who was not a nice character, was a centaur. [1 mark]
4. Nessus was killed – it was written – by heroic Heracles. [1 mark]
5. Nessus also poisoned Heracles (which was very sad). [1 mark]
6. Another creature – also from Greek myths – is the Sphinx. [1 mark]
7. The Sphinx, in a play by Sophocles, asks people riddles. [1 mark]
8. Only one man (who was called Oedipus) got its riddles right. [1 mark]

Try these

Position and punctuation of parentheses will vary.

1. For example, Centaurs (who were half man, half horse) were wild. [example]
2. For example, Giants – not to be confused with Titans – also feature in myths. [1 mark]
3. For example, Harpies, another kind of mythical monster, were huge birds with human faces. [1 mark]
4. For example, In one myth, Heracles (the son of Zeus) must complete twelve tasks that seem impossible. [1 mark]
5. For example, In another, Charybdis – a sea monster – creates a deadly whirlpool. [1 mark]
6. For example, In a different myth, Perseus defeats a Gorgon (which had hair made of snakes). [1 mark]

Now try these

1.–6. Open-ended questions: accept any three sentences with appropriate and correctly punctuated parentheses added. [3 marks per question]

Punctuation Unit 4

Get started

1. We visited a theme park last weekend; it was great! [example]
2. We arrived early; it was about two o'clock. [1 mark]
3. The weather made things even better: it was very sunny. [1 mark]
4. We went on loads of rides; there were so many things to do there. [1 mark]
5. The Spinning Star was the best ride: it was so fast! [1 mark]
6. We nearly forgot lunch; we had it late. [1 mark]
7. We took things more slowly in the afternoon: we were getting very tired. [1 mark]
8. I was exhausted by teatime: it was such a long day. [1 mark]

Try these

Accept dashes in place of colons or semi-colons in some (but not all) sentences.

1. Mary read the map: she's good at directions. [example]
2. The queues were massive; it was frustrating. [1 mark]
3. There was so much to do; we raced around! [1 mark]
4. I went on a roller coaster; I was nearly sick. [1 mark]
5. Emil didn't come on with us: he was scared. [1 mark]
6. We had to look after him: he's my younger brother. [1 mark]
7. We had a great time together; I will remember that day for a long time. [1 mark]
8. I kept an eye on my watch: we were meeting Mum again at five. [1 mark]

Now try these

1. Open-ended question: accept any appropriate main clause that serves as a reason or example. [1 mark]
2. Open-ended question: accept any appropriate linked main clause that has equal weight. [1 mark]
3. Open-ended question: accept any appropriate main clause that serves as a reason or example. [1 mark]
4. Open-ended question: accept any appropriate linked main clause that has equal weight. [1 mark]
5. Open-ended question: accept any appropriate main clause that serves as a reason or example. [1 mark]
6. Open-ended question: accept any appropriate linked main clause that has equal weight. [1 mark]

Punctuation Unit 5

Get started

1. Some things scare me: dogs, which are loud; spiders; and mean people. [example]
2. I made sure I prepared for the party: sent out the invitations; bought the food; and made large, bright decorations. [3 marks]

Year 6: Pupil Book answers

3. I have so much homework: practising my times tables; reading long, difficult chapters; and learning my spellings. [3 marks]
4. I have three chores: tidying my room; visiting Gran, who's old; and dusting. [3 marks]
5. I've got some really good friends: Tom, who's my next-door neighbour; Karin, from school; and my cousin Sameer. [3 marks]
6. I picked Mum's favourite flowers: daisies; forget-me-nots, which are my favourites too; and buttercups. [3 marks]
7. I love word games: crosswords, which we find in newspapers; word-searches; and hangman, which I play with my uncle. [3 marks]

Try these

1. adventures; long, old historical dramas; and comedies. [example]
2.–8. Open-ended questions: accept any appropriate lists correctly punctuated with semi-colons. At least one list item in each question should be a phrase including a comma, and the semi-colon before 'and' should be kept. [1 mark per question]

Now try these

1. Open-ended question: accept any appropriate introduction correctly punctuated with a colon. (For example, My scarf has lots of colours:) [1 mark]
2. Open-ended question: accept any appropriate introduction correctly punctuated with a colon. (For example, I packed for our trip:) [1 mark]
3. Open-ended question: accept any appropriate introduction correctly punctuated with a colon. (For example, I bought stationery for school:) [1 mark]
4. Open-ended question: accept any appropriate introduction correctly punctuated with a colon. (For example, I had these things in my pockets:) [1 mark]
5. Open-ended question: accept any appropriate introduction correctly punctuated with a colon. (For example, They offer lots of sports at school:) [1 mark]
6. Open-ended question: accept any appropriate introduction correctly punctuated with a colon. (For example, There isn't much in my town:) [1 mark]

Punctuation Unit 6

Get started

1. dance group, [example]
2. I'll try at school. [1 mark]
3. Snowball the mouse *or* Walter the cat, [1 mark]
4. board games. [1 mark]

Try these

Award marks for correctly punctuated and presented bullet-pointed lists; punctuation will vary.

1. Animals in a zoo:
   - giraffes
   - zebras
   - hippos. [example]
2. For example, These things are in my bathroom:
   - bath;
   - our towels, which are soft;
   - toothbrushes. [5 marks]
3. For example, There are several ice-cream flavours:
   - chocolate
   - mint
   - strawberry [5 marks]
4. For example, Shades of blue:
   - navy
   - sky
   - royal [5 marks]
5. For example, There's a lot of traffic:
   - lorries,
   - cars,
   - bicycles. [5 marks]
6. For example, Tania has plenty of stationery:
   - pens;
   - crayons;
   - notebooks, with lines. [5 marks]

Now try these

1.–6. Open-ended questions: accept any appropriate bullet-pointed lists with introductions that follow the three main rules and two guidelines. [5 marks per question]

Spelling

Unit 1

Get started

Nouns: caution [1 mark]; infection [1 mark]; space [1 mark]; grace [1 mark]; avarice [1 mark]
Adjectives: infectious [example]; conscious [1 mark]; fictitious [1 mark]; cautious [1 mark]; spacious [1 mark]

Try these

1. spacious [example]
2. malicious [1 mark]
3. nutritious [1 mark]
4. pretentious [1 mark]
5. contentious [1 mark]

1. voracious [example]
2. superstitious [1 mark]
3. avaricious [1 mark]
4. gracious [1 mark]
5. cautious [1 mark]

Now try these

Accept sentences where the target word is spelt correctly and the context is correct. [9 marks: 1 mark per sentence]

Year 6: Pupil Book answers

Unit 2
Get started
Correct: artificial [example]; quintessential [1 mark]; confidential [1 mark]; facial [1 mark]; superficial [1 mark]
Incorrect: parcial [1 mark]; unoffitial [1 mark]; potencial [1 mark]; antisotial [1 mark]

Try these
1. crucial [example]
2. potential [1 mark]
3. martial [1 mark]
4. special [1 mark]
5. beneficial [1 mark]
6. essential [1 mark]
7. substantial [1 mark]
8. partial [1 mark]

Now try these
1. crucial [example]
2. partial [1 mark]
3. official [1 mark]
4. special [1 mark]
5. potential [1 mark]
6. essential [1 mark]
7. martial [1 mark]
8. substantial [1 mark]
9. beneficial [1 mark]
10. social [1 mark]

Unit 3
Get started
-ance / -ancy: infancy [example]; occupancy [1 mark]; expectancy [1 mark]; observance [1 mark]
-ence / -ency: residence [1 mark]; currency [1 mark]; fluency [1 mark]; emergence [1 mark]

Try these
Adjective: negligent [example]; magnificent [1 mark]; extravagant [1 mark]; elegant [1 mark]; urgent [1 mark]; convergent [1 mark]
Noun: negligence [example]; magnificence [1 mark]; extravagance [1 mark]; elegance [1 mark]; urgency [1 mark]; convergence [1 mark]

Now try these
1. licence [example]
2. confident [1 mark]
3. magnificent [1 mark]
4. urgency [1 mark]
5. intelligence [1 mark]
6. decency [1 mark]
7. inelegant [1 mark]; elegant [1 mark]
8. evidence [1 mark]; intelligent [1 mark]

Unit 4
Get started
1. applicably [example]
2. comfortably
3. acceptably
4. understandably
5. noticeably
6. fashionably

Try these
1. considerable [example]
2. collapsible [1 mark]
3. variable [1 mark]
4. manageable [1 mark]
5. responsible [1 mark]
6. imaginable [1 mark]
7. sensible [1 mark]
8. changeable [1 mark]

Now try these
1. arguably [example]
2. eligible [1 mark]
3. forcible [1 mark]
4. pliable [1 mark]
5. irreplaceable [1 mark]
6. negligible [1 mark]
7. submergible [1 mark]
8. illegible [1 mark]
9. tangible [1 mark]

Unit 5
Get started
1. proffered
2. buffered
3. pilfered
4. differed
5. deferred

-fer is stressed when the suffix is added: deferred [2 marks]
-fer is not stressed when the suffix is added: proffered [1 mark]; pilfered [2 marks]; buffered [2 marks]; differed [2 marks]

Try these
Add -ing: conferring [example]; transferring [1 mark]; referring [1 mark]; deferring [1 mark]; differing [1 mark]; inferring [1 mark]
Add -ence: conference [example]; transference [1 mark]; reference [1 mark]; deference [1 mark]; difference [1 mark]; inference [1 mark]

Now try these
1. inferred [example]
2. suffered [1 mark]
3. preferring [1 mark]
4. differed [1 mark]
5. preferred [1 mark]

236

Year 6: Pupil Book answers

6. offered [1 mark]
7. referring [1 mark]
8. conferring [1 mark]
9. transferring [1 mark]
10. deferred [1 mark]

Unit 6
Get started
1. ultra-angry [example]
2. co-own
3. anti-ageing
4. re-educate
5. re-enter
6. de-ice
7. re-elect
8. co-ordinate
9. co-operate
10. pre-election

Try these
1. pre-election [example]
2. re-enter [1 mark]
3. re-accumulate [1 mark]
4. nonsense [1 mark]
5. re-educate [1 mark]
6. antifreeze [1 mark]
7. defrost [1 mark]
8. co-educate [1 mark]
9. co-ordinate [1 mark]
10. rebound [1 mark]

Now try these
Accept sentences where the target word is spelt correctly and the context is correct. [9 marks: 1 mark per sentence]

Unit 7
Get started
Words that follow the rule: niece [example]; friend [1 mark]; receive [1 mark]; conceive [1 mark]
Words that do not follow the rule: protein [1 mark]; caffeine [1 mark]; seize [1 mark]; weird [1 mark]; either [1 mark]; neither [1 mark]

Try these
1. niece [example]
2. chief [1 mark]
3. believe [1 mark]
4. deceitful [1 mark]
5. hygienic [1 mark]
6. ceiling [1 mark]
7. mischief [1 mark]
8. siege [1 mark]
9. receive [1 mark]
10. fields [1 mark]

Now try these
Accept sentences where the target word is spelt correctly and the context is correct. [10 marks: 1 mark per sentence]

Unit 8
Get started
1. ruph [example]
2. stough, stuph [2 marks]
3. coff [1 mark]
4. bau [1 mark]
5. wough [1 mark]
6. corough [1 mark]
7. dow [1 mark]
8. threu [1 mark]
9. troff, troph [2 marks]
10. blough [1 mark]

Try these
1. brought [example]
2. borough [1 mark]
3. ought [1 mark]
4. plough [1 mark]
5. thought [1 mark]
6. trough [1 mark]
7. rough [1 mark]
8. boughs [1 mark]
9. although [1 mark]
10. drought [1 mark]

Now try these
Accept sentences where the target word is spelt correctly and the context is correct. [10 marks: 1 mark per sentence]

Unit 9
Get started
1. sto**m**ach [example]
2. su**b**tle [1 mark]
3. **w**rinkle [1 mark]
4. recei**p**t [1 mark]
5. conde**mn** [1 mark]
6. **r**hyme [1 mark]
7. colum**n** [1 mark]
8. **k**nickers [1 mark]
9. bom**b** [1 mark]
10. clim**b** [1 mark]

Try these
1. whale, wail [example]
2. plum, plumb [1 mark]
3. gnaw, nor [2 marks]
4. write, right [2 marks]
5. kneel [1 mark]
6. not, knot [2 marks]
7. gnome [1 mark]
8. answer [1 mark]

Year 6: Pupil Book answers

9. island [1 mark]
10. limb, limp [2 marks]

Now try these
1. knight [example]
2. sword
3. while
4. gnarled
5. wrestled
6. knee
7. stomach
8. solemn
9. knuckles
10. gnashed
11. knew
12. what

Unit 10
Get started
1. weary [example]
2. proceed [1 mark]
3. wary [1 mark]
4. desert [1 mark]
5. affect [1 mark]
6. precede [1 mark]
7. effect [1 mark]
8. dessert [1 mark]
9. complement [1 mark]
10. compliment [1 mark]

Try these
1. complimented [example]
2. proceeded [1 mark]
3. affected [1 mark]
4. preceded [1 mark]
5. proceeds [1 mark]
6. deserted [1 mark]
7. desserts [1 mark]
8. precedes [1 mark]

Now try these
Accept sentences where the target word is spelt correctly and the context is correct. [10 marks: 1 mark per sentence]

Unit 11
Get started
1. guessed [example]
2. guest [1 mark]
3. herd [1 mark]
4. past [1 mark]
5. led [1 mark]
6. lead [1 mark]
Accept all correct definitions. Approximate definitions:
7. herd: a group of animals [example]
8. For example, passed: move in a specified direction [1 mark]

9. For example, lead: a soft, heavy metal [1 mark]
10. For example, heard: to perceive through one's ear [1 mark]

Try these
1. guessed [example]
2. lead [1 mark]
3. guest [1 mark]
4. heard [1 mark]
5. passed [1 mark]
6. led [1 mark]
7. herd [1 mark]
8. past [1 mark]

Now try these
Accept sentences where the target word is spelt correctly and the context is correct. [9 marks: 1 mark per sentence]

Unit 12
Get started
1. licence [example]
2. prophesy [1 mark]
3. devise [1 mark]
4. license [1 mark]
5. advise [1 mark]
6. practise [1 mark]
7. advice [1 mark]
8. device [1 mark]

Try these
Accept all correct definitions. Definitions should approximate the following:
1. practice: (noun) a custom or procedure [example]
2. advise: (verb) [1 mark]: to recommend or suggest [1 mark]
3. prophecy: (noun) [1 mark]: a prediction of the future [1 mark]
4. licence: (noun) [1 mark]: a permit to do something [1 mark]
5. prophesy: (verb) [1 mark]: to say what will happen in the future [1 mark]
6. devise: (verb) [1 mark]: to plan or invent by careful thought [1 mark]
7. practise: (verb) [1 mark]: to repeat something in order to improve [1 mark]
8. license: (verb) [1 mark]: to permit someone to do something [1 mark]
9. advice: (noun) [1 mark]: recommendations or suggestions [1 mark]
10. device: (noun) [1 mark]: a machine or tool used for a specific task [1 mark]

Now try these
Accept sentences where the target word is spelt correctly and the context is correct. [10 marks: 1 mark per sentence]

Year 6: Pupil Book answers

Unit 13
Get started
Accept all valid synonyms. Synonyms may include the following:
1. outline [example]
2. For example, primary [1 mark]
3. For example, walkway [1 mark]
4. For example, standard [1 mark]
5. For example, island [1 mark]
6. For example, series [1 mark]
7. For example, audibly [1 mark]
8. For example, breeze [1 mark]
9. For example, endorsed [1 mark]
10. For example, motionless [1 mark]
11. For example, bran [1 mark]
12. For example, envelopes [1 mark]

Try these
1. cereal [example]
2. allowed
3. stationery
4. isle
5. principal
6. aloud
7. aisle
8. serial
9. stationary
10. principles

Now try these
Accept sentences where the target word is spelt correctly and the context is correct. [10 marks: 1 mark per sentence]

Unit 14
Get started
Nouns: mourning [example]; ascent [1 mark]; bridle [1 mark]; descent [1 mark]; father [1 mark]; profit [1 mark]; morning [1 mark]; prophet [1 mark]
Verbs: mourning [example]; bridle [1 mark]; father [1 mark]; profit [1 mark]
Adjectives: bridal [1 mark]; farther [1 mark]
Adverbs: farther [1 mark]; morning [1 mark]

Try these
Accept all correct definitions. Definitions should approximate the following:
1. assent: an agreement or to agree [example]
2. For example, steel: a hard, strong metal [1 mark]
3. For example, morning: the beginning of the day [1 mark]
4. For example, dissent: to disagree [1 mark]
5. For example, steal: to take without permission [1 mark]
6. For example, mourning: a state of grieving arising from loss [1 mark]
7. For example, ascent: a journey upwards [1 mark]
8. For example, whose: belonging to which person [1 mark]
9. For example, descent: a journey downwards [1 mark]
10. For example, who's: a contraction of **who is** or **who has** [1 mark]

Now try these
Accept sentences where the target word is spelt correctly and the context is correct. [16 marks: 1 mark per sentence]